Banquet of the Word

Bible Study Based
on the Sunday Readings

by Thomas Welbers

Published by
Resource Publications, Inc.
160 E. Virginia St. Suite 290
San Jose, CA 95112

Editorial Director: Kenneth Guentert
Production Editor: Scott Alkire
Mechanical Layout: Geoff Rogers and Sharon Montooth
Cover Design: Kevin Heney

Nihil Obstat:
Very Rev. Charles E. Miller
Censor Deputatus

Imprimatur:
Most Rev. Roger M. Mahony
Archbishop of Los Angeles

September 26, 1985

ISBN 0-89390-073-7
Library of Congress Catalog Card Number 86-060891
Printed and bound in the United States 5 4 3 2 1

TABLE OF CONTENTS

Table of Contents

YEAR B

Table of Contents

SEASON OF THE YEAR

YEAR C

ADVENT-CHRISTMAS SEASON AND RELATED FEASTS

Table of Contents

ALL YEARS

OTHER SOLEMNITIES AND FEASTS OF THE LORD

FOREWORD

Presiders, homilists, lectors, and liturgy planners have plenty of books and periodicals aimed at them to provide commentary on the Sunday liturgical readings. They don't need another one.

But the average Catholic Christian who hears the Church's call to study, pray, and live the Scriptures within the frameword of the Sunday liturgy finds few guides. Most Bible study aids treat one book at a time or pursue particular themes throughout the Bible text.

This book was conceived from a conviction that Bible Study for Catholics most properly takes place in resonance with the rhythm of the celebration and life of the Church. It was born out of nearly ten years' experience with just such Bible study groups at Our Lady of Lourdes Church in Northridge, Holy Name of Jesus Church in Los Angeles, and the Catholic Newman Center in Long Beach. I gratefully dedicate this book to the members of those communities who helped bring it about.

Thomas Welbers
Long Beach, California
September 30, 1985
Memorial of St. Jerome

INTRODUCTION

BIBLE AND LITURGY AND LIFE

The Bible is at home in the liturgy.

The Bible was born when God's people perceived his active presence among them, and gathered together to acknowledge and celebrate his saving work in them.

Most books of the Bible came from oral traditions — stories, teachings, laws, and songs that were told and sung when God's people gathered for worship. They were written down so they could be kept alive through continued proclamation in the liturgical assembly. This is true for both the Jewish Scriptures (Old Testament) and for the Christian Scriptures (New Testament). Throughout Jewish-Christian history, God's word in Scripture has most deeply touched life in the celebration of liturgy.

Before Jesus, in the times when the Jewish Scriptures were being formed, people gathered to hear the law, to recall the heroes and events of the past, to listen to the words of the prophets, and to sing psalms. Through this living word they were put in touch with their origins and identity. God's saving work of the past was recalled in a way that made it alive in the present. Putting these words down in writing was something secondary; the written word existed principally to serve and preserve the living, spoken word.

In Jewish traditions, prayer, especially liturgical prayer, arose from this living recollection of God's saving events for his people in their history. In remembering past events, especially at mealtime, expressions of praise for who God is and thanks for what he had done unfolded into petitions that God would accomplish now for his people what he did for them in the past. This particular way of praying, called the *berakah* or blessing, was the ancestor of the Christian eucharistic prayer, the heart of the Mass.

After Jesus, the events of his life and his teachings continued to be told over and over when his followers gathered to worship and to celebrate the breaking of the bread. These stories came from the faith of the earliest Christians — the apostles and disciples — and were preached and carefully preserved and collected in order to nourish the faith of Christians as they sought to live the kingdom of God announced by Christ. The four Gospels were written between forty and seventy years after the death and resurrection of Jesus, and were made possible because the early Christian communities continued to remember Jesus whenever they gathered in his name.

Even the letters of the Christian Scriptures, especially those of Paul, were destined to be read in liturgical assemblies. Paul addressed the problems of the early Christian churches in the light of the faith-teaching he had already given them. Since these letters were public documents addressed to the whole community, it was only natural that they be shared publicly in the liturgical assembly. The fact that many (though by no means all) of Paul's letters to churches were saved and eventually found their way into the recognized body of Scriptures shows that they were shared from church to church and kept alive through repeated proclamation in the liturgical assembly.

Having been born of the living faith of God's people, the Scriptures have continued to nourish that faith by putting Christians of all times and places in touch with their origins and heritage. Many early Christian writers, as well as the Second Vatican Council, referred to two tables in the liturgical celebration — the table of the word and the table of the eucharist (see the *Constitution on Divine Revelation*, 21). Both were seen as equally important sources of nourishment for God's faithful people. The bread of the word is presented in the proclamation of Scripture and broken open in the homily to feed the members of the assembly just as the bread of the eucharist is brought and placed on the altar table, blessed in the eucharistic prayer, broken, and shared in communion.

We of the late twentieth century need to remember that prior to the sixteenth century when the printing and distribution of books made near-universal literacy possible, the only contact with Scripture that most people could have was in public proclamation, and that usually meant liturgical proclamation. Private reading, as well as private interpretation, of the Bible was simply an impossiblity for at least three-fourths of our Christian history. In its origin and its history the Bible has consistently been a public book, nourishing the shared and living faith of a Christian people, not just of individual Christians.

Throughout this *Banquet of the Word* we will consistently use the terms "Jewish (or Hebrew) Scriptures" and "Christian Scriptures" in place of "Old Testament" and "New Testament." As Christians, we need to recover an awareness that the Jewish tradition is not "old" in the sense of antiquated or obsolete, but is truly the foundation of our faith. The event of Jesus' coming did not destroy or invalidate God's original promise and saving presence to the Jews but fulfilled it and made it universal for all times and places. The only Bible that Jesus and the first generations of Christians knew was the Jewish collection of scriptural books. Inspired apostolic writings, while cherished and carefully preserved in their own day, were gathered together in collections recognized as Scripture by all Christian churches only in second and third centuries.

THE LECTIONARY

The word "Lectionary" refers primarily to the selection and arrangement of the Scripture readings for the liturgy rather than the book from which the Scripture is proclaimed. A Bible itself, preferably a large and dignified one, would be the most appropriate book from which to proclaim the liturgical readings at Mass.

The present Lectionary is one of the glories of the liturgical reform following the Second Vatican Council. Before Vatican II, only a few passages from the Bible were read over and over again year after year. The Council directed that the readings be so arranged that the "treasures of the Bible be opened more lavishly" in the liturgy (see the *Constitution on the Liturgy*, 51). Both biblical and liturgical scholars worked together to draw up a reformed Lectionary; it was completed in 1970. Several principles guided their work:

First, to assure that a substantial portion of the Bible would actually be read, a three-year cycle was adopted. Trying to cover the whole Bible, or even just the important parts, in one year would have meant excessively long readings or the omission of many significant sections.

Second, for Christians the Gospels stand at the heart of the Bible, therefore they are also at the heart of liturgical proclamation. The three-year cycle is based on the Gospels of Matthew, Mark, and Luke — with John reserved for special times.

Third, if the Gospel passage is the climax of the readings, two additional readings are called for, the first usually from the Jewish Scriptures and the second from the non-Gospel Christian Scriptures.

Fourth, the first reading from the Jewish Scriptures should have some relationship to the Gospel. This enables Catholic Christians to hear and study these readings in the light of our belief that God's revelation to his chosen people, the Jews, finds its fulfillment in Christ.

Fifth, the second reading, is to be a semi-continuous reading from the letters of the Christian Scriptures. Thus one week's selection would begin more or less where the previous week's left off.

Thus the Lectionary provides an ideal framework for Bible study. It both assures basic coverage of the entire Bible over the course of three years and it keeps study of the Bible in tune with the rhythm of the Church's life and the liturgical year.

THE LITURGICAL YEAR

The liturgical year establishes the rhythm of the Christian life. The high points of the year are the two major seasons, Lent-Easter being the most important, and Advent-Christmas being secondary. Each of these seasons is made up of a period of preparation and a season which prolongs the celebration of the feast itself. The remainder of the year is called "Ordinary Time" in many official Church documents, but the Lectionary more aptly calls it the "Season of the Year."

During the major seasons, the readings are chosen to shed light on the mystery that is being prepared for or celebrated. Often the selection of these passages goes back into the usage of the early Church, and so they reflect the insights of many centuries of faith. The Gospel of John, because of its concentration on the development of faith and its theological reflections on the divinity of Jesus as manifested in his death and resurrection, has traditionally been given pride of place in these seasons.

The Season of the Year begins after the Advent-Christmas season, is interrupted for the Lent-Easter season, and resumes after Pentecost. The Gospel narrative proper to each year of the three-year cycle begins after Christmas season with the events following the baptism of Jesus, and continues throughout the year with the life and teachings of Jesus as found in that Gospel.

A number of feasts supplant the Sunday celebration, some regularly and others only when Sunday falls on a particular date. The rules for this are rather complex, and a good calendar will tell you what is celebrated when, so there is no need for us to go into detail. It is enough to note that only feasts of major significance are allowed to displace the regular Sunday cycle. We should try to see these feasts as enhancing rather than interrupting the rhythm of the year.

LITURGICAL BIBLE STUDY

The word of God in the Bible continues to nourish our faith. In the years of reform and renewal following Vatican II, Catholics have begun to rediscover the Bible's significance in understanding and living their faith. Bible study has recently become an important part of Catholic life, both for individuals and for parishes. At the same time, the major Protestant churches are experiencing a renewal of liturgical life, especially in more frequent and wholehearted celebration of the eucharist. Now Catholics and Protestants are both gain-

764

805

ing a new appreciation of the relationship between the scriptural word and the liturgy.

Unfortunately, this renewed interest in Bible study among Catholics has often not taken into account the close relationship of the liturgy and the Bible. Both our liturgical celebrations and our Christian lives are the poorer for it.

The liturgy provides the natural connecting link between the Bible and Christian life. What we celebrate in the liturgy is intended to unfold in our life of faith day by day. Not only homilists and lectors need to study the Sunday Scripture readings in preparation for Mass; it is an important element of everyone's particpation. In order to celebrate well, we must prepare well to hear and respond to the Scripture to be proclaimed. If we do not read and study and pray over the Sunday Scriptures during the week in preparation for the Mass, we rob the proclamation of its power and starve our faith of its rightful nourishment.

PROCLAMATION AND MINISTRY

Proclamation speaks primarily to the heart, not the head — heart as the center of our being rather than just an emotion. It makes the word of God a living and active reality within the liturgical assembly. The liturgy of the word challenges and stimulates us to renew and deepen our commitment to new life in Christ. Proclamation seeks a response, a "yes" that is not merely spoken but lived in a new way. The word of God holds up a mirror in which we see not only ourselves, but ourselves in God's presence. And God's presence in his word is the standard by which we measure ourselves and change our hearts to live in his presence. The appropriate response to proclamation is discipleship.

Comprehension and retention are not primary values in proclamation as they are in Bible study or reading. The passage to be proclaimed must already have been read and studied, it must already be present in mind and heart, for its proclamation to be effective. The word in the liturgical celebration calls forth an echo in the life of the assembly; it stimulates the growth of what must already be present. Some will argue in favor of following the text in a missal or a missalette along with the lector or deacon because following the printed word promotes greater retention and understanding. Perhaps so, but the it also locks each person in a purely personal and individual relationship with the printed word, and reduces the act of proclamation itself to secondary importance. In the liturgy, the focus of attention is on the living word proclaimed by the person who at this moment is ministering to the whole assembly in Christ's name. The assembly is unified in its attentiveness to the word, and is empowered as well to respond as one body.

It should be obvious that careful preparation — reading, study, and prayer — must precede both the proclamation and the hearing of the proclaimed word, or else the Scripture will lose its own proper power. We have so many weak celebrations of liturgy not because the word itself has failed but because we have lost faith in its potency and do nothing to enable it to shine forth.

1. THE MINISTRY OF THE ASSEMBLY

We often think of liturgical ministry as something done "by someone up there" at the chair or ambo or altar. The primary liturgical ministry — the one on which all other ministries depend — is that of the assembly. All who gather for worship have a responsibility to minister in faith to one another. Attentiveness and wholehearted response is contagious within the assembly. You manifest your faith in the power of the word by your attentiveness to it, and you thereby support the faith of those around you.

Effective presiding by the priest and effective proclamation by the lector depends in large measure on how well the congregation ministers to them by its attention and responsiveness. A lector who must face a crowd of indifferent faces every Sunday morning soon loses much of the incentive to proclaim well and almost cannot help but succumb to routine performance. A congregation prepared by study and prayer to receive God's word can hardly fail to bring forth the best in their ministers.

2. THE MINISTRY OF PRESIDING

The priest's liturgical role of presiding reflects the role of the priest as presider in the life of the community. Often the liturgical ministry of presider is weakened by failure to bring this reality into preparation for liturgy. Although special times must be set aside for collecting and composing the homily and other parts of the liturgy, this work is nourished by day-by-day interaction with the community.

The homily is not the fruit of isolated research and study, but comes properly from immersion in the Scriptures in union with members of the community. The homily is not an explanation of the proclaimed word, it is an unfolding of the power of the word in one's own life and in the life of the community. It is not a teaching, but a call to bring the word to life. Ideally, the homily should develop within the context of the presider's involvement in the total liturgy planning process, which begins with studying the Sunday Scriptures with the liturgy committee. At very least, homilists should be part of Bible study groups — not necessarily the leaders — composed of people of the parish, in which they can expand their own horizons and can derive a clearer sense of their needs and the community's needs in relation to the word.

3. OTHER MINISTRIES

Members of the liturgy committee should begin their preparation for the Sunday liturgy by immersing themselves in the assigned Scripture texts. Those who compose the prayer of the faithful or are responsible for the music in the liturgy need to become familiar with the content of the Sunday readings so it can illuminate their specific concerns: how can this liturgical assembly present its needs in prayer or respond in song in the light of the word they have just heard?

Lectors need to study not only the particular passages they will proclaim, but the other readings as well, including the Gospel, in order to grasp the fullness of the message. Otherwise they cannot proclaim the word as a living reality within them, but only as words coming from a printed page.

Music ministers have the difficult task of putting the "queen of the arts" to the service of the community's worship. They have devoted their lives and their hearts to acquiring skill and competence in an art which they are now required to place in a position of servant. The servanthood of ministry is never easy, and it can be accomplished only in union with Christ the Servant.

The role proper to liturgical music ministers requires more than just reading over the Sunday Scriptures to get an idea of the theme in order to pick appropriate songs. They need to be first of all actively participating members of the Christian community that draws nourishment from the proclaimed word. Music that is truly the servant of the Church's worship grows out of the community's struggle to listen to the word of God as it speaks to all aspects of life. At very least, music ministers need to be in communication with other liturgical ministers and join with them in reflecting on the Sunday readings.

Ministers to the sick bring not only the eucharist but also the word of God to the sick and shut-ins in their care. Their ministry is primarily to keep alive the bonds of unity between the rest of the community and the person who has been isolated by sickness. Realizing that they embody the life and activity of the parish for the sick person, ministers to the sick should be prepared to share reflections on the Sunday readings as they bring communion from the Sunday eucharist.

The Christian Initiation of Adults envisions a process that introduces the catechumens to the rhythm of the Church's life through the Sunday liturgical proclamation of Scripture. Their dismissal after the liturgy of the word is not so much a deprivation of the remainder of the community's liturgy as a call to their own liturgy which continues immersion in the proclaimed word of God in a way that nourishes their journey.

The Sunday Scriptures also have a central place in the classroom. If the goal of Catholic schools and religious education programs is to form children and adults in the art of Christian living in the world, the liturgical proclamation of God's word provides the fundamental source for this formation just as the liturgical year establishes the environment in which it takes place.

STUDYING AND PRAYING THE SUNDAY SCRIPTURES

The Lectionary and the liturgical year provide a framework for Bible study, not a straight-jacket. There are many creative possibilities within this framework, especially for those who already have some familiarity with the Bible and the liturgical year.

The liturgical selections should never be studied alone in complete isolation from the rest of the Bible. It is always important to pay attention to the context, parallels, and cross references, as well as those sections that may have been omitted from any given reading.

The Gospel is the last of the three Scripture readings, and therefore the climax of the liturgical proclamation of the word. In study and preparation, however, the Gospel should always be considered first because its message sets the theme of the liturgy of the word, and of the whole celebration.

The first reading is from the Jewish Scriptures (except during Easter season) and it nearly always helps us to understand the journey in faith of the people God first prepared to receive and share the Good News. Usually, the particular passage is chosen to shed light on the Gospel reading, but it often relates thematically to other passages in the Jewish Scriptures which can be studied with profit and which in turn show the development of thought and faith before Jesus.

The responsorial psalm is not really a part of the Scripture proclamation, but makes use of the words of Scripture to embody the assembly's response to the first reading. In liturgical Bible study, however, this psalm together with its response-verse can serve as the opening or closing prayer to the session.

The second reading is from a letter in the Christian Scriptures and gives us a glimpse of the way the Gospel event was appropriated and lived by the disciples and the earliest Christians. Although not chosen specifically to correspond with the Gospel passage of any Sunday, this reading often can be found to say more to the thematic content of the Gospel than is usually supposed. The concrete message of the Gospel always benefits from being put in a broader context, and we can hear it better with ears that are sharpened by the experience and advice of the apostolic letter writers.

Within the framework of liturgical Bible study it is still possible and at times desirable to study a single book at a time. Choose a book that is being proclaimed during the present liturgical cycle or season, and study it with reference to the season and the liturgical proclamation. This may be especially appropriate after having already gone through the three year cycle, and having acquired a good familiarity with the Bible as a whole and the rhythm of the Church's year.

HELPFUL HINTS FOR BIBLE STUDY

All Bible study begins with reading the Scripture passage and reflecting on it. There is no substitute for reading it aloud — even privately. The Bible came from oral traditions and was written down specifically to be read aloud. The printed word serves the spoken word, and is fulfilled in speaking and hearing. Reading aloud involves the body and activates the senses; it slows us down to pay closer attention to what we are reading. It allows us to play with the meaning, to discover different ways of emphasizing words to bring out nuances of meaning that we would miss otherwise. Hearing our own voice sharpens our senses to listen to others' voices in reading.

When we approach Scripture, it is important to realize that we come in contact with our whole heritage as a Christian people. First of all, we are a people, not a group of isolated individuals, and we cannot relate to God outside of our identity as a people, as his Church. Second, we are a people with a past, and we cannot relate to God apart from that past. God revealed himself through the events of our ancestors' history, and in touching them we are touching him. We should not be so concerned with trying to hear God speaking directly to us through the Scripture, but should learn to appreciate our heritage of faith as mediating his presence here and now.

Let the passage you are studying lead you. Ask yourself questions about it, and try to answer them by using a good Bible diction-ary and/or a commentary. Explore related passages with the help of a concordance.

In discussing the Bible, try to define three levels of meaning. First, come to grips with the meaning in itself. What did the Biblical author intend to say? What is the historical context? What actually happened and what did it mean to the people of that time? Then share what the passage means to you. How can the ancient ex-perience illuminate your life here and now? What in your own ex-perience echoes the patterns you discovered in the Biblical passage? Finally, explore what this passage can say to us as Church. We have to challenge ourselves to get beyond the purely personal and see ourselves as part of the community. How does this Bible passage en-rich our Christian living and call forth a deeper commitment to the kingdom of God here and now? The questions at the end of each section in this book are designed to help move from through these layers of meaning.

An exercise called "clustering" can be quite helpful in group Bible study to get sharing or discussion started. After reading the passage aloud, reflect on it for a few minutes in silence. Each person should have a pencil and a blank sheet of paper, and begin to write down words that come to mind. These may be key words from the text itself or words that the reading suggests, such as feelings or re-lated thoughts. It is important that these words not be put down in a column or outline fashion, but be scattered more or less at random around the page. After the words stop coming to mind, draw a heavy circle around whatever word seems key or most important. Then spend a few moments connecting the words with circles and arrows in whatever relationships they seem to suggest.

After about five minutes of this activity, enough people begin to develop insights and confidence to begin sharing. It also focuses discussion on the content of the reading and helps prevent wander-ing into concerns not pertinent to the reading.

The success of this exercise depends upon involvement of all the senses in the act of writing on paper as well as a shift into a global, non-linear mode of thinking (sometimes called "right brain") encouraged by the random clustering of words, as opposed to the logical ordering of concepts. "Clustering" may seem somewhat simplistic and superficial, but it does work in practice. Do not expect it, however, to be what it is not. It is not a Bible study method as such, it is only a technique to encourage the type of thinking that leads to sharing within a group. (For more on this "right brain shift" and "clustering", I recommend Gabriele Lusser Rico, *Writing the*

Natural Way, J.P. Tarcher, Inc., Los Angeles, 1983.)

Prayer is always a response to God who has taken the initiative to speak to us first. Reading, reflection, and study of the Scriptures should never be far from praying the Scriptures. Personal prayer outside the liturgy nourishes prayer within the liturgy, and liturgical prayer establishes the pattern for the prayer of the rest of the week. In liturgy, we listen and we respond. In life, we make that response active and concrete. In studying and praying the scriptural word, we say "yes" to that word in our private moments. In celebration, our personal "yes" becomes one with the Church's and Christ's "yes."

TOOLS

Any work requires its own tools, and Bible study is no exception. There are many types of tools, mostly books, that will prove helpful and even essential to both individuals and groups engaged in studying the Bible. Most of the fears and questions that intimidate beginners can be addressed by knowing and making use of some of the resources available. Here are various categories of tools that you should consider, both for individual and for group study. The prices given reflect the retail cost at the time of this writing (summer 1985) as well as I could determine it. They are given more for purposes of comparison than as an assurance of what you will pay.

1. A CALENDAR.

The first question asked by most who want to study the Sunday readings is, "How do I find out what they are?" This is really two questions: "Which Sunday (or feast) are we preparing to celebrate?" and "What are the Scripture readings proper to that celebration?"

The answer to the first can come as simply as finding a good Catholic calendar — the kind that are sold or given away in most churches around Christmastime. Not all calendars, however, are clear on which year of the three-year cycle it is, so here is a table that will last you till the millenium:

Year A		Year B		Year C
1987		1988		1986
1990		1991		1989
1993		1994		1992
1996		1997		1995
1999		2000		1998

Don't forget that the liturgical year begins with the First Sunday of Advent, so, for example, Year A 1987 actually begins November 30, 1986.

I know that suggesting an ordinary religious calendar seems a little too obvious, but usually the questions with the obvious answers are the ones that block us at the very beginning of a venture.

2. A BIBLE.

A beginning student of the Bible has to face a bewildering variety of versions and decide which one to buy. There are three things to look for: (1) Is it a faithful translation? (2) Is it in contemporary readable English? (3) Does it have explanatory introductions and notes? Out of many good versions and editions, three can be especially recommended for for our purposes.

The *New American Bible* (NAB) is the official Catholic translation in the United States and is the one most commonly used in parish Sunday liturgies. The NAB is recommended as a first choice mainly because it is what you will usually hear in church. Most scholars regard it to be a faithful and accurate translation of the original texts. The English is fairly idiomatic, but sometimes a bit clumsy and inelegant for reading aloud. The introductory material and notes are fairly good. The NAB is available from several publishers, but perhaps the least expensive editions with the very clear type are the "St. Joseph" editions from the Catholic Book Publishing Company. Prices begin about $6.95 for a paperback edition, but I would recommend the larger hardbound student's edition for about $12.00.

The *New Jerusalem Bible* (JB), published by Doubleday, is based on a very famous French translation with excellent and extensive commentaries, notes, and cross references. The complete hardbound edition runs $24.95. Avoid the cheaper "Reader's Edition" which gives only the text and omits the helpful notes.

The *Oxford Annotated Bible with the Apocrypha*, published by Oxford University Press, uses the highly regarded Revised Standard Version (RSV) and also gives a variety of excellent study helps. It runs $24.95.

For more casual reading only, the *Good News Bible* or *Today's English Version* (TEV), published in a Catholic edition with the Deuterocanonical books (Apocrypha) is excellent, and a good buy as well. Available by mail order from the American Bible Society (P.O.

Box 5601, Grand Central Station, New York, NY 10163) for $3.50 soft cover or $4.00 hardbound. It is also sold in bookstores, but is much more expensive. This is a good Bible to keep by your bedside or in the office or wherever you might find yourself with some reading time.

Not particularly recommended are two Protestant versions popular among conservative evangelicals, the *New American Standard Bible* (NASB) and the *New International Version* (NIV). They are not bad, but the others we have recommended are better for our purposes.

Definitely not recommended are the *King James* (KJV) and the *Douay* versions and the so-called *Living Bible* (also called *The Way*). The King James and Douay are four hundred years old and the language of that time does not speak well today, even though many people still like its "churchiness." If you are reading for understanding rather than just musty feelings, avoid these. The *Living Bible* is a recent work (1971) but it is a paraphrase, not a translation. In other words, the author sought to retell the Bible text in other words. Usually these "other words" reflect a fundamentalist Protestant interpretation that even most mainline Protestants do not agree with. It also comes in an "approved" Catholic edition, but mere "approval" does not remove its flaws! The *Living Bible* may be useful as a second or third Bible version in order to get the flavor of a certain kind of interpretation, but it should not be used as the basic text for serious Bible study.

3. INTRODUCTIONS.

These are books about the Bible, usually addressed to beginners or those who need to return to the basics — as we all do from time to time. They are designed to take you by the hand and lead you through the background territory you need in order to know to approach the Bible with some degree of familiarity, understanding, and confidence. They are important both for individuals and groups because they usually answer the questions that make first-timers feel awkward and old-timers impatient. Out of many good ones available, I would recommend three:

(1) Robert R. Hann, *The Bible: and Owner's Manual*, Paulist Press, 1983, $5.95. This book assumes that you don't know anything about the Bible, and therefore jumps right into the questions you were afraid to ask. This is a book you should devour from cover

to cover but hide from your friends (or else mail it to them anonymously). You don't want them to know you're that ignorant, but secretly you suspect they have the same questions.

(2)   Gerhard Lohfink, *The Bible: Now I Get It!*, Doubleday, 1979, $7.95. Described as "an entertaining look at the Bible for people who think they know it already," this book picks up where the "Owner's Manual" leaves off. It is a popular study of what contemporary scholarship says about the various forms of literature that make up the books of the Bible and how to interpret them.

(3)   Wilfrid Harrington, O.P., *The New Guide to Reading and Studying the Bible*, Michael Glazier, 1978, $7.95. Harrington is a distinguished scholar who covers much the same territory as the above two books in a readable but more concise and less entertaining way — not necessarily an advantage.

4.   CONCORDANCES.

If you are doing any work with the Bible you cannot live without a concordance. This is an index to all the words (or at least major words) found in the Bible, giving the verses and quotes from the lines in which they are found. You need a concordance find that passage you only half remember that could be somewhere in Matthew — or maybe it was Exodus, or Ephesians. It also can help to search for themes. If you want explore, for example, the "kingdom of God," you can find all the passages that use the word "kingdom," as well as "reign," "rule," and "dominion."

The best buy is the hardcover *Concordance to the Holy Bible* published by the American Bible Society and sold by them (see address above) for $3.25. It is not exhaustive, but it is a handy size and complete enough to be useful, with 4,700 keywords and 70,000 references. It uses the KJV which in this case is not a disadvantage. Highly recommended.

The next step up is a big one, both in price and weight. *Nelson's Complete Concordance of the New American Bible*, 1977, is an exhaustive concordance based on the NAB. If you want to pay $39.95 and lug around a 1274-page book that weighs almost eight pounds, this is the one to buy rather than the other exhaustive concordances, such as Young's or Strong's, of similar size and cost.

5.   DICTIONARIES.

There are many Bible dictionaries on the market, including tiny pocket books scarcely worthy of the name. A Bible dictionary should be more like a small encyclopedia, treating each word in some depth. Most reviewers seem to agree that the best all-around buy for the average-to-serious Bible student is the popular John L. McKenzie, S.J., *Dictionary of the Bible*, Macmillan, 1965, $13.95 paperback. It's a good-sized book, but not overwhelming. The fact that it has been around for twenty years and is still regarded as one of the best testifies to its reliability and accessibility.

6.   COMMENTARIES.

A commentary is simply what the name implies — a running commentary that provides background information to help understand the text as you are reading it. Most commentaries also contain articles that treat of various aspects of Scripture study. The best of them are the work of a large number of experts and reflect the findings of recent scholarly research.

One of the most useful and accessible one-volume commentaries to the whole Bible is *The Interpreter's One-Volume Commentary on the Bible*, Abingdon, 1971, $22.95. Also recommended, but considerably more expensive, are *A New Catholic Commentary on Holy Scripture*, Nelson, 1969, $34.95, a work of English authorship, and *The Jerome Biblical Commentary*, Prentice-Hall, 1968, $57.95, a comprehensive and detailed work by American Catholic scholars. Familiarly known as the JBC, you may find it worth the price, but I would suggest you use it in a library before investing. A somewhat simpler and much less inexpensive one-volume commentary on the whole Bible is Willliam Neil, *Harper's Bible Commentary*, Harper and Row, 1962, $6.95.

There are also many multi-volume commentaries that treat only one or a few books of the Bible in each volume. They range from the very expensive and somewhat controversial and as yet incomplete Anchor Bible, $15.00 to $25.00 per volume, to the relatively inexpensive Collegeville Bible Commentary Series, published by Liturgical Press at $2.50 each. In between are series published by Michael Glazier, Doubleday Image Books, and many more. The value of these multi-volume sets is that certain numbers may be outstanding, but it is not worth getting a whole set. The cost of even the Collegeville series can quickly mount up to more than the much larger and more comprehensive one-volume commentaries.

7.   GOSPEL PARALLELS.

A Gospel parallel is perhaps not as essential as a concordance or a good commentary, but it is a handy thing to have, especially for liturgical Bible study. It lines up the Gospels texts in vertical parallel columns so you can see at a glance which Gospel has what and where the similarities and differences are. The Lectionary is arranged so that frequently only one of several parallel texts are read in the liturgy, so it is helpful to be able to compare them.

The least expensive and best is Kurt Aland, *Synopsis of the Four Gospels*, English Edition, American Bible Society, 1982, $5.95. You have to order it by mail, see address above under "Bibles." Most stores carry Burton H. Throckmorton, Jr., *Gospel Parallels: A Synopsis of the First Three Gospels*, 1979, $9.95. Both can be recommended. A companion to Throckmorton's Gospel Parallels, Neal M. Flanagan, O.S.M., *Mark, Matthew, Luke: A Guide to the Gospel Parallels*, Liturgical Press, 1978, $4.95, sheds light on the why's and how's of Gospel parallels.

While we are on the subject of parallels, Fred O. Francis and J. Paul Sampley, *Pauline Parallels*, Fortress, 1984, $29.95, is as intriguing as it is expensive. It's a very handy way to discover the ways that Paul's thought is related from one letter to another.

8.   MORE ...

The tools we have listed represent just the beginning and a very small part of the resources that are available as you probe more deeply into study of the Bible. Two books that may help the search for more treasures in the Biblical field are Erasmus Hort, *The Bible Book: Resources for Reading the New Testament*, Crossroad, 1983, $12.95; and Iris V. Cully and Kendig Brubaker Cully, *A Guide to Biblical Resources*, Morehouse-Barlow, 1981, $4.95. The former is a bit more serious and scholarly; the latter covers the basic territory but also delves into resources for children's study as well as the Bible in arts and literature.

Exploring the Bible is an image of exploring the Divinity itself: the deeper you probe the more you discover new riches that beckon you. Perhaps that's why we will always be left less than satisfied in this life ... and why heaven needs to be eternal.

YEAR A
ADVENT-CHRISTMAS SEASON
AND RELATED FEASTS

AWAKE!

Gospel: Matthew 24:37-44

The liturgy of the beginning of Advent calls for watchfulness in preparation for the Lord's coming. In Christmas we not only celebrate the coming of the Son of God in time, but, aware of his presence with us now, we also look forward to his final coming. The one thing that is certain about this coming in fulfillment is the impossibility of predicting the time — even from signs, all of which are easily subject to many different interpretations (v 36). Therefore the coming of the kingdom must be the object of constant attention. The ultimate sin is immersion in the ordinary affairs of this world to the exclusion of what is beyond (vv 37-39).

The "being taken" and "being left" of vv 40-41 refers to a coming to light of the inner state of a person's soul — the basic orientation of life — which is not evident from ordinary occupations. The watchfulness required is not one of mere passive waiting, but of attentive and constant preparation (vv 43-51).

First Reading: Isaiah 2:1-5

This prophecy of the messianic kingdom helps us to understand something of the nature of the present-day existence and growth of the reign of God in relation to its future fulfillment in the final coming of Christ. Jesus the Messiah came to restore rightness to humanity — it is our responsibility to participate in and promote that rightness. All efforts to bring about peace, justice, and true prosperity that can be shared by all people are in some way related to bringing about the kingdom just as all exploitation, greed, oppression, and violence are opposed to the kingdom and delay God's vision of fulfillment.

Responsorial Psalm: Psalm 122:1-2, 3-4, 4-5, 6-7, 8-9

God's order is fulfilled in peace, and work for peace is expressed and fortified in prayer. Response: "I rejoiced when I heard them say: let us go to the house of the Lord."

Second Reading: Romans 13:11-14

The coming of Jesus Christ in time marked the beginning of the "final age" of the world. Therefore for the past two thousand years we have been living in "the last days." The sense in which to undersand the urgency of time is not to concentrate on the brevity of time left, but to realize that the moment which is once past does not return. The past is dead and the future is out of our hands; so the present moment is of decisive and urgent importance. Night clothes are no longer proper in the light of day, especially since day is a time of battle with the forces of evil. The vices of v 13 are the clothing of night. Jesus Christ himself is the clothing (armor) of the day — the day which opens onto the eternal day.

Questions for thought, discussion, and prayer:
1. What does it mean to "put on the Lord Jesus Christ"?

2. Discuss the "unconcern" of Mt 24:39 as the greatest possible sin.

SECOND SUNDAY OF ADVENT — YEAR A

REFORM!

Gospel: Matthew 3:1-12

John the Baptist needed no introduction to the Jewish Christian communities that were Matthew's original audience. In fact, there is evidence that his influence extended far beyond the Jordan locality and the times of his life and preaching — his disciples turned up many years later in Ephesus as witnessed by Acts 19:1-5. The Gospels intentionally portray John in a way that resembles Elijah (see 2 Kgs 1:8) to show that he continues, in fact completes, the prophetic tradition.

Listen to the proclamation of John with fresh ears. The word "reform" is so much a part of our religious vocabulary that we can easily shortcut its meaning. John speaks of reform in terms of road building, a scene we can identify with today. Both the need for good roads in order to give access to all places remote as well as near, and the planning and labor that go into their building and repair, can tell us of the necessity of reform as preparation to allow the Lord to enter our lives. And the kind of work required gives us a strong image — clearing the debris of worldly attachments that hinder access, as well as widening the path of welcome to the Lord.

Put yourself in the place of the people who approached John the Baptist. Why did you come? How hard is it to confess your sins? What does bathing in the Jordan river mean to you? Who are the Pharisees and Sadducees, and why would John speak so harshly to them? Do we deserve those words too?

Repentance — turning one's life around — comes from the individual person's intention, but only God can complete it by offering entry into a family relationship with him. The Holy Spirit and fire, along with harvest winnowing as an image of judgment, speak of God's power to accomplish what John's preaching and baptism can only allude to.

First Reading: Isaiah 11:1-10

The work of the Holy Spirit goes beyond individual desires for personal salvation. Reconciliation even of deeply divided antagonists is the fruit of the Spirit in the fullness of God's kingdom. This reading compels the Christian to share in the spirit of reconciliation, and to rise above a self-centered concern with only his or her own righteousness. God's kingdom is not brought about until all people are at peace with one another.

Responsorial Psalm: Psalm 72:1-2, 7-8, 12-13, 17

This coronation song extols the qualities of the ideal monarch, whose reign is the sign of God's reign. Of course, then, it speaks of Christ. Response: "Justice shall flourish in his time, and fullness of peace for ever."

Second Reading: Romans 15:4-9

This reading brings Isaiah's prophecy into the time of Christian fulfillment. Reconciliation of all peoples is the meaning of Christ's mission. God is to be glorified only by one heart and one voice rising from humankind. The unity of Jews and Gentiles in Christ is a symbol that impels us to promote the same unity in Christ among all people, overcoming barriers of distance and prejudice.

Questions for thought discussion, and prayer:
1. What does John the Baptist's detachment from everything people consider essential to "good living" signify? Who are some contemporary prophets who convey the same message by their way of life?

2.   What does God's reign mean? How can we translate it into today's language?

ARE YOU THE ONE, OR DO WE LOOK FOR ANOTHER?

Gospel: Matthew 11:2-11

Today's Gospel reading presents to us the consummation of John the Baptist's mission which was shown in its full bloom in last week's Gospel. John's whole purpose in life was to prepare for and point to Jesus as Messiah. Here we find a paradox that contains a strong lesson for us. A careful reading of the scriptural evidence indicates that John the Baptist never really knew Jesus. He never became one of his followers, and even after Jesus began his ministry, John continued to preach and to baptize and to instruct his own disciples. It would seem that the events surrounding Jesus' baptism, striking though they were (see Mt 3:13-17), were not conclusive to an observer like John. His question from prison (vv 2-3) was an honest inquiry, and shows John concerned to fulfill his task even in the face of uncertainty.

The lesson for us is that John knew his mission, and he faithfully fulfilled it to the end without ever being privileged to see fully or participate personally in the fruits of that mission. He was not even able to confirm from his own experience that he was on the right track.

Experience, however, is uppermost in what Jesus presents as his credentials to John's disciples (vv 4-5). He does not try to prove his identity by claims and arguments. He simply says, "What do you see and hear? Judge for yourself."

The paradox of the greatest and the least, which concludes this Gospel passage, gives a foretaste of Jesus' later teaching about true greatness in the kingdom of God (see Mt 18:1-4; 20:20-28). Healing the sick, strengthening the weak, sharing the good news with the poor — all characteristics of the messianic reign — are continued in our day by those who make themselves least through selfless service.

First Reading: Isaiah 35:1-6,10
This prophecy speaks in beautiful poetic images of the restoration of God's people in their return from exile. This renewal of life and nationhood is depicted as a new exodus, because the original exodus from Egypt, nearly a thousand years before, was the primal "salvation event" for Israel — all God's saving deeds afterward fall into the same pattern of liberation, and are seen as extensions of the one great saving event. The particular care toward the weak and the unfortunate — they are the first to come into the new kingdom — is a typical way of emphasizing that God's concern reverses human priorities and interests. For the Christian, this restoration becomes real today through commitment to serve others in Christ's name. Service on behalf of the poor, the oppressed and the helpless is not an optional nicety — it is the heart of what it means to be a Christian.

Responsorial Psalm: Psalm 146:6-7, 8-9, 9-10
This psalm of praise echoes the qualities of God's compassion and power as depicted in the Isaiah reading. Response: "Lord, come and save us."

Second Reading: James 5:7-10
Patience is a virtue proper to the restoration of the kingdom of God. It is not passive waiting or idleness, but rather calls for perseverance in the active work of healing through reconciliation.

Questions for thought discussion, and prayer:
1. Discuss the thoughts and feelings of John the Baptist in prison. What sort of faith does it take to remain detached from seeing the results of your lifetime dedication? What does this say to your own life?

2. Christmas is often an occasion to extend a hand to those who are in need. What can you do to continue that same spirit of service throughout the year?

THEY SHALL CALL HIM EMMANUEL

Gospel: Matthew 1:18-24

Christian tradition gives us several interpretations of the dilemma Joseph faced when he discovered Mary's pregnancy. His uprightness could be seen as devotion to Mary in not wanting to expose her to shame and disgrace. It could also be interpreted as devotion to the Jewish law in refusing to take a presumed adulteress as his wife. Finally, this uprightness could be a direct act of humility before God in hesitating to identify himself with what he perceived as the work of the Holy Spirit.

We need not decide which of these interpretations is correct — they all have some basis in tradition and some merit. However, if we consider the ambiguities in Joseph's dilemma that are common to all of these interpretations, we can find a mirror for our own Christian response to God's presence in life.

The heart of the matter — the area where Joseph can be our model — is his fidelity and openness to God's will within an uncertain situation. The Gospel message is often presented as bringing certainty to our questions and doubts, sometimes at the price of oversimplifying and distorting its meaning and creating a blind and false sense of security. Today's picture of Joseph groping and struggling is a healthy corrective model.

First Reading: Isaiah 7:10-14

Ahaz was the young king of Judah facing the threat of the northern kingdom of Israel allying with powerful Syria. His rule in danger, Ahaz was engaging in political manuevers for survival. Isaiah encouraged him to rely on God, not on other nations, for strength. The king was hesitant even to ask for a sign of God's favor. The prophet gave one anyway — a young maiden's child whose name would be "God with us." Most likely, this statement refers to Hezekiah, son of the king's wife, who would rule Judah, and would be a sign that God had not forsaken his people.

The import of the sign, then, is less a prediction of the virgin birth (the Hebrew words do not necessarily imply "virgin" in the strict sense) but an affirmation that the sign of God's care is already present. Ahaz need not look for special omens or portents. We too can find the same advice meaningful in our lives: look to the ordinary for the signs of God's saving presence.

Responsorial Psalm: Psalm 24 1-2, 3-4, 5-6
This psalm was sung by worshipers as they approached the temple in Jerusalem, the sign of God's dwelling among his people. Response: "Let the Lord enter; he is the king of glory."

Second Reading: Romans 1:1-7
The Christian community at Rome was composed primarily of Jewish converts whose families had migrated to Rome generations earlier. Paul had not yet visited the city when he wrote this letter, nor had he been involved in their conversion or instruction. In the introduction to his letter to them, which comprises our reading, he affirms his claim as an apostle to non-Jews in particular by pointing to the mission he shares with all apostles — to proclaim the Gospel. He also expresses the link between the incarnation and the paschal mystery: in Jesus, the Son of God became a man precisely to die and rise so that we might have life through him.

Questions for thought discussion, and prayer:
1.   Faith may be less a matter of certainty in truths than of steadfast trust in uncertainty. Discuss the pros and cons of that statement.

2.   How do you think Joseph felt in his dilemma? How can he be a model for your own life?

THE SOLEMNITY OF CHRISTMAS — YEAR A, B, AND C

THE BIRTH OF
THE UNCONQUERED SUN

The Birth of the Unconquered Sun was originally a pagan Roman feast celebrating mid-winter and looking forward to the lengthening of sunlight that would lead to spring. The transformation of this festival into the Christian celebration of the Incarnation was appropriate — the seasonal renewal of the sun speaks clearly of the birth of the True Light, Jesus Christ, the Word of God become one with us in flesh.

THE MASSES OF CHRISTMAS

Each of these Mass texts reveals a particular dimension of the mystery we celebrate on this day. Taken as a whole, they comprise a richly varied tapestry of faith and tradition. The VIGIL MASS sums up the spirit of Advent by addressing the human origins of Jesus as the fulfillment of the scriptural messianic hopes embodied in the history of the Jewish people. The MIDNIGHT MASS presents Christ as the light which dispels the darkness of the world. The MASS AT DAWN shows Jesus as God's savior sent for our sakes, while the MASS DURING THE DAY focuses on the incarnation as the fullness of God's Word become flesh among us.

* * * * * * *

VIGIL MASS

Gospel: Matthew 1:1-25

Matthew begins his Gospel by giving Jesus the title of Christ — the Messiah, the Anointed One — and therefore asserts that Jesus is the fulfillment of the messianic hopes of Jewish tradition. In this genealogy, which shows many traces of artificial construction, Matthew wants to demonstrate that Jesus is of the royal line of king David, and highlight the importance of Joseph in the lineage, even though he is not the father of Jesus in a physical sense.

Although ancestry is always traced through the male line, Matthew takes pains to include four women in his list. Each is a sinner or a foreigner: the incestuous and deceitful Tamar (v 3, see Gn 38); Rahab, the Canaanite prostitute (v 5, see Joshua 2:1-21; 6:22-25); Ruth, a young Moabite widow (v 5, see Ruth, especially 4:17); and Bathsheba, the adulterous wife of Uriah (v 6, see 2 Sam 11-12). It is not merely ancient sexist prejudice that prompted Matthew to include women in this way. He wanted to affirm the Jewish origins of Jesus, and yet show from Jewish history that God's promised salvation includes all, even those traditionally excluded: women, foreigners, sinners. As the Son of David, Jesus is at the same time truly one of us in being a son of sinners as well.

The outcome of Joseph's dilemma (vv 18-19 — see the Fourth Sunday of Advent, Year A) was that God clearly revealed to him that his role would be to give the child a claim to Davidic ancestry. V 25 affirms the virginal birth of Jesus, but has no bearing, one way or the other, on the Church's tradition that Mary remained perpetually a virgin.

First Reading: Isaiah 62:1-5

Just as the source of a bride's happiness is her husband's presence, so the happiness of God's city comes from the Lord's presence (vv 4b-5). The marriage-image of God and his people foreshadows both the perfect union of divinity and humanity in Christ himself, and the relationship of Christ to the Church as his bride.

Responsorial Psalm: Psalm 89:4-5, 16-17, 27, 29

This psalm elaborates upon God's promises to David (2 Sam 7:8-16) that we see fulfilled in Jesus Christ. Response: "For ever I will sing the goodness of the Lord."

Second Reading: Acts 13:16-17,22-25

Paul begins his sermon to the assembled Jews in Antioch by considering God's call of their ancestors to be his own people (vv 16-17) — a theme which echoes the first reading. Then he recalls the promises made to David (v 22) fulfilled in Jesus (v 23), and finally presents John the Baptist as the forerunner, calling people to prepare for Christ by change of heart (v 24). Aside from announcing the kingdom of God, John had no function on his own, and must of necessity yield to Jesus.

* * * * * * *

MIDNIGHT MASS

Gospel: Luke 2:1-14

The fact and meaning of the birth of Christ are more important than whether or not the historical details are accurate. Luke was more concerned with conveying the full reality and significance of the event than with reporting mere happenings. There is, for example, no other evidence of the world-wide census of v 1, but Luke's intention is not to talk about a census. He uses, or perhaps invents, this detail to emphasize that Jesus' messiahship follows and yet surpasses the line of king David. Absolute poverty, as a necessary condition for taking part in the kingdom of God, is constantly emphasized by Luke. The most ordinary and lowly persons and things — shepherds, stable, cloth wrappings — make up the sign of the most extraordinary event in history. As the human poverty serves to highlight the richness of God's power, so the darkness of night brings into relief the light-giving and glorious nature of this birth.

First Reading: Isaiah 9:1-6
  Among ancient peoples, darkness symbolized bondage and slavery — often the eyes of captives were put out, leaving them able to do heavy physical work, but making independent activity or escape impossible. Further, the land of the dead was called "sheol," which may be derived from a word meaning "dusk," and was certainly thought of as a place of shadowy, enslaved half-existence. Light, then, represented new life, and more importantly, liberation. The hoped-for liberator was given names which summed up the best qualities of past kings: "God-hero" and "Father-Forever" like David, who unified the nation through victorious struggles and established the royal dynasty from which the Messiah would come (v 5); "Wonder-Counselor" and "Prince of Peace" like Solomon, the wise king who brought peace and prosperity to the nation.

Responsorial Psalm: Psalm 96:1-2, 2-3, 11-12
  This psalm invites all peoples throughout the world to praise God's glory. Response: "Today is born our Savior, Christ the Lord."

Second Reading: Titus 2:11-14
  The first part of this chapter gives moral advice that any good teacher might have given in those days. But since the birth of Christ, all human values are elevated, and a morally good life becomes a witness to the presence of God. Moral living in itself has no value beyond the purely natural, but in God's power it is transformed into freedom from inner slavery and death.

* * * * * * *

MASS AT DAWN

Gospel: Luke 2:15-20
  This reading, which continues the passage from the previous

Mass, concentrates on the shepherds' discovery of the infant Jesus. The revelation of this birth is made first to the shepherds, who are not only poor, but also people who live on the fringes of society, and are rejected and ignored by "proper folk." In simplicity, the message is verified (v 18) and the value of the event is realized (vv 19-20). The poverty of Jesus' birth (and life) is not merely a quality to be admired, but a way of life to be put into practice in order to follow him truly.

First Reading: Isaiah 62:11-12

The coming of the Savior as bridegroom transforms the identity of his people. They are no longer "Abandoned" but "Cherished." A change in name signifies a real change in being. The new name in this reading, "Frequented," indicates an abundance of population — the full richness of humanity call to God's love.

Responsorial Psalm: Psalm 97:1, 6, 11-12

This psalm glories in the victory of the Lord over false gods and all forces of evil. Response: "A light will shine on us this day: the Lord is born for us."

Second Reading: Titus 3:4-7

The Lord's Spirit permeates our whole being, and so morality is not merely keeping rules, nor just a way to promote human well-being, nor even a way to please God, but rather it is the way to fulfill truly the will of God by being most fully what we are. By moral behavior and good works, we become perfected in what we already are — members of Christ's body — and this is fulfilled in eternity.

* * * * * * *

MASS DURING THE DAY

Gospel: John 1:1-18

"Word" means far more in this Gospel than it means in our common everyday language. So often, for us, a word is something empty and unreal. The world of media and advertising has cheapened words into near non-existence. Not so in the world of John, the author of this Gospel. The Greek world, to which John wrote, understood "word" as an idea communicated. A word is part of myself that I share with you. The Hebrew world, from which John came, added an element of challenge. A word not only communicates to me, it does something to me. It moves me. It has the power to change me.

The Word of God, therefore, is his perfect idea of himself — so perfect that we can in truth speak of it as having a personality in every way equal to God — God's perfect self-idea as communicated. Yet this Word must be clothed in language we can understand if the act of communication is to be complete. This language is humanity itself. And here lies the key to understanding the teaching that Jesus is both God and a man. If he were God alone, but only a make-believe man, the communication would be unreal. God, whatever of himself he might be sharing, would not be speaking our language, and we would not be able to grasp him. It would be an idea without a voice, or with a false voice. If he were only a man — even a very special, most perfect man, but not God — the communication would be empty. An eloquent voice, perhaps, but no content. Spend a lot of time with this reading. It is better understood if contemplated — allowed to penetrate mind and heart — rather than explained or analyzed.

First Reading: Isaiah 52:7-10
This reading reflects the power of the word in Hebrew understanding. The news of salvation does not merely speak about a fact, it makes the event itself happen. Thus, in the very telling and hearing of the word, "Your God is king," God is acknowledged and accepted as king, and his power transforms his people from ruin and destruction to victory and peace.

Responsorial Psalm: Psalm 98:1, 2-3, 3-4, 5-6
This hymn of praise celebrates the victory God has accomplished for his people. Response: "All the ends of the earth have seen the saving power of God."

Second Reading: Hebrews 1:1-6
The letter to the Hebrews looks back on all Jewish religious tradition and interprets it in the light of the event of Christ's coming. Its first part concentrates on the greatness of Christ which surpasses that of the angels (the greatest powers imaginable) and the Jewish patriarchs (the greatest human beings). This reading repeats in different words the same understanding given by the Gospel. Note especially the first part of v 3.

Questions for thought, discussion, and prayer:
1. Describe the particular character of each Mass as it sheds light

on the mystery of the Incarnation.

2.   Is your understanding of the meaning of Christmas any different after having studied these readings than it was before? In what ways?

FEAST OF THE HOLY FAMILY — YEAR A

FAMILY MODEL

Gospel: Matthew 2:13-15, 19-23
   Often Jesus, Mary, and Joseph are pictured as a "model" family in terms that impossible for any real family to identify with — the virginal relationship of husband and wife, a harmony unmarred by normal disagreements and tensions, and a child-God who never protested being washed behind the ears. The down-to-earth picture in this Gospel speaks directly to situations that are faced in some way by the majority of families in our society today: poverty, displacement, alienation, and fear. Joseph, Mary, and Jesus are a model family because they experienced the same struggles we encounter.

First Reading: Sirach 3:2-6, 12-14
   These teachings on family life reflect both the incomplete Jewish concept of afterlife and the culture of a primitive agricultural people. Respect for one's parents is the only way to promote the respect of one's children, and therefore to insure that one's name would live on in descendants. Further, only a family comprising several generations living in harmony has the inner resources to be an independent unit in a society. Cut off from one's parents or children, a major part of the support of life is gone, and chances of survival are less. Children were seen as a blessing because they contributed to the total resources of the family.

Responsorial Psalm: Psalm 128:1-2, 3, 4-5
   In this psalm prosperity is seen as the reward of virtue, but true prosperity lies not in worldly possessions but in peace of heart. Response: "Happy are those who fear the Lord and walk in his ways."

Second Reading: Colossians 3:12-21

The heart of this passage is the very first phrase — "you are God's chosen ones, now live accordingly!" All the practical advice that follows flows from this overwhelming realization. Unfortunately, the message we often convey to our children is just the opposite: by our attitudes and our actions we tell them that being good, or at least staying out of trouble, is more important than loving God. No wonder they reject us! Be on fire first with a sense of God's love, then you have the only solid foundation for morality. For a few words on vv 18-19, which can cause problems for our understanding today, see the comments on Eph 5:21-32, Twenty-First Sunday, Year B.

Questions for thought, discussion, and prayer:
1. What have we lost when individual families can seldom claim any support from a larger family unit?

2. Is it possible to avoid giving children the sense that they are a liability rather than an asset until they are grown and "on their own"?

SOLEMNITY OF MARY, MOTHER OF GOD, JANUARY 1 — YR A, B, C

THE EIGHTH DAY

Eight speaks of eternity. The seven days of the week signify natural completion of time, so seven-plus-one embodies the first and never-ending day of the fulfillment beyond time. It is, therefore, quite appropriate that the New Year should begin on the eighth day of our celebration of God become man with us. Today is also World Day of Prayer for Peace. The proper, official title of this day in the Church calendar is the Solemnity of Mary, Mother of God, a title which embraces all other titles and feasts of Mary, and defines her role in God's plan of salvation. As mother of Christ, she is therefore mother of the whole body of Christ, the Church.

Gospel: Luke 2:16-21

This is almost the same reading as the dawn Mass on Christmas, but the slight change in verse selection shifts the emphasis from the visit of the shepherds (introduced by v 15) to the life and mission of Jesus. The circumcision of v 21 signifies his participation in the covenant God had made with his people in ancient days and pledged his active cooperation as a Jew with God's power to renew all things. As Messiah, Jesus embodies all that it means to be a Jew and brings the covenant with God into a new dimension of universality, making God available to all people, not just a chosen race.

First Reading: Numbers 6:22-27

This blessing of vv 24-26 was usually spoken by the Hebrew priests over the people at the end of liturgical ceremonies. It implies both God's favor (v 25) and an active conformity to his will (v 26). In this reading it serves as a remembrance of Christ as the enduring blessing of God.

Responsorial Psalm: Psalm 67:2-3, 5, 6, 8

This psalm expresses the universality of God's saving love. Response: "May God bless us in his mercy."

Second Reading: Galatians 4:4-7

This message is put in simple terms, and yet is so difficult to grasp and realize. What Jesus Christ is, as the Son of God, his Spirit makes us to become.

Christian, recognize your dignity as a son or daughter of God . . and live in accord with it!

Questions for thought, discussion, and prayer:
1. How is Mary a sign of God's favor to all people?

2. Is this an appropriate feast for New Year's Day? Why or why not?

SOLEMNITY OF THE EPIPHANY — YEARS A, B, AND C

THE WISE STILL SEEK HIM

Gospel: Matthew 2:1-12

This story about the mysterious wise men fires up our imagination so that we often get lost asking unimportant questions about details rather than trying to understand the deeper meaning. Remember that these Gospel stories about Jesus' early life were recorded in the light of the experience of his death and resurrection, and took their final shape in the life of the early Church. Looking backwards, this story anticipates Jesus' rejection by the Jewish leaders contrasted with his manifestation to and acceptance by pagan peoples.

The prophecy quoted in v 6 (adapted from Micah 5:1 and 2 Sam 5:2) points to Jesus as fulfilling the messianic hope symbolized by king David. More significantly, the entire story echoes the coming of the Queen of Sheba to Solomon (1 Kg 10:1-13), and shows Jesus as the "new Solomon" whose wisdom draws even the wisest of the world to humble submission.

Second Reading: Isaiah 60:1-6
Jerusalem is situated on a hill above a deep valley (the Kidron Valley) to the east. Imagine the poet-prophet sitting on the Mount of Olives across the valley, watching the city glow radiant in the light of dawn. This passage was written during the restoration of the ruined city after the captivity in Babylon, and the prophet dreams that the former glory (vv 1-4) and prosperity (vv 5-7) — such as king Solomon had achieved — would again belong to the Jewish people. This dream was never fulfilled literally, but was more than fulfilled in reality by the coming of Christ.

Responsorial Psalm: Psalm 72:1-2, 7-8, 10-11, 12-13
This psalm looks backward to the reign of king Solomon, characterized by the greatest peace, prosperity, power, and justice Israel had ever known, and forward in hope to another king who would be like Solomon. Response: "Lord, every nation on earth will adore you."

Second Reading: Ephesians 3:2-3,5-6
The mission of the Church, to call all humankind into union with God, is called a "mystery" by Paul. Its truth is not immediately evident because different cultures and mentalities seek their own privilege and importance to the exclusion of others. God wills that these barriers be broken down, and all men and women without exception come to know his love. The Church's mission is not so much to guard the faith as to open up its treasures to all.

Questions for thought, discussion, and prayer:
1.   Contrast the wise with the powerful. How do the things they hold important influence (or control) their behavior? How do the things you hold important influence (or control) your behavior?

2.   Do you feel that your faith is a gift or an obligation? Do you feel it is your business alone, or something to be shared?

SECOND SUNDAY AFTER CHRISTMAS — YEARS A, B, AND C

THE WORD
DWELLING AMONG US

The Mass proper to the Second Sunday after Christmas is celebrated only when the Solemnity of the Epiphany remains on January 6 and falls on a weekday. In the United States, the Epiphany is always transferred to a Sunday, and so these readings will not be used. Nevertheless, a commentary on them is included for completeness and for their contribution to a fuller understanding of the mystery of the incarnation we celebrate in the Christmas season.

Gospel: John 1:1-18
See the commentary for Christmas Mass during the Day, pages 32-33.

First Reading: Sirach 24:1-4, 8-12
This beautiful hymn in praise of wisdom is similar to Proverbs 8, but wisdom is seen here more clearly in terms of God's presence among his people. Wisdom dwelling in a tent anticipates the language and imagery of Jn 1:14, and recalls the tabernacle or meeting tent of Ex 24 and 40 as the dwelling place of God. God's wisdom is identified with his word (vv 2-3), his creative power (vv 5-6), and his redeeming and loving presence (vv 8-12).

Responsorial Psalm: Psalm 147:12-13, 14-15, 19-20
This is the second part of a two-part psalm that praises God for his goodness toward the people he has chosen as his own. Response: "The Word of God became man, and lived among us."

Second Reading: Ephesians 1:3-6, 15-18
This blessing-introduction to this letter unfolds the theme of God's choice of a people being an act of sharing his wisdom with them. Jesus Christ is the unfailing sign that God has chosen us — all who believe in his name have that assurance as God's adopted children. And through Christ God enlightens us to realize the gift of his election and to understand its value.

Questions for thought, discussion, and prayer:
1.   What is wisdom? How is wisdom distinct from other qualities such as understanding or knowledge?

2.   What does your understanding of the meaning of "word" contribute to your understanding of Jesus?

FEAST OF THE BAPTISM OF THE LORD — YEAR A

FULFILL GOD'S COMMANDS

Gospel: Matthew 3:13-17
A comparison of the different accounts of Jesus' baptism in the four Gospels reveals the development of early Christian faith and understanding of the significance of this event in the salvific mission of Jesus.

In Mark, the earliest and simplest account, Jesus goes to John, is baptized by him, and at that point receives the Spirit of his mission (Mk 1:9-11).

Matthew's Gospel was written with a sharp eye toward discovering the roots of Jesus' messiahship in the Hebrew Scriptures. Mt 3:1-12 presents John the Baptist as the new Elijah who was expected to come before "the day of the Lord" (see Mal 4:5). John's garments and life-style recall what was remembered about Elijah's (see 2 Kgs 1:8). The dialog of vv 14-15 is Matthew's unique contribution to the baptism account. In the same breath it emphasizes the superiority of Jesus over John (and over the whole Jewish order) and shows Jesus' concern to respect and fulfill the Jewish law and practice.

Luke's story, written for Christians of non-Jewish origins, plays down the role of John in the baptism itself in order to emphasize the coming of the Spirit and the prayer of Jesus (Lk 3:15-22). The Gospel of John (1:29-34), focusing on the divine origins of Jesus rather than on his human or Jewish roots, alludes to Jesus' baptism by John, but avoids explicit mention of it.

First Reading: Isaiah 42:1-4, 6-7
The Spirit of Jesus' ministry, which the Gospels associate with Jesus' baptism in the Jordan, fulfills the role of the Spirit-filled servant in Isaiah. The people of Israel saw a reflection of their own mission to the world in this portrayal of the chosen servant, but we must see this image as a pale foreshadowing of the mission of Christ — and of the continuation of his body, the Church.

Responsorial Psalm: Psalm 29:1-2, 3-4, 9-10
This psalm meditates upon the power and glory of the Lord in the awesome natural forces of a violent storm. Response: "The Lord will bless his people with peace."

Second Reading: Acts of the Apostles 10:34-38
Peter's teaching to Cornelius and his family revolves around two main points: (1) progress from knowledge of Jesus to faith in him as the Anointed One (equals Christ equals Messiah); and (2) the portrayal of Jesus' Spirit and his resurrection as the pattern for the Christian's own possession of the Spirit and final resurrection.

Questions for thought, discussion, and prayer:
1. What do the symbolic elements of water, wind (or breath), and fire say to you?

2. Discuss the similarities between the working of the Spirit in Jesus' life as recorded in the Gospels, and in your own life.

YEAR A
LENT-EASTER SEASON

REND YOUR HEARTS
NOT YOUR GARMENTS

Gospel: Matthew 6:1-6, 16-18

The readings of Ash Wednesday establish the theme of Lenten penance — a call to interior conversion. The Gospel passage is from the sermon on the mount where Jesus reveals the basic ethic of his kingdom. His concern is to bring observance of the law from a mere external act into the inner realm of intention. Jesus' new commandments here are nothing more than an interiorization of the old. Almsgiving (works of charity), praying, and fasting are the three fundamental practices of any religious life, and they must spring from the heart and go hand in hand with each other. Almsgiving without prayer and fasting lacks a spiritual dimension. Prayer without fasting and charity is an exercise in self-expression, navel-gazing, or wishful thinking. Fasting without charity and prayer becomes self-centered physical conditioning.

First Reading: Joel 2:12-18

Almsgiving, prayer, and fasting are not purely individual religious matters. "Me and God" exercises quickly become egocentric. Our relationship with God is always mediated through the community, and anything that has to do with that relationship cannot escape being part of our relationship with our brothers and sisters. As a people, we do charity, we pray, and we fast together (vv 15-16). What we do in private, as the Gospel counsels, must serve to nourish our community activity as well as personalize it.

Responsorial Psalm: Psalm 51:3-4, 5-6, 12-13, 14, 17

The verses chosen from this great psalm of David's repentance emphasize the spirit of inner conversion as not only emptying oneself of sin but filling one with joy. Response: "Be merciful, O Lord, for we have sinned."

Second Reading: 2 Corinthians 5:20-6:2

The conversion-journey of catechumens preparing for Easter

initiation gives a foundation and motivation for the Lenten practice of the rest of the community. It is up to the already formed Christian community to accompany them on their journey, to welcome them, to give them an example of reconciliation (5:20-21), and to share a sense of urgency in responding to God's call (6:2).

Questions for thought, discussion, and prayer:
1. What sort of "Lenten penance" could both follow Jesus' command of secrecy and still benefit the whole Christian community?

2. What is the significance of ashes in expressing conversion?

FIRST SUNDAY OF LENT — YEAR A

SIN AND GRACE IN THE WORLD

Gospel: Matthew 4:1-11

Matthew's Gospel firmly roots the beginning of Jesus' ministry in Jewish history and tradition to show that in his person he sums up and brings to perfection all God's saving works of the past as well as the total human response to what God has done. Thus he is the new Moses, both as leader of God's people undergoing the forty-day fast (see Ex 34:28; Dt 9:9-18) and as representative of the people being tempted during their desert wandering.

The temptation to turn stones into bread recalls the Israelites' demand for food (Ex 16:1-3; Dt 8:2-5). In both instances, the real temptation is to settle for something less than the authentic nourishment found in the word and will of God.

The second temptation calls to mind the demands of the Israelites in the desert for a sign in Ex 17:1-7 (see also Dt 6:16; Num 14:22; Ps 95:9). In overcoming this temptation, Jesus shows that true confidence in God rises above the need for marvelous signs.

The third temptation is to replace the true God with earthly gods — that is, to settle for anything less than God himself. Read the injunctions against false worship in Ex 23:20-33; 34:11-14; Dt 6:12-15. These had to be repeated so often because the Israelites were continually compromising their worship of God by paying allegiance to the gods of their neighbors as well. Jesus rises above this, and reinstates the proper order of all reality — the Lord God is supreme above all.

These temptations represent all possible obstacles to Jesus' ministry, and show that through his life he was eminently successful in overcoming them. Lent is the time in which we prepare to welcome new life into the Christian community — the catechumens who today in the rite of election enter their final stage of preparation for baptism, confirmation, and eucharist at the Easter Vigil. Through our own renewal of life in penance, we join with the elect in appropriating this same victory over temptation and obstacles in our own lives.

First Reading: Genesis 2:7-9; 3:1-7

The basic temptation and sin of humankind, represented in the serpent and forbidden fruit, is attempting to achieve by one's own effort what is reserved to God, and thus setting oneself up as one's own god in opposition to him.

A fundamental pattern of human growth is reflected here: adolescent innocence passes to adult knowledge at the cost of transgression. This human predicament is at the heart of what we call original sin. In the pattern of salvation, we see God's action more as calling us back to a restoration of goodness rather than as simply preserving original innocence.

Responsorial Psalm: Psalm 51:3-4, 5-6, 12-13, 14, 17

This is David's song of repentance after he had sinned by the adultery with Bathsheba and the murder of Uriah (see 2 Sam 11-12) — a sinful act followed by a deceitful and violent cover-up, which reflects the pattern of the Genesis sin. Response: "Be merciful, O Lord, for we have sinned."

Second Reading: Romans 5:12-19

The effect of the primal sin is that we humans cannot break the hold of sin by our own efforts alone. Innocence lost cannot be restored except by God's intervention. We are chained and held captive by sin — our own and that of others — and we are powerless to break out. Jesus, in his own human life, did break this pattern by submission to the power of his Father, and he became the source of our ability to follow him in this submission and so to share in the same power. Adam, in his pride, represents our own impotence to overcome prideful self-centeredness. But Christ, as the new Adam, overcame temptation and thereby enables us to do the same.

Questions for thought, discussion, and prayer:
1. Even religious people are tempted to use God for their own ends. How can we recognize this tendency and overcome it?

2. Discuss what is meant by "reign of sin" and "reign of grace."

SECOND SUNDAY OF LENT — YEAR A

THE VISION

Gospel: Matthew 17:1-9

All the readings of the Sundays in Lent for Cycle A have particular significance in the preparation of the elect for baptism. In the primitive Church, as well as in the recently restored liturgy, Easter is the special time for the baptism of adults, and Lent is the period of final and intensive preparation. For those who are already Christians, Lent should be a time when we become more aware of our baptismal calling, and get ready to renew our baptismal commitment along with the newly initiated at Easter.

The transfiguration of Jesus describes in strikingly symbolic terms the awareness of Jesus' disciples of the true nature of his mission — not to be an earthly hero-messiah, but to be the source of final and eternal salvation to those who believe in him. The victory over the anti-mission temptations of last week's Gospel is here communicated to the disciples in a vision which looks forward to Jesus' final enthronement in glory.

The other Synoptic Gospels relate this same event with minor changes in wording (Mk 9:1-7; Lk 9:28-36). These variations indicate the particular emphasis each evangelist gives to the meaning of the event. In Matthew's narrative here, Jesus is portrayed as the new Moses. Writing for Jewish Christians, Matthew wanted to convince them that the law of Moses had been completed by the law of Christ. Details added by Matthew recall Moses on Mount Sinai: (v 1) six days later — Ex 24:15-16; (v 2) the radiance of Christ's face — Ex 34:29-35; (v 3) Moses is mentioned before Elijah. Also the voice from the cloud and the command of the Father recall the giving of the law to Moses on the mountain. Following upon the disciples' awareness of the true meaning and mission of Christ, there is only one obligation: "Listen to him!"

First Reading: Genesis 12:1-4

Abram came originally from Ur in the Chaldean land, present-day Iraq. It was then an extremely fertile area, and had one of the most advanced cultures of the day (17th century B.C.E.). Abram, the Father of the Israelite people, was called out of paganism to be the founder of a people faithful to the One True God.

Abram's name is significant: one whose father (Ab) is great (ram). God's call to him was to leave the greatness of his father's house, and to establish an even greater house. Thus, greatness is the theme of this blessing. This surpassing greatness of his descendants was fulfilled in the mission of Christ, to bring all peoples to share in God's glory.

Responsorial Psalm: Psalm 33:4-5, 18-19, 20, 22

This psalm gives voice to the loving and trusting response of one who has heard and answered God's call. Response: "Lord, let your mercy be on us, as we place our trust in you."

Second Reading: 2 Timothy 1:8-10

God's call is put in terms appropriate to second generation Christians, living a settled life in community under the leadership of an "overseer" ("bishop" translates to *episcopos* in Greek which means one who watches over). This call, which echoes the one to Abram, is not to a new land or a new people, but to a new life — a life made possible because Jesus has conquered death and holds out saving grace to all people.

Questions for thought, discussion, and prayer:

1. Why did Jesus resist Peter's desire to stay on the mountaintop? What does that say to our own desire to settle down and to stop growing?

2. How does God's favor transform us? And transform the world through us?

LIVING WATER

Gospel: John 4:5-42

This is the day of the first scrutiny of the elect preparing for Easter baptism. The purpose of this rite, celebrated publicly at Sunday Mass, is to assist the elect in their process of final preparation: Lent is their period of purification and enlightenment. They — and the whole Christian community with them — are invited to examine their lives in the light of this Gospel passage to discover new insight into what is weak and in need of strengthening, and what is strong in need of affirming. In short, we are asked to thirst for living water, and respond to Jesus' revealing and healing presence just as the Samaritan woman did.

There are several themes in this story that are woven together like multicolored threads in a beautiful fabric. Careful reading and attentive thought are needed to begin to discover its meaning.

Jesus, tired and hungry, asks his disciples for bread (v 8). When they bring it, he teaches them about the deeper nourishment of God's will (vv 31-34). Likewise he asks the Samaritan woman for water because he was thirsty (v 7) and then he tells her about his own living water (vv 13-14). Note that he offers eternal bread and living water only to those who seek bread and water for others — even for enemies (remember that as a Jew, Jesus was an enemy of the Samaritans). When we extend ourselves to fill others' needs, Jesus reveals himself through them (see Mt 25:31-46).

Jesus turns from the differences between Jewish and Samaritan forms of worship to speak of genuine worship in Spirit and in truth (vv 20-24), and he tells his disciples to look at the fields ready for harvest as a sign of the spiritual harvest of humankind ready for God's self-revealing love.

Finally, note that as the Samaritan woman gradually becomes aware of who Jesus is, she also becomes aware of her own identity (vv 16-19, 29, 39).

First Reading: Exodus 17:3-7

Jesus' presentation of himself as living water provides the link connecting this reading with the Gospel. The dissatisfaction and quarreling of the Israelites in the desert contrasts with the growth and acceptance of faith by the sinful Samaritan woman. "Massah" means "a testing" and "Meribah" means "quarreling." The attitude of the Israelites here is basically pagan: "What's the use of believing in God if he doesn't fill our needs?" In other words, testing God means trying to make him our own servant.

Responsorial Psalm: Psalm 95:1-2, 6-7, 8-9
This psalm is a call to praise God in joyful fidelity, aware that it is we who must be tested before him, not him by us. The concluding verses look back to the unfortunate incident in the desert of Israel's past as an example of how not to respond to God. Response: "If today you hear his voice, harden not your hearts."

Second Reading: Romans 5:1-2, 5-8
Chapter 5 is a transition section in this letter, summing up the doctrine of justification by faith which precedes it, and leading into the concrete demands of the Christian life which follow. Paul begins by considering our present experience of justification by faith as the source of peace and hope (vv 1-2). Then he finds in this present reality two signs of God's eternal love: the presence of the Holy Spirit, and Jesus' death for our sakes (vv 3-8).

Questions for thought, discussion, and prayer:
1. How does knowing Jesus help you to know yourself? How does knowing yourself help you to know Jesus?

2. What is the meaning of water in these readings? Discuss its significance in Scripture, in the sacramental life of the Church, and in your own life's experience.

FOURTH SUNDAY OF LENT — YEAR A

NOW I CAN SEE!

Gospel: John 9:1-41
This Gospel story, the healing of the man born blind and the ensuing controversy, parallels and develops the patterns of salvation and revelation we saw in last week's Gospel. Like the Samaritan woman, the blind man seems to have been in a position of pre-faith

— open to faith, but not yet knowing what direction to take or how to profess it. Note that the man does not even ask to be healed — Jesus does it on his own initiative. Restoration of physical sight is thus tte beginning of a process that leads to faith rather than the result of an act of faith. Note also the steps of that process: first, uncertainty (vv 11-12) followed by an unformed and indistinct faith — "he is a prophet, there is something special about him" (v 17); then, growth through common sense and struggle with adversity (vv 24-34); finally, Jesus himself leads him to a full profession of faith (vv 35-38).

The basic pattern shown here is that Jesus leads one who is open from the natural state of spiritual blindness to faith in him. This is contrasted with the willful lack of sight in others. Some, like the Pharisees, are so blinded by their own interpretations and ideas of self-importance that they fail to recognize the true light. But blind also are those, like the parents, who are afraid to "get involved" because the light is a threat to them — it means giving up something of their own security.

This story speaks to the progress of the elect who are celebrating the second scrutiny today in preparation for their Easter sacramental initiation: the healing touch of Christ is perceived first, then search combined with a struggle against adversity and rejection by the world, finally the full act of faith through baptism (v 13).

First Reading: 1 Samuel 16:1, 6-7, 10-13

This is a prophetic, and perhaps somewhat legendary, account of the beginning of David's reign through the anointing by Samuel. Later hindsight into God's dealings with his people would see the definitive hand of God in the events of David's succession to the throne of Israel. Saul had proven himself unworthy, and so God cut off his line of descendants and chose a new king — David. This account emphasizes that it was truly God's choice, not anyone else's, by the consistent rejection of the more promising brothers, and the final selection of the youngest and least of them. Subsequent history was to see David's reign as pregnant with meaning for the promised Messiah.

Responsorial Psalm: Psalm 23:1-3, 3-4, 5, 6

This psalm is one of the most familiar to all Christians, and picks up the theme of the shepherd in the first reading. The office of leadership of God's people, symbolized by a shepherd, is also a symbol of God's lordship. Response: "The Lord is my shepherd, there is nothing I shall want."

Second Reading: Ephesians 5:8-14
     The theme of light overcoming darkness is one of the most consistently recurring motifs in early Christian literature. The point emphasized by Paul here is that the traces of pagan living should not continue to find a place in the Christian lives of new converts. Baptism introduces an absolute break with the darkness of the past; there can be no question of looking back to past ways and habits. The new light does away with all darkness.

Questions for thought, discussion, and prayer:
1.   What is light? Discuss what light means to you. How is the cure of blindness like growth in faith?

2.   The Lord's ways are not our ways. Discuss how this statement is shown in these readings.

COME FORTH!

Gospel: John 11:1-45
     Today is the third and final scrutiny of the elect preparing for Easter baptism. Together with them, we examine our own lives in the light of the struggle between life and death, and the challenge to make Jesus' victory over death our own.
     Jesus is approaching the final journey to Jerusalem and his own death. The disciples seem quite hesitant to go with him, recognizing the danger (vv 8,12,16). Yet Jesus is intent on reaffirming life, and will show that death itself is the road to victory over death.
     Jesus' delay until Lazarus is dead emphasizes his power over death even when death has apparently won its victory. It is also paradoxical that Jesus' own death is hastened by his bringing Lazarus back to life (vv 46-53; 12:9-11).
     Although Jesus is completely in control of the situation, it is not easy. His emotions (v 33) may not be simply sympathy for Lazarus and his family, but more significantly, evidence that Jesus is also confronting the inevitability of his own death in much the same way that everyone must grapple with this ultimate reality. He does this again with greater immediacy and passion at Gethsemane.

Superficial human fascination might prompt us to ask, "What's it like to die and come back?" This sort of question is simply beneath consideration by John in his Gospel. In the light of the fulfillment of our relationship with Christ, to make decisions on a shallow idea of "what it's like" risks missing the whole point of "what it is." Christian life is not an "advance taste" of paradise, but rather a coming to grips with the meaning of life itself. Even in the grasp of death, Jesus is the source of life.

First Reading: Ezekiel 37:12-14

This brief passage concludes the famous vision of Ezekiel of the dry bones being covered again with flesh and restored to life (37:1-14).

The prophet was writing during the Babylonian exile, and the vision refers to the restoration of the people in their own land (centered on Jerusalem) upon their return from captivity. Secondly, from our perspective, the whole event of return from exile and re-establishment is a prefigure of the resurrection.

The breathing of the spirit into the dead recalls the gift of life in creation (see Gn 2:7) and looks forward to the fullness of the Spirit poured out upon the Church following the resurrection of Jesus.

Responsorial Psalm: Psalm 130:1-2, 3-4, 5-6, 7-8

This is a song of hope that has traditionally been associated with the funeral liturgy and the Church's prayer for the dead. Even in the midst of the "depths," faith still enables the believer to trust that God will fulfill the life that he has given. Response: "With the Lord there is mercy, and fullness of redemption."

Second Reading: Romans 8:8-11

The contrast between "flesh" and "spirit" is one of the key themes in Paul's thought (Rom 7-8; Gal 5:13-26).

"Flesh" characterizes the path of the self-sufficient person who refuses to look beyond what it perceptible to the senses. "Living according to the flesh" means taking oneself alone as the basic principle and goal of existence. It means isolation from God and therefore from true reality.

"Spirit" is looking beyond oneself and being open to communion with God. "Living according to the spirit" means accepting the presence and direction of God's Spirit, and therefore becoming one with true reality.

Questions for thought, discussion, and prayer:
1.   Put yourself in the place of the various characters in the Gospel story, and describe your feelings — the disciples, Mary, Martha, Lazarus, the bystanders, the enemies of Jesus.

2.   Discuss in the light of your own experience the meaning of "resurrection" in Christian faith; also the words "flesh" and "spirit" as Paul uses them.

PASSION/PALM SUNDAY — YEAR A

HOSANNA!

Gospel for the Procession with Palms: Matthew 21:1-11
     This Gospel passage tells of Jesus' final entry into Jerusalem to fulfill his messianic mission. He enters, not as a conquering hero, but in poverty — without kingly display and on a borrowed beast of burden, reflecting the quote from Zech 9:9. But it is clear that he is recognized as Messiah, and the branches and greeting (from Ps 118:26-27) speak of the glorious enthronement of God in the holy city (Jerusalem), which is one of the elements of the feast of tabernacles (booths) in Lv 23:40 and Neh 8:12-18.

Gospel of the Mass: Matthew 26:14-27:66
     The Passion according to Matthew. The word "passion" can signify both a deep, strong emotion and intense prolonged suffering. The root meaning of the word is "to undergo something."
     In this long narrative of Jesus' suffering and death, Matthew has two characteristics peculiar to his entire Gospel to watch out for: (1) he is more attentive to details than the other Gospels, and (2) the details are presented specifically as fulfilling the Hebrew Scripture. Writing for Jewish Christians, Matthew is always careful to present Jesus as the fulfillment of God's revelation in Jewish history.
     The "story line" of the passion narrative may be divided into four sections:

(1)   the Lord's supper and prayer in the garden (26:14-46);
(2)   the arrest, the religious trial, and Peter's denial (26:47-75);
(3)   the civil trial and the sentencing (27:1-31);
(4)   crucifixion and death (27:32-66).

First Reading: Isaiah 50:4-7

In Isaiah there are four "servant songs" which depict the Messiah as the faithful suffering servant of the Lord who is rejected by the people and yet saves them through that very act of suffering (Is 42:1-4; 49:1-7; 50:4-11; 52:13-53:12). Although the original intention was probably to identify a prophet or leader, or even the nation of Israel itself, as the servant, we can see the perfect fulfillment of these prophecies in Jesus Christ.

In this third song, the suffering servant speaks of his ability to endure pain and insults in his mission because of his trust in God's help and protection. This is not mere passive endurance but an active seeking of God's will and conformity to its demands of integrity and fidelity. Hearing God's word is the source of his strength (v 4), and this openness to God enables the true servant to see an echo of God's word in all events. (See also the first reading of the Twenty-Fourth Sunday of the Year.)

Responsorial Psalm: Psalm 22:8-9, 17-18, 19-20, 23-24

This prayer of a man oppressed by his enemies and feeling abandoned by everyone was on Jesus' lips in his final moments before death (Mt 27:46). The details of this psalm reflect the plight of the suffering servant in Isaiah, and strikingly prefigure some of the events of Jesus' passion. Two Gospels (Mt 27:46 and Mk 15:34) indicate that this psalm was on Jesus' lips as he hung on the cross. Note that the second part of the psalm (vv 23-32) expresses confidence and praise that God does hear those who call upon him. Response: "My God, my God, why have you abandoned me?"

Second Reading: Philippians 2:6-11

Paul quotes a hymn professing faith in the lordship of Jesus that was probably already familiar to his readers. He gives the passion (or better, passage) of Jesus as the pattern for Christians — Jesus emptied himself; God the Father raised him up, and enthroned him as Lord.

An overemphasis on the suffering of Jesus can lead us into a spiritual dead end. When reading or contemplating the story of Jesus' passion, we have to remember that we are looking through eyes that witnessed the resurrection as well. Pain in itself is purposeless. It takes on meaning only in view of a goal that rises above it. The passion can make sense only as the passage to new life. This reading lends perspective to Passion Sunday and Good Friday: we are not concentrating on death alone but on the mystery of life that overcomes death.

Questions for thought, discussion, and prayer:
1.   What is humility? How can Jesus' passion be a pattern for our own lives? How can your attitude be that of Christ?

2.   Discuss the qualities in persons you know that make them "servants of the Lord."

THE SACRED TRIDUUM

Easter does not happen without Good Friday. Conversely, the death of the cross leads to the resurrection without fail. The union of these two mysteries — death and resurrection — is not optional for the Christian. Their celebration together is at the very center of our faith and hope. Good Friday is not a dead end, and Easter's new life comes only at the end of the pathway of the cross. The Sacred Triduum — the three days beginning Holy Thursday evening — should be considered one feast, not three distinct feasts. The passage of Jesus Christ through death to new life is the fulfillment of many death-life passages in the history of the Jewish Scriptures, and is in turn the pattern for our own death-life passage.

* * * * * * *

HOLY THURSDAY: MASS OF THE LORD'S SUPPER — YEARS A, B, AND C

Gospel: John 13:1-15
      John's Gospel does not give the narrative of the institution of the eucharist, but does tell the meaning of it in Jesus' farewell words to his disciples (Jn 13-17). His crucifixion and death manifest his love of them "to the end" — and this very love is continued and shared through the eucharist. Jesus' washing of his disciples' feet serves as an introduction to his discourse — it is a summary which probes the heart of the eucharist: as I have done for you, you must do for others.

First Reading: Exodus 12:1-8, 11-14

The paschal lamb, whose blood is a sign and cause of salvation to all who partake of it, foreshadows the sacrifice of Christ, who leads his people to life through his giving himself up to death.

Responsorial Psalm: Psalm 116:12-13, 15-16, 17-18

This was the prayer of a faithful Jew who had recovered from a serious illness. The second part of the psalm speaks of how to return thanks concretely, and is an image of the eucharist (which means "thanksgiving"). Response: "Our blessing-cup is a communion with the blood of Christ." (See 1 Cor 10:16.)

Second Reading: 1 Corinthians 11:23-36

In recalling the words of Jesus, Paul emphasizes that when we celebrate the eucharist as he commanded, we are proclaiming the death of the Lord by uniting ourselves fully to him in his sacrificial death. The way we live our lives in union with him makes his sacrifice present to the experience of others.

Questions for thought, discussion, and prayer:
1. Reflect: often it is more difficult and challenging to allow oneself to be loved than it is to give love.

2. What does "remembrance" mean?

* * * * * * *

GOOD FRIDAY: CELEBRATION OF THE LORD'S PASSION — YR A, B, C

Gospel: John 18:1-19:42

The Passion according to John. In his narrative of Jesus' passion and death, John is less concerned with the details of Jesus' physical suffering than with those things which reflect his divinity and glory. In each stage, Jesus is shown to be fully in control of the course of events, actively giving himself rather than passively submitting. (This is not true of the other Gospel accounts.) The water and blood from Jesus' side represent the pouring forth of Jesus' life and spirit sacramentally (19:34) in eucharist and baptism, and its continuation in the Church, represented by the beloved disciple and Mary (19:25-27).

First Reading: Isaiah 52:13-53:12
        The fourth and most important of the servant songs presents the paradox of salvation: it is in the "affliction unto death" of the servant (representing the nation of Israel, Jesus, and the Church as well) that the overwhelming power of God becomes evident.

Responsorial Psalm: Psalm 31:2, 6, 12-13, 15-16, 17, 25
        This is a prayer of confidence in God's power to save even in the midst of terrible distress when that salvation is nowhere evident. Response: "Father, I put my life in your hands" (Lk 23:46).

Second Reading: Hebrews 4:14-16; 5:7-9
        Jesus Christ is the perfect mediator with God the Father because he partakes of both natures. He fully stands for humanity, and so is able to act in our name. Yet he is also united with God the Father, and is able to draw us into that union.

Questions for thought, discussion, and prayer:
1. In what ways can we say that we are healed by Christ's sufferings?

2. How are we "set free" by the cross and resurrection of Christ? (Fourth memorial acclamation of the eucharistic prayer of the Mass.)

* * * * * * *

THE EASTER VIGIL — YEAR A

There are seven readings from the Jewish Scriptures, and it is strongly recommended that all be proclaimed in a leisurely and reflective liturgy of the word. However, a minimum of three must be chosen. All of these readings recall the great events of God's saving power.
        Since the heart of the Easter Vigil celebration is the sacramental initiation of new Christians into the Church, it is important to explore the baptismal connotations of these readings. God continues his creative and saving action now through immersion into the death and resurrection of Christ symbolized by immersion into the baptismal waters.
        (1) *Genesis 1:1-2:2* — God's power is shown first of all in the

creative act, which is depicted as a victory over chaos and darkness. In the center of creation are man and woman in the image of God, and they are given the charge to care for and continue the work that God has done. In observing the seventh day as the sabbath rest, God's people imitate their Creator. This account makes no claims to be a scientific or historical description of the physical origins of the universe, but rather is a poetic celebration of God's life-giving word.

(2) *Genesis 22:1-18* — Abraham's sacrifice of Isaac is not an act of whimsy on God's part, but rather a strong manifestation of Abraham's faith that God is not capricious but is faithful to his word even in face of apparent contradiction. Note that God allows Abraham to go to the brink of the sacrifice before stopping him. Fidelity to God's word and will is no guarantee of comfort or certitude every step of the way, but we can be assured that the final outcome will be life-sustaining and humanly fulfilling.

(3) *Exodus 14:15-15:1* — The passage of the Israelites out of Egypt through the sea and into the land of promise foreshadows Christ's passage through death to his risen life, as well as the Christian's passage in faith from the darkness of sin though baptism to new life in Christ.

(4) *Isaiah 54:5-14* — The union of marriage is an image of God's love of his people. Not even sin can change God's love. God remains faithful, and sin evokes God's compassion and mercy more than his anger. This reading embodies the particular character of this night — to rediscover the signs of God's faithful and enduring love in the events of our heritage.

(5) *Isaiah 55:1-11* — God's gift of new life overwhelms us beyond our powers of comprehension. See the Eighteenth, Twenty-Fifth, and Fifteenth Sundays of Year A for a more detailed commentary on this reading.

(6) *Baruch 3:9-15,32-4:4* — We do not earn the new life that is God's gift, but we must live in accord with it. In knowing God, we touch the Source of all wisdom.

(7) *Ezekiel 36:16-28* — Ezekiel was a priest as well as a prophet — a rare combination at at time when priests were mostly temple functionaries more concerned with making a profit off the externals of sacrifice than with authentic worship. His prophetic book is filled with concrete images derived from liturgical worship. Here a ritual cleansing, looking forward to baptism, is seen to express a new spirit.

Reading from Christian Scriptures: Romans 6:3-11

Baptism is insertion into the death of Christ. It demands com-

mitment in faith to live in union with his death, and is therefore the
pledge of sharing the new life of his resurrection. (See the Thirteenth Sunday of Year A.)

Gospel: Matthew 28:1-10
Matthew's telling of the resurrection of Jesus makes conscious
use of the great manifestations of God in the Hebrew Scriptures —
earthquake, angel, terror — and so emphasizes that resurrection is
not merely survival after death, but a new order of being brought
about by the renewing action of God's power.

The Gospel accounts emphasize witness in describing the discovery of the resurrection. The early Church was faced with a need
to express these events clearly to give an account of their faith in the
risen Jesus. It could not be merely an invention of the women whose
only purpose was to care for the corpse. The words of the formula of
faith, "he has been raised up," are spoken by an angel, a messenger
of God, in Matthew. (Other Gospels leave the identity of the messenger more mysterious.) Witness of this is carried to the disciples
by the women, and they in turn carry it to the world (which in this
account may be symbolized by Galilee, hence the instruction to go
there).

Questions for thought, discussion, and prayer:
1.   How may the resurrection of Jesus be spoken of as a renewal of
creation?

2.   What is "passage"? Reflect on the meaning of this word for the
events of your own life.

EASTER SUNDAY — YEARS A, B, AND C

ALLELUIA!

Gospel: John 20:1-9
Throughout his Gospel, John calls attention to growth in faith
through a step-by-step encounter with Christ. In this account of the
resurrection, Peter and the disciple, thinking that Jesus' body has
been removed, rush to investigate the empty tomb. In seeing the cir-

cumstances, they begin to believe. But this faith has yet to be confirmed and deepened by a return to the Scriptures to see them in the new light of the Spirit, and completed in personal encounter with the risen Lord.

The Church and every Christian now have at their disposal two testimonies of the resurrection: the ancient Scriptures read now in and by the Church under the guidance of the Holy Spirit, and the witness of the apostles handed down in living tradition. Further, the Christian faithful encounter the risen Christ personally in the sacraments and in "the least of his brethren" (see Mt 25:31-46).

First Reading: Acts 10:34, 37-43

This is one of several discourses of Peter to Jewish crowds, showing how the apostles fulfilled the command to preach the Gospel. This sermon consists of a summary of the life, death, and resurrection of Jesus, with the conclusion that salvation comes through faith in him. Although the Gospels speak of Jesus rising from the dead by his own power, the Acts and the letters of Paul usually speak of God raising Jesus from the dead. (The references are quite extensive — Acts 2:24, 32; 3:15, 26; 4:10; 5:30; 10:40; 13:30-37: 17:31; Rom 4:24, 25; 6:4, 9; 8:11; 10:9; 1 Cor 6:14; 15:4, 12-20; 2 Cor 4:14; Gal 1:1; Eph 1:20; Col 2:12; 1 Th 1:10; 1 Pet 1:3, 21.) This is to emphasize that Jesus established the pattern of our own resurrection: we submit to the ultimate reality of death and it is God's power that raises us up.

Responsorial Psalm: Psalm 118:1-2, 16-17, 22-23

This is a hymn of thanks to God as Savior of his people, and it looks toward the enthronement of the Messiah as Lord for ever. Response: "This is the day the Lord has made; let us rejoice and be glad."

Second Reading: Colossians 3:1-4 or 1 Corinthians 5:6-8

Each of these readings, in its own different way, focuses on the new life that is God's gift in the resurrection. Colossians concentrates on the promise of future fulfillment in eternity. Corinthians on the change of heart that the presence of the risen Christ now requires. (It alludes to the matzo — unleavened bread — of the passover that was made in Jewish households after the last year's old yeasty dough fragments were thrown out as part of a ritual spring cleaning.)

Questions for thought, discussion, and prayer:
1.   How can we give witness to the resurrection by our actions?
Can you give examples of how others show the risen Christ in their
lives?

2.   What is faith? Why does God expect faith? Wouldn't it be better
if the evidence of Christ's resurrection were clearer and more convincing?

AS THE FATHER
HAS SENT ME . . .

Gospel: John 20:19-31
The risen Jesus appears in a new form of existence. His
"glorified body" is presented as not having the physical limitations
of the human body, and yet is truly physical and can be touched.
However, the Gospel writers do not show Jesus as merely proving
his resurrection by his presence, but as leading his disciples into
deeper faith and understanding in preparation for their going forth
to establish the Church. In commissioning them to continue his mission, he is empowering them to make him present in body to all
peoples of all ages.
The peace of Jesus' greeting is the commonly used Hebrew
word, "Shalom." He speaks it, however, as far more than a mere
greeting ("my peace, not as the world gives it," Jn 14:27). Jesus'
"Shalom" is his promise that his Spirit will restore order and harmony to all creation (Jn 14:26).
The Church commonly holds this imparting of the Holy Spirit
(vv 22-23) to be the institution of the sacrament of penance. But
more than that, Jesus shares the fullness of his victory over evil and
sin with his disciples. In the power of the Spirit, we become able to
carry out his command: "As the Father has sent me, so I send you"
(v 21). Jesus intends those words literally, but it takes strong faith
for us as Christians to recognize our own dignity in them, as well as
the dignity of our brothers and sisters.
Jesus seeks the disciples' faith (vv 20, 26-29), but also em-

phasizes that faith is more than merely seeing and touching his glorified body. Faith sees the presence and work of Christ in his people, the Church.

The manifestation of Jesus to Thomas, who wanted proof, had deep significance as the concluding incident of John's original Gospel (chapter 21 is a later appendix). Faith cannot be proven by external convincing evidence. Instead, it comes only as a gift to those who seek it. Faith is born and grows through an understanding of the Scriptures and a personal encounter with Christ in the life of the Church. The Church, in proclaiming faith in Jesus as risen Lord can point only to the witness of our heritage and our present life.

Note that in John's Gospel there is no record of a departure or ascension. John wished to emphasize that it is the same risen Christ who continues to live and work in his Church throughout all time.

First Reading: Acts 2:42-47
During Easter season each year, the first reading is from the Acts of the Apostles rather than from the Jewish Scriptures. In this book, the Holy Spirit is seen forming the early Christian community after Christ's image.

This reading tells of the shared life of the early Jerusalem community. We see the beginnings of the Mass in the twofold religious act of going to the temple (for Scripture and prayer — the remote origin of our present-day the liturgy of the word) and breaking bread (the eucharist) at home. The witness of their lives of love and praise in the Spirit was itself a drawing power for others (v 47).

Responsorial Psalm: Psalm 118:2-4, 13-15, 22-24
This hymn of praise recounts God's deliverance of his faithful servant from death, and sings to God's glory. Vv 22-24, while referring to the oppressed nation of Israel directly, also gives a beautiful summary of God's power raising Jesus to life and establishing him as Lord of all creation. Response: "Give thanks to the Lord for he is good, his love is everlasting."

Second Reading: 1 Peter 1:3-9
The entire letter of 1 Peter may have been a baptismal instruction for newly baptized Christians in the early Church. These verses, which quote a hymn (vv 3-5), clearly indicate that baptism is a rebirth into the life of the risen Christ, which commits us to share in his death by the trials we endure (vv 6-7), but to do so joyfully because of the promise of salvation. Vv 8-9 reflect the faith Jesus

speaks of to Thomas in the Gospel (Jn 20:29). We will continue reading from this letter throughout Easter season this year.

Questions for thought, discussion, and prayer:
1.   How is faith in the risen Jesus manifested in the community life shared by Christians? How do forgiveness and mutual support express and deepen faith?

2.   In the light of these readings, discuss what might be the greatest gift of the Holy Spirit.

THEY RECOGNIZE HIM IN THE BREAKING OF THE BREAD

Gospel: Luke 24:13-35

In Luke's Gospel, the miraculous aspect of the resurrection is almost taken for granted. The women (vv 5-8), the two disciples (vv 25-26), and the Eleven (vv 38, 44-45) are chided for not having expected it, so obvious and inevitable was God's plan. For Luke, as for John, the Christian life is a day by day continuation of the power of the resurrection.

This event reflects the pattern of developing faith through instruction, a faith that is climaxed in the recognition of Jesus in the eucharist. It is idle to speculate whether what Jesus did in vv 30-31 was really the eucharist. The point is that Luke saw this as reflecting the ordinary experience of the Christian — in the breaking of the bread we come to know Jesus.

One does not keep this knowledge merely to oneself. Once their eyes were opened, the disciples had to share it in joyful praise with the others (vv 33-35). And in their returning to share what they received, all were led to a still deeper understanding (vv 36-39).

First Reading: Acts 2:14, 22-28

Eight missionary sermons by the apostles are recorded in Acts. This is the first one given by Peter to the crowds on Pentecost. It is interesting to compare these sermons with one another (to Jews —

2:14-41; 3:12-26; 4:9-12; 5:29-32; 10:34-43; 13:17-41; to Gentiles — 14:15-17; 17:22-31.) They all have nearly the same basic structure: (1) an introduction, (2) an account of Christ's death and resurrection seen as fulfilling Hebrew Scriptures, (3) a proclamation of Christ's enthronement as Lord, and (4) a summons to conversion. Note that the heart of these sermons is already found in the instructions of Jesus to the two disciples in the Gospel reading, Lk 24:25-27.

In referring to the Hebrew prophecy, Peter is not interested in proving the resurrection as a fact — this is done by living witnesses (v 32). The Christian life itself, lived under the power of the Spirit of the risen Christ, is the proof. Peter seeks rather to clarify its meaning. The resurrection of Jesus truly fulfilled the messianic hopes of God's people, and so fulfills his promises to us.

Responsorial Psalm: Psalm 16:1-2, 5, 7-8, 9-10, 11

This psalm is an expression of king David's own commitment to the Lord who had chosen him and established his throne. As David is a "preview" of Christ, this psalm, quoted in the above reading from Acts, vv 25-28, is fittingly placed in the mouth of Christ as well as his followers. Response: "Lord, you will show us the path of life."

Second Reading: 1 Peter 1:17-21

The key to this passage is the preceding verse (v 16): "Be holy, for I am holy." As Christians, we are not holy by our own effort or merit, but solely on account of Christ, in whom we have been reborn through baptism. What we are unfolds, then, in what we do.

This passage alludes to the passover ritual of the Jews, in which the blood of the lamb was the price (or condition) of their deliverance from slavery in Egypt.

Questions for thought, discussion, and prayer:
1. How does the presence and power of Christ in the eucharist relate to the other ways he is present — in his people, in his word, in those who serve others?

2. How does your own awareness of the risen Christ influence your life?

MY SHEEP RECOGNIZE MY VOICE

Gospel: John 10:1-10

This Sunday may be called "Good Shepherd Sunday" because the Gospel selections for all three years of the cycle come from Jn 10, in which Jesus compared his own ministry to the work of a shepherd. For now, read the whole chapter to get a complete picture.

In response to the objection of the Pharisees to Jesus' challenge to their self-importance in 9:40-41, Jesus alludes to the role of the shepherd and gives criteria for true authority: (1) his followers recognize him (10:1-10); (2)   he gives his life for them and they are united to him (10:11-18 — next year's reading); and (3) this recognition by faith is God's gift (10:27-30 — following year's reading).

In this passage, the true shepherd is contrasted to a thief. The oriental custom was for several flocks belonging to different shepherds to share the same grazing land, and to be put into a common enclosed area for the night, so they could all be watched by one shepherd while the others slept. In the morning, the sheep would recognize their own shepherd by voice, and each flock would gather naturally around him, to be led out to pasture. A thief, however, could only break in and steal — no sheep would recognize and follow him.

In changing the image to compare himself to the gate, Jesus describes the results of confidence in his authority. There is only one gate to the safe enclosed area where the sheep are protected. Therefore, it is easy to guard, and only legitimate shepherds can gain access. Jesus is the only one who can delegate others to care for his flock in his name. Thieves can get in only by violence — breaking down the walls. They may be recognized for what they are by their ambition and deceit.

First Reading: Acts 2:14, 36-41

Today's reading continues the first missionary sermon of Peter to the crowds of Jews on Pentecost, which we began last Sunday. The invitation to put faith in Jesus as Messiah (v 36) leads to the question of what to do about it (v 37). Peter's answer (v 38) reflects the process of initiation as developed in the early Church, and re-emphasized today in the restored rite of adult initiation. (1) Faith leads to a change of heart, which must be tested by a sincere reform of life. (2) The outward expression of faith, ratified by the acceptance of the Christian community and by the power of God, is baptism in the name of Jesus for the forgiveness of sins. (3) The gift of the Holy Spirit confirms the follower of Christ in the life of the "promise" (v 39) because he orients the believer to participation in the life and mission of the community of Christ's body. (4) The center of this life is participation in the eucharist — thanksgiving and praise in the "breaking of the bread" (vv 42-46).

Responsorial Psalm: Psalm 23:1-3, 3-4, 5, 6

Recall that David was a shepherd boy before his call to be a warrior-king (1 Sam 16), and even in his military and political exploits he preserved a shepherd's simplicity and perspective. Response: "The Lord is my shepherd: there is nothing I shall want."

Second Reading: 1 Peter 2:20-25

Many early Christians were from the poor and oppressed classes, and they were exhorted to take Christ's submission to violence as their example. This was not to condone unjust institutions of slavery and oppression, nor was the intention to propose a non-violent plan to reform society. The counsel concerns instead the individual's own way of living within a situation he or she cannot change. The challenge of the risen Christ to the Christian community is to transform the world, but this can be accomplished only if the individual accepts the challenge to live as Christ in his or her own circumstances.

Questions for thought, discussion, and prayer:

1. How are you healed by Christ's wounds?

2. Does the image of a shepherd still speak to our society today? What other images could be used?

I GO TO PREPARE A PLACE FOR YOU

Gospel: John 14:1-12

Today, and for the next few weeks, we shall read excerpts from John's account of Jesus' farewell teaching at the last supper, in which he speaks about his continued presence with his disciples.

Reference to the many dwelling places of the Fathers's house emphasizes his desire to be with us, to make his abode in our hearts if we allow him. "Place" is less a physical location than the sense of "room": God has room in his life for us; what sort of room do we make for him?

Thus Jesus as the "way" is the perfect pattern of one who has made room for God in human life. Jesus in his humanity fully acknowledged and accepted the presence of divinity in him to the point of total self-giving.

Thus we can come to the Father only by following his way. "Way" is not so much a "road" or a "path" as a "manner" or "ability." Jesus is saying, "I have submitted to God the Father; this is how you do it. You can do it, for I am with you."

Just as the faithful servant reflects his master, a faithful lover reflects his beloved, or a child reflects the parent, so Jesus reflects the Father perfectly. Jesus, the Son of God, is not the Father, and yet can say, "The Father and I are one."

First Reading: Acts 6:1-7

The perfect unity of the early Jerusalem Christian community (2:42-47; 4:32-35) was perhaps more idealized than real. This section reveals developing tensions and jealousies between Christians of differing Jewish origins. There were probably many unrecorded conflicts, also painful, that had to be solved in the power of the Spirit. Note that the authority of the Twelve is clearly recognized, but was exercised communally, with the community's acceptance. This passage also shows a developing diversity of ministry. Those with different gifts complement each other rather than compete.

Responsorial Psalm: Psalm 33:1-2, 4-5, 18-19
This is a song of trusting praise — the Lord has been faithful in the past, and so he will continue to be faithful. He recognizes his own, those who hope in him, and will preserve them in sharing his life. Response: "Lord, let your mercy be on us, as we place our trust in you."

Second Reading: 1 Peter 2:4-9
This section forms the introduction to the practical considerations of the Christian way of life in the light of Christ's resurrection.
The "living stone" (v 4) alludes to the first covenant, founded on Mount Sinai which could not be approached under pain of death (Ex 19:23). As the chosen people of the old covenant were established upon Sinai, so the chosen people of the new covenant are founded upon Christ (vv 9-10). The other allusion, which corresponds to the Gospel reading, is that of God's dwelling, no longer centered in a stone temple, but now is the temple of the spirit, the heart that accepts God's presence as Christ did.

Questions for thought, discussion, and prayer:
1. How do we see the Father in Christ? Where do we now see Christ?

2. How can we learn from the experience of the Church through history to handle the conflicts within the Church today?

SIXTH SUNDAY OF EASTER — YEAR A

IF YOU LOVE ME, OBEY . . .

Gospel: John 14:15-21
Love unfolding itself in action is the heart of this reading's message. Obedience as the sure sign of love (vv 15, 21) reflects God's command in the Jewish Scriptures (Dt 6:4-6; 11:1). Jesus here is actually demanding the same sort of love from his followers that God deserves.
The word "paraclete" of v 16 has a number of meanings, all of which convey the idea of someone who represents — or even con-

tains in some way — another person, as an advocate, spokesperson, teacher, or witness. "Another Paraclete" expresses a continuity between the activity of Christ and of his Spirit in the Church. What Christ accomplished, his Spirit would continue.

The return of Jesus in vv 18-19 is not so much the promise of his return in fullness at the end of the world, but his continued presence within his Church. This presence will be expressed and realized by his faithful disciples, but not seen nor understood by those who have no faith and are "of the world." Thus, in ordinary life, the Christian experiences union with Christ, just as Christ is one with the Father (v 20). The bond of this union is love: the love of God, which is the Spirit, and the corresponding love of the disciple, which is obedience.

First Reading: Acts 8:5-8, 14-17

In Luke's story of the step-by-step spread of the faith from the first Jerusalem community to the entire world, the conversion of the Samaritans is a logical intermediate stage. They were of Jewish origin, but regarded as heretical traitors, and therefore could be considered "half-Gentile." The preaching of Philip (himself a Greek-Jewish convert, and a deacon, see 6:5) and the signs which accompanied his message inspired in the people a rather emotional manifestation of faith (v 8) and triumphantly overcame a blatant display of magical opposition (vv 9-13).

The laying of hands by Simon Peter and John (vv 14-16), although reflecting something of the origins of confirmation and/or "baptism in the Holy Spirit," was mainly a sign of the acceptance of the Samaritan Christian community by the Jerusalem community, which would of course involve a sharing or recognition of the same Spirit. (Acceptance into the fullness of the life of the Spirit-filled community by the bishop is the foundation of confirmation as a sacrament.)

This incident shows the unifying gift of the Spirit as promised in the Gospel overcoming natural enmity to unite diverse and hostile people as one in Christ. It must have taken considerable courage for the apostles to take this step because they probably faced strong opposition from many Jewish Christians.

Responsorial Psalm: Psalm 66:1-3, 4-5, 6-7, 16-20

This psalm commemorates the deliverance of Israel from her enemies, and witnesses to all nations the Lordship of Israel's God. Response: "Let all the earth cry out to God with joy."

Second Reading: 1 Peter 3:15-18
The hope of the Christian should be evident by his or her life-style. Are we today noticeable in society by the goodness of our lives? And further, how ready are we to give an account of just what and why we believe? Defensiveness and argumentation about religion accomplish little, but we should be ever ready to present a good explanation of what we believe to those who are searching for faith.

Questions for thought, discussion, and prayer:
1. Discuss the relationship between love and obedience.

2. How can you give an account of your faith and hope in Christ?

THE SOLEMNITY OF THE ASCENSION — YEAR A

I AM WITH YOU

Gospel: Matthew 28:16-20
Through his death-resurrection passage, Jesus has been given lordship over heaven and earth by the Father. In turn, he shares this power with the Church, the community of his disciples. The early Church was very conscious that it was living and acting, growing and expanding by the power of the risen Jesus.

Baptism is entry into the new mode of life of the risen Lord. A person passes through the waters of Christ's death-passage to share his Spirit and power. Baptism "in the name" of the three Divine Persons is not just a formalized invocation of them, but a making present of their life and power. Baptism immerses the Christian into the life-sharing relationship of the Father, Son, and Spirit.

The presence of Jesus makes effective the whole life and activity of the Church. In the power of Jesus, Christians live in a way that attracts and forms disciples. In his power they go forth and make him present in the world.

First Reading: Acts 1:1-11
The Ascension is seen in the Christian Scriptures as the point of transition from Christ's activity as Savior to the continuation of

his mission by his disciples as the "saving community."

Both the conclusion of Luke's Gospel and the beginning of his Acts of the Apostles narrate the same event, but each has a different emphasis. Both stress the witness of the apostles to continue throughout the world what Jesus began in Jerusalem. The Gospel account, however, looks back to the death and resurrection of Jesus as the content of this witness, and penance and forgiveness of sins as the result (Lk 24:46-48). The book of Acts looks forward to the coming of Christ in fullness (the restoration of Israel) as the content, and the fulfillment of God's rule over humanity as the result (vv 6-8).

Luke's Gospel account ends on a note of joyful resolution — as a result of the Ascension of Jesus, the apostles are depicted in almost "happy-ever-after" terms (Lk 24:53). The beginning of Acts, however, is filled with tension and anxiety to get about the business of witnessing — "why do you stand here?"

Responsorial Psalm: Psalm 47:2-3, 6-7, 8-9

This processional song of exaltation proclaims God's rule over all the peoples of the earth Response: "God mounts his throne to shouts of joy; a blare of trumpets for the Lord."

Second Reading: Ephesians 1:17-23

The Ascension celebrates the exaltation of Christ rather than merely his departure. Enthroned at God's right hand, he is more than just the object of our worship — he is the source of our new creation. His position is not so much that of domination as that of sharing life.

Questions for thought, discussion, and prayer:
1. What does this feast mean to you?

2. Are you more comfortable thinking of Christ as exalted Lord whom you worship, or as the head of the body of which you are a member? Why?

SEVENTH SUNDAY OF EASTER — YEAR A

THE GLORY OF THE LORD

Gospel: John 17:1-11

Jesus' farewell words to his disciples in John's Gospel conclude in chapter 17 with a prayer for them and for all believers. The "glory" Jesus speaks of is the fulfillment and manifestation of God's work in the world. Thus, in doing God's will, he does not merely give God glory, but that very action is God's glory because it can be accomplished only by God's power. Glory is the passage of Jesus through death to resurrection.

The faith of the disciples leads them to share in Jesus' glory — God's power enables them to follow Jesus in his death and so into his resurrecion. This is the road to belonging to Christ and to the Father.

First Reading: Acts 1:12-14

These few lines depict the interval between Jesus' ascension and the coming of the Holy Spirit as a time characterized by unity and prayer. The upper room appears to have been a sort of headquarters during this time, and the number one hundred and twenty gathering there (v 15) shows that there must have been a lot of coming and going. Their attitude seems to have been one of alert confidence rather than fear, as they had before (see Jn 20:19).

Luke's emphasis on Jerusalem as their gathering place and the spread of the word from there after Pentecost, seems to reflect the role of Jerusalem a the center of the restored universe in Isaiah 60 and Psalm 87.

The prayer of the disciples is one of watchful and active searching for God's will and saving power in the real events, rather than mere passive waiting for God to do something.

Responsorial Psalm: Psalm 27:1, 4, 7-8

This psalm reflects the trustful seeking that would have been the prayer of the disciples before Pentecost. Response: "I believe that I shall see the good things of the Lord in the land of the living."

Second Reading: 1 Peter 4:13-16

Persecution is the lot of anyone who makes Christ center of his or her life. As Christ suffered, we should expect the same. This type of suffering, however, is not punishment, but purification. "Fire" in Scripture usually conveys a purifying action — as the refiner's fire separates the slag from the pure metal.

Questions for thought, discussion, and prayer:

1. What does the word "glory' mean to you?

2. How can Jesus' prayer be a model for your own prayer?

THE SOLEMNITY OF PENTECOST — YEARS A, B, AND C

THE FIRE OF GOD'S SPIRIT

On Pentecost, we Christians celebrate the final day of the great feast of Easter, the day marked by the coming of the Holy Spirit upon the apostles to empower them to continue and bring to completion the work of Christ. The ancient Jewish feast of pentecost foreshadowed this Christian feast as the commemoration of the giving of the law on Mount Sinai. For the faithful Jew, observance of the law was the way of fulfilling the covenant (celebrated at passover) in daily life.

One set of readings is given for the evening before the feast itself (the vigil), and these convey a sense of anticipation. The readings of the feast day speak of fulfillment. Our consideration of all the readings will enable us to see the theme of Pentecost completeness developed in them. Jesus' resurrection from the dead, enthronement at the Father's right hand, and sending of the spirit are all aspects of one saving act of God. The new life of glory that belongs to Jesus in his resurrection is ours through the coming of the Spirit.

VIGIL MASS

Gospel: John 7:37-39

Jesus is the pivot point of history, the fulfillment of all past expectation (v 38), who promises to be the source of life for all time. Note in v 39 that the Gospel author connects the resurrection and glorification of Jesus with the coming of his spirit — the Spirit is the gift of Jesus who passed through death, and is raised to glory. By the power of the Spirit, the disciple becomes a source of living water (living water means the saving word) just as Christ himself (see 4:14).

Chapters 7 and 8 in John (except for the adulteress story, which was added later) form one unit culminating in Jesus' clear statement of his divinity in 8:58.

First Reading: there is a choice among four.

Genesis 11:1-9 depicts the fragmentation and alienation in human relationships that comes as a result of greed and self-interest. The confusion of tongues symbolizes the deeper disunity of heart caused by sin, while the many tongues of Pentecost (Acts 2:5-12) signal the unity of humankind restored in the Spirit.

Exodus 19:3-8, 16-20 recalls the Hebrew origins of Pentecost, the command to live in accord with the Covenant. This is not an order expecting blind obedience or an empty hope, but is based on the experience of God's having already shown his saving love to his people.

Ezekiel 37:1-14, the famous vision of the dry bones being joined together again and enfleshed with new life, speaks of restoring the unity of the Israelite nation, which had become disintegrated and corrupt. However, we can see the fulfillment of this strikingly vivid image in the new life of the risen Christ that is the Spirit's gift to humanity. (See also the commentary of the first reading for the Fifth Sunday of Lent, Year A.)

Joel 3:1-5 paints a different and more personal picture than Ezekiel. The action of God's Spirit lifts his people out of the ordinary, and challenges them to face the fullness of God's work.

Responsorial Psalm: Psalm 104:1-2, 24, 25, 27-28, 29, 30

Different verses from the same psalm are chosen for the vigil and the feast day. The psalm, a hymn of praise to God for the creative work of his Spirit, depicts the goodness of creation, summed up in life and nourishment, as speaking of renewal in God's Spirit. The verses chosen for the vigil emphasize the hunger of God's people for the life he gives them. Response: "Lord, send out your Spirit, and renew the face of the earth."

Second Reading: Romans 8:22-27

Our present condition of weakness and lack of perfection gives evidence of our need for redemption. But the life of the Spirit enables us to rise above these present limitations, and so his activity is the guarantee of future fulfillment. The Spirit is also the source of our prayer, the only sure foundation from which we can address God. We have now, imperfectly and initially, what will be fulfilled and perfected in eternity.

MASS OF THE DAY

Gospel: John 20:19-23

John portrays Jesus giving his promised gift of the Spirit in the evening of the day of his resurrection, and thus shows clearly that the Spirit is the fulfillment of the presence of the risen Christ in his followers. The Spirit is to continue Jesus' mission of reconciliation, the heart of which is not preaching, but living what one preaches — in a word, forgiveness.

This forgiveness of sins should not be taken in a narrow legalistic sense, but should be seen as the entirety of God's saving power which is his gift to the Church. The Christian community's success or failure will be measured only by the degree to which its members are reconciled to one another — in other words, love. Forgiveness is the catalyst that enables reconciliation and love to happen.

We are not vending machines for God's forgiveness. Our forgiveness of one another is the perceptible and genuine sign that God's forgiveness is happening. This unconditional love and forgiveness is the distinguishing mark of a true Christian (Jn 13:34-35) because it is beyond unaided human powers (Mt 5:38-48) and therefore is a sign of the Spirit's presence. Forgiveness and love are not merely ethical precepts, they are the overflow of the new life that is God's gift.

First Reading: Acts 2:1-11

Just as the Jewish feast of Pentecost, celebrated fifty days after Passover, was seen as the completion of the covenant, so the coming of the spirit is celebrated as the completion of the new covenant accomplished in the Easter mystery of Jesus' death and resurrection. As narrated in Acts, the Holy Spirit is the source of the mission of witness to the resurrection and lordship of Jesus, which characterizes the entire life of the Church. In graphic and symbolic detail, this passage emphasizes the power of the Spirit impelling the disciples to go forth and preach the Word of Life to all people (v 4), and the universal effect of their mission (vv 5-11). With good reason the

Acts of the Apostles is sometimes referred to as the "Gospel of the Holy Spirit."

Responsorial Psalm: Psalm 104:1, 24, 29-30, 31, 34
These verses simply praise God for his eternal deeds, and thus foreshadow the new creation in the Spirit. Response: "Lord, send out your spirit, and renew the face of the earth."

Second Reading: 1 Corinthians 12:3b-7, 12-13
The diversity of gifts is not only the source of our glory as a Christian community, but unfortunately is also the reason why we need reconciliation — it is difficult to recognize and accept another's uniqueness as a gift. Often we view others' gifts with suspicion as a threat to our own. The Spirit gives this diversity of gifts (v 11), and we must allow the Spirit to open our eyes to see the unity in this diversity, and to proclaim the lordship of Jesus (v 3).

Questions for thought, discussion, and prayer:
1. How do you recognize the Spirit's activity in the Church? in your own life? in the lives of others?

2. How are peace and forgiveness important characteristics of the Christian life?

SOLEMNITIES OF THE LORD FOLLOWING EASTER SEASON

SOLEMNITY OF THE HOLY TRINITY — YEAR A
(SUNDAY AFTER PENTECOST)

FATHER, SON, AND SPIRIT

Gospel: John 3:16-18
This brief section is from the dialogue of Jesus with Nicodemus, which unfolds the relationship of baptism to faith. Read all of chapter 3 carefully to get the context. (It is likely, though not certain, that vv 13-21 are John's commentary on the words of Jesus rather than a quotation of them directly.) The whole chapter continues what John the Baptist alluded to in 1:33.
Jesus, as the revelation of the Father, vv 11-16, echoes for us the beginning of the Gospel of John — Jesus is God's Word made flesh. Why did God reveal himself in this way? The only possible

answer is love — he loves us and wants to share his life with us, and this is how he shows it (vv 16-17).

Acceptance and belief, as the condition for salvation, are contrasted with rejection and "love of darkness" as bringing condemnation. The situation of those who have not had the opportunity (as far as we are able to know) to accept or reject Christ is simply not referred to here. This moral imperative is for those who hear the word of Christ, but it also involves a serious obligation on the followers of Jesus to make that word known. It does not, however, give us the right to judge the salvation or condemnation of anyone else.

First Reading: Exodus 34:4-6, 8-9

A person's name identifies him or her. Here YAHWEH (which means "He Who Is") is affirmed as Israel's God. This name (see Ex 3:14) points to the oneness of God in distinction to the many gods of other nations. Jesus, in turn, reveals this same one God to be a Trinity of distinct Persons, sharing their family life with us in knowledge and in love.

Note that a few Bibles, especially the Jerusalem Bible, consistently use the proper name, Yahweh, for God whenever it appears in the Hebrew text. Others, like the New American Bible, translate it more familiarly as "the Lord."

Responsorial Psalm: Daniel 3:52, 53, 54, 55, 56

These verses are from the magnificent song of the three young men in the fiery furnace, giving voice to the praise of all creation to Yahweh as Lord of all. Response: "Glory and praise for ever!"

Second Reading: 2 Corinthians 13:11-12

The Christian Scriptures, especially the writings of John and Paul, speak of the three divine Persons as intimately sharing their family life with us. And so Christian love, which overcomes obstacles and difficulties, is the sign of union with and in the family life of God.

Questions for thought, discussion, and prayer:
1. Do the names by which we call God say more about him or about ourselves? Why?

2. What do the titles Father, Son, and Spirit say about our relationship with God and with one another?

THE BREAD OF LIFE

Gospel: John 6:51-58

The entirety of Jn 6 focuses on the eucharist. The nearness of the Passover (v 4) ties the occasion both to the celebration of God's deliverance of his people in the past, and to the fulfillment of Jesus' sacrifice in his death and resurrection. The multiplication of loaves and the walking on water unite Jesus' power as the Son of God to the elements of nature — his is not a dominating and manipulating power but a perfecting and liberating power. The elements — bread, wind, sea — in obedience to him become more truly what they already are: instruments of grace.

Those miracles are a prelude to Jesus' teaching about himself as "bread of life," of which this passage is the concluding section. The word "flesh" is unmistakable in its concrete meaning. Jesus is no longer speaking metaphorically of "food" — as in "I am the bread of life" (vv 35, 48) — but now is calling his disciples to participate intimately in the incarnation itself. The word "incarnation" means "enfleshment," and Jesus' words here recall the beginning of John's Gospel: "The Word became flesh and made his dwelling among us" (1:14). Jesus is "God-in-the-flesh" fully and really.

These words are not "merely symbolic," but neither are they merely literal. They are symbolic in the fullest sense of the word. To eat and drink, as the action of the eucharist, is the sign of the intimacy of union with the human and divine Christ in the sacrament, as well as the means to it. This action brings us into the family relationship of the Trinity (v 57). By uniting with Christ totally ("in the flesh") we share in the same life-receiving relationship he has with the Father.

Obviously, "flesh" here does not refer to the corrupting tendencies of lower nature, as St. Paul uses the term. (See Rom 8; Gal 5.) Instead, the flesh encompasses the total humanity of Christ as the dwelling place (Jn 1:14) of the divinity.

First Reading: Deuteronomy 8:2-3, 14-16

God is closest to his people in times of suffering and trial — just when he seems farthest away! In the midst of "the test" he sustains those who are faithful to him by the continuance of his creative Word. This type of sustenance is symbolized by the manna. God's work is not finished in creation alone; he remains active in history, bringing his creation to perfection.

We can no more "test" God than we can prove his existence. He is fidelity itself, and what is self-evident is incapable of test or proof. On the other hand, God has the right to test us, so that through trial we may be led to the perfection that he seeks for us. The faithful, tried and true, become the strongest evidence for God's existence and his fidelity.

Responsorial Psalm: Psalm 147:12-13, 14-15, 19-20
These verses, from the second half of a two-part song, praise God for his goodness to his people. Response: "Praise the Lord, Jerusalem."

Second Reading: 1 Corinthians 10:16-17
Pagan mystery religions held that the worshiper who shared in a sacrificial meal participated in the power of the god being worshiped. St. Paul both compares and contrasts this to the Christian eucharist. Sharing the one loaf and the one cup of the eucharist make us one with the whole Christ. And this participation cannot be half-hearted, divided among other "gods" as well. The union signified and brought about in the eucharist must permeate every aspect of our lives.

Questions for thought, discussion, and prayer:
1. How is sharing Christ's body and blood in communion an act which affirms our union with one another as well?

2. Discuss the eucharist as the continuation of "God-with us" — Emmanuel.

WISDOM IN POVERTY

Gospel: Matthew 11:25-30

The two parts of this reading — Jesus' prayer to his Father and his invitation to his followers — share a common focus: poverty. The hymn-like prayer echoes the song of Daniel in Dn 2:20-23, praising God for giving his wisdom to those who empty themselves of their own wisdom. The vision of Dn 7:13-14 sees God placing all things into the possession of the Son of Man. Jesus, in making himself one with the poor and the worldly unwise — the "merest children" — is free to depend on the Father and receive all from his hand.

Those who "find life burdensome" are those who labor under the yoke of the law, expecting to find salvation in meticulous outward performance of detailed prescriptions. Often this gives rise to wearying inner tensions and anxieties because of unrealistic demands and expectations. Jesus' poverty of spirit — the "yoke" of his teaching — cuts through legalistic entanglements and returns us to basic simplicity of outlook and life.

First reading: Deuteronomy 7:6-11

The Deuteronomy telling of the covenant was actually written about six hundred years after the event took place, and reflects the perspectives of the situation shortly before the Babylonian exile. God's people had weakened and lost faith, were fragmented, and on the verge of destruction. In recalling the origins of the law to them (Deuteronomy means "second law"), the author relates Moses' words in a way that emphasizes God's free love in choosing to make them his nation — it was not any merit or glory of theirs. Yet this freely given love demands their acceptance and response, and the destruction that they are facing is the consequence of not having kept his commandments. Although God gives his love freely, we are partners in his plan to keep his love alive for all creation.

Responsorial Psalm: Psalm 103:1-2, 3-4, 6-7, 8,10

This psalm praises God's overwhelming love and forgiveness toward those who turn to him. Response: "The Lord's kindness is everlasting to those who fear him."

Second Reading: 1 John 4:7-16

Our love for one another is the only valid proof that God is with us. This is the conclusion of the simple wisdom of the Gospel. Intellectual arguments do not convince others of the truth of what we say; only our actions can do that. The work of the spirit is not only within our heart individually, as though he were our own personal dynamo. The Spirit's greatest work is making and solidifying the connections between us that make possible a community that puts love into practice.

Questions for thought, discussion, and prayer:

1. What is the difference between Christ's wisdom and worldly wisdom? How can a spirit of worldly wisdom infect even our religious attitudes?

2. Discuss how to prove to the world that God exists.

YEAR A
SEASON OF THE YEAR

THIS IS GOD'S CHOSEN ONE

Gospel: John 1:29-34

Unlike the other three Gospels, John's does not record the event of Jesus' baptism in the Jordan, but alludes to it in the words of John the Baptist (v 33). John the Gospel-writer did not want to say anything that might seem to subordinate Jesus to John the Baptist, so he portrayed the latter's role as only as giving witness to Jesus. Up to this point, John the Baptist emphasized that his mission was one of preparation. Now is the moment when he could point to Jesus and say, "This is God's chosen One" (v 32). The sign by which John recognized him became the key point of his testimony — the descent of the Spirit in the form of a dove (v 32). The dove symbolized love and represented the nation of Israel in the Jewish Scriptures (see Ps 74:19; Is 60:8; Hos 11:11; also numerous references in the Song of Songs).

The expression "Lamb of God" is a play on words in the original Aramaic language that the Baptist and Jesus spoke. "Lamb" and "servant" are the same word: *talia.* So the use of this expression refers back to both the suffering servant of Isaiah's prophecy (see Is 42:1-4; 49:1-7; 50:4-11; 52:13-53:12) and to the lamb of the paschal sacrifice whose blood saved the first-born of Israel (see Ex 12).

John's words may also stem from the same tradition that finally found expression in the book of Revelation, in which the Lamb is the central character. Read and reflect upon the passages about the Lamb: the scene of heavenly worship in Rev 4:1-5:14; the wrath of the Lamb, Rev 6; salvation from the Lamb, Rev 7ff; the victory of the Lamb, Rev 17:14; the new Jerusalem as the bride of the Lamb, Rev 19:5-9; 21:9-27.

First Reading: Isaiah 49:3, 5-6

This passage reflects the call of the prophet as servant of God. His role is not merely to announce, but to be in person the point of contact between God and humankind. Christ was the definitive insertion of God's presence into human history, and this presence is continued through the Church, charged with the mission of transforming all humanity into Christ's body.

Responsorial Psalm: Psalm 40:2, 4, 7-8, 8-9, 10
Originally the thanksgiving of one who had been rescued from danger of death, this psalm expresses readiness to do God's will, and to praise God by proclaiming his power and mercy. Response: "Here am I, Lord; I have come to do your will."

Second Reading: 1 Corinthians 1:1-3
The letters to the Corinthians reveal many serious problems that plagued the early Christian communities: divisions in leadership, factions among the members, and reversion to pagan immorality. These problems confront Christians in every age, and are very much alive today. At the beginning of his letter, Paul affirms the foundation of the solution: awareness that we are consecrated a holy people in Christ. If we truly realize our dignity in our relationship with him, we must act accordingly.

Vv 4-8, which emphasize the total giftedness of the Christian life, are read on the First Sunday of Advent, Year B.

Questions for thought, discussion, and prayer:
1. How can you proclaim in your own life: "Now I have seen for myself and can testify, 'Jesus is God's chosen One'"?

2. How can an awareness of your relationship with Christ influence your thoughts and actions?

THIRD SUNDAY OF THE YEAR — YEAR A

THE KINGDOM OF HEAVEN IS AT HAND

Gospel: Matthew 4:12-23
The relationship between the ministry of John the Baptist and Jesus is the focus of this reading. Jesus saw the necessity of beginning his ministry in union with John, and even signified this union by undergoing his baptism (Mt 3:13-17). It was only after John's arrest that Jesus showed real independence and embarked on his own ministry. Thus it is clear that Jesus did not break with the Jewish tradition represented by John, but built upon it and fulfilled it.

Jesus began his ministry by repeating John's call to repentance (v 17), but whereas John emphasized personal conversion (see Mt 3:1-12), Jesus' preaching began to center on the presence already of the kingdom of God, and its meaning and demands (see Mt 5ff).

John stayed in one place, the Jordan valley near the Dead Sea, and imposed a baptismal rite of purification upon all who wanted to follow him. His message was for an elite group of the "purified" who came to him accepted his way. Jesus, however, became a wandering preacher, conveying his message to everyone everywhere, even to the borderlands of Israel, where many Jews had been influenced by the "darkness" of paganism (vv 15-16, 23-25). Jesus went forth into the heart of humanity, into the roughest and earthiest of trades and situations, and invited followers from all social classes and occupations. He showed concretely that his message was not to be restricted to a chosen few.

First Reading: Isaiah 8:23-9:3

Darkness and light in this oracle have several layers of meaning. Often the eyes of captives and slaves were put out, and captivity itself was a "living death," as though one were already dwelling in sheol, the land of shadows after death. Light not only symbolizes freedom happiness, and glory, but also is needed for finding one's way, for direction on a journey. This light applies to Christ, the ultimate object of these prophecies, because he comes with new life, and a new way of life. In darkness one can see neither the goal nor the road to it. Light enables one to keep the goal in sight, and find one's way on the road to it.

Responsorial Psalm: Psalm 27:1, 4, 13-14

These psalm verses offer further reflections on the theme of light, almost in the sense of "seeing is believing." To see the Lord in his goodness is proof of his love, and is itself the reward of fidelity. Response: "The Lord is my light and my salvation."

Second Reading: 1 Corinthians 1:10-13, 17

The Christian community at Corinth had lots of problems, and Paul's letters there provide some of his strongest teaching. The factions which plagued this community were set up on the basis of allegiance to whomever had the strongest influence on these individuals. Disciples of Peter would tend to be Judaizers, while those of Paul would likely be missionary and charismatic. Apollos, as a Greek native, would probably appeal to those of a more philosophical bent, while there may have also been some in the community who had known Jesus personally, and they might have felt superior to the others. Paul's message is simply that these secondary and incidental things must not be allowed to overshadow our basic unity in Christ.

Questions for thought, discussion, and prayer:
1. What is the meaning of "the Kingdom of heaven is at hand"?

2. What does the call to reform mean in your life each day?

FOURTH SUNDAY OF THE YEAR — YEAR A

BLESSED ARE YOU

Gospel: Matthew 5:1-12
In the plan of Matthew's Gospel, Jesus proclaims the kingdom of the new covenant and its requirements while seated on a mountain. This parallels the establishment of the Jewish covenant on the mountain — Mount Sinai (see Ex 24:12-18). Matthew 5-7 comprises the famous "sermon on the mount," which is a collection of various sayings and teachings of Jesus that lay the foundation for the kingdom of God.

Many interpretations of the beatitudes are possible, but it is best to see them as reflecting basic Christian attitudes which manifest themselves in one's way of life, rather than as specific commands or counsels. The word "blest" simply means "happy" or "fortunate." It is an affirmation that one is on the right track and truly a part of the kingdom. (See also the Gospel for the Solemnity of All Saints, November 1.)

First Reading: Zephaniah 2:3; 3:12-13
This prophet, writing after Isaiah but before the Babylonian captivity, foresaw the coming of destruction but also realized that spiritual strength would enable some to survive. The self-sufficient proud would not be able to withstand, but the humble, the spiritually "poor" who rely on God, would be the saved remnant who in turn would be instruments of salvation for others. (See also the Third Sunday of Advent, Year C, for a more detailed introduction to this book.)

Responsorial Psalm: Psalm 146:6-7, 8-9, 9-10
This psalm describes in a concrete way the faithfulness and protection of God for those who trust in him. Response: "Happy the poor in spirit; the kingdom of heaven is theirs."

Second Reading: 1 Corinthians 1:26-31
Paul, continuing the advice begun in last week's reading, shows that human wisdom of itself is incapable of really knowing God's person and plan. (Note that the preceding section, vv 22-25, emphasizing the wrongheadedness of human standards of wisdom, is read on the Third Sunday of Lent, Year B.) God has revealed himself in the foolishness of poverty and the cross. It is there that true human dignity and worth are recognized.
These words condemn the "wisdom" of the proud, which causes divisions among the people of God who are called to unity in Christ. This is the worldly wisdom that seeks reasons to say, "I am better than you" or "I can do it myself, I don't need any God." In no way can these words be interpreted to condemn genuine wisdom that seeks truth and understanding, whether through science or theology. There is no criticism here of putting God's gift of intellect to the service of God's gift of faith.

Questions for thought, discussion, and prayer:
1.   Discuss the qualities that you find in people you admire that reflect the beatitudes.

2.   Reflect upon what Paul means by "boasting in the Lord" in the light of the whole message of these readings.

FIFTH SUNDAY OF THE YEAR — YEAR A

YOU ARE SALT AND LIGHT

Gospel: Matthew 5:13-16
The beatitudes concern the inner attitudes that must belong to a Christian as one who is part of the kingdom of God, but now the images of salt and light make it clear that Christianity demands more than a personal feeling or an individual moral code. Salt and light are important because of what they do, the effect they have on something else. So also, the disciple of Christ is not called merely for

his or her own sake, but to accomplish a change in the world.

If Christians concentrate only on their own personal salvation and do not flavor and preserve the world around them (as is the function of salt), and if they do not cast a light of truth into the lives of their associates, they are — in the words of Jesus — good for nothing.

Salt, for the ancients, was a very precious commodity. It was quite essential for health in a hot, dry climate. It not only added graciousness and flavor to meals, but was needed to preserve food. Yet because it had to be dug out of remote and inaccessible areas, such as around the Dead Sea, and transported long distances, salt was valuable and very carefully guarded. At times it was used as a means of exchange and payment — "salary" in its word-origins means "salt-pay."

Light, of course, is a recurring image for truth and wisdom throughout the Scriptures. Light is not merely to be seen and enjoyed, but to be used — to allow us to see other things as they are, and to find our way through life.

Look at these same verses in other Gospels. Mark's version is probably the closest to the original sayings of Jesus. In Mk 9:49-50, salt is an image of the effect that Christ's words will have in the hearts of those who receive him, while in Lk 14:34-35, it refers to the whole-hearted dedication of a disciple. Light in Mk 4:21 designates the power of Jesus' teachings. Here in Matthew, however, both salt and light refer to the effect that the disciples' lives must have on others.

First Reading: Isaiah 58:7-10

The Gospel theme of "what you are must overflow into what you do" is echoed in this discourse on the nature and results of true fasting. Any religious act that is done from false motives is a perversion and a lie. False fasting may be done either for show or for self-perfection. True fasting gives up what one holds dear — not merely food alone — for the sake of sharing with those in need.

Responsorial Psalm: Psalm 112:4-5, 6-7, 8-9

This song extols the virtues of the truly good person — he or she is an example and inspiration to all. Concern for others and generosity are their own reward and seen as the source of salvation. Response: "The just man is a light in darkness to the upright."

Second Reading: 1 Corinthians 2:1-5

True wisdom cuts to the heart of all things and sees them as they truly are. Wisdom is not the same as knowledge or understanding. Rather, wisdom is the ability to give proper perspective to what we know and understand. The power of the Spirit, which is the source of wisdom, enables us to view every element of our lives in relation to Christ crucified, and therefore in relation to the kingdom of God.

In this passage, Paul remembers his first visit to Corinth. After he had suffered a stunning defeat at Athens where he attempted to use human wisdom to explain the Christian way and to win over the pagan philosophers, he went to Corinth chastened by a keen sense of his own inadequacy. After a brief initial rejection, his preaching was immensely successful because he focused on the paradox of a crucified Savior rather than on rational explanations for faith. (See Acts 17:16-18:11.)

Questions for thought, discussion, and prayer:
1.   What is light and what does it do? What is salt, and what does it do? Do these images still have value and strength in today's world? How do these images speak to you in your own life?

2.   What does Paul mean by contrasting worldly wisdom with the power of God? Is there such a thing as spiritual wisdom?

SIXTH SUNDAY OF THE YEAR — YEAR A

BUT I SAY TO YOU . . .

Gospel: Matthew 5:17-37
From the Christian viewpoint, both human ethics and the Jewish biblical law are incomplete reflections of God's revelation to humankind. Christ's fulfillment of the law and the prophets did not merely consist in making ancient predictions come true or in giving a new set of commandments. He laid a totally new foundation for human life and behavior. The Christian is to be like Christ, and his or her behavior is to be in accord with this new reality.

The "old law" — not just the prescriptions of the law of Moses, but the whole way of conceiving law itself — sought to establish the conditions by which a person might enter and develop a relationship with God. Its orientation may be summed up: "If you do this, you shall be God's people." The "new law" of Christ — in reality a new way of looking at all facets of human life — looks first to the person's identity as a member of the kingdom of God, and then speaks of what one must do because of what one is. Its orientation is: "You are God's people, therefore you must act in accord with what you are."

The old style of law concerns itself with the action only — it cannot really touch the heart. In each of these "new commandments," Jesus moves from external action — murder, adultery, perjury — to the intention behind the act, and he says: "That is where the true basis of sinfulness lies." Laws against murder and other forms of violence against others treat the symptoms only. The root cause of evil that must be addressed in the light of God's kingdom is internal: conscious and intentional contempt and hatred for the other person. The injury begins in the heart, and there it must be stopped.

Similarly, adultery begins not merely with unsought fantasies but with the intention that says, "Yes, I will act on these desires." Thoughts and feelings in themselves are unintentional and therefore not yet sinful. When they become intentions, lust as sinful passion begins to bloom.

First Reading: Sirach 15:15-20

This brief reading is part of a meditative instruction on wisdom and how to live as a wise person. Here the author is reflecting on the meaning of law as a guide to one's life, and he shares the important insight that reward and punishment (life and death) are not something given or imposed from outside but are the real consequences of one's moral choices. Those who choose the good are truly seeking life, and those who choose evil are thereby embracing death. The roots of this passage are in both Gn 1:27 and Dt 30:11-20.

Responsorial Psalm: Psalm 119:1-2, 4-5, 17-18, 33-34

This longest psalm in the Bible praises God's law as the way of life for his faithful people. Response: "Happy are they who follow the law of the Lord."

Second Reading: 1 Corinthians 2:6-10

This letter of Paul to the Corinthians had the purpose of calling them back to the unity and integrity of they life they had chosen as Christians. His instruction on wisdom, which forms the basis of the advice and commands of the rest of his letter, reminds them to have their vision firmly fixed on the fulfillment of God's promises in the glory of the kingdom.

Questions for thought, discussion, and prayer:
1.   Do you see these new commandments of Christ as something that makes you free or something that restricts your freedom? Discuss why?

2.   What is the difference between God's wisdom and worldly wisdom?

SEVENTH SUNDAY OF THE YEAR — YEAR A

LOVE YOUR ENEMIES

Gospel: Matthew 5:38-48
      In actual practice, the Hebrew "law of retaliation" (see Ex 21:23-24; Lv 24:18-21), demanding "an eye for an eye and a tooth for a tooth," was seldom if ever taken literally. It was a vivid image of the obligation of equivalent compensation for an injury rather than a license to inflict the same injury in return. Jesus' law, however, sets up forgiveness and love, rather than insistence upon one's own rights, as the principle of operation in his kingdom.
      His whole "new law" is summed up in the final sentence of this reading: "Be perfect as the Father is perfect." This does not mean "playing God," which is to impose one's own personal whims as the law of the universe. It does mean doing what God does, and that is to love all his children with one mind and heart.
      The inevitable consequence of this command to take God's perfection as our own is the obligation to love our enemies. It is precisely in this that Jesus' teaching rises above every other system of ethics or morality. It is also precisely in this that Jesus' teaching is most ignored by those who profess to be his followers!
      Everybody recognizes the need to love others, but everybody draws lines limiting that love to family, friends, fellow citizens, "good people," "our own kind," etc. The central but difficult challenge of Jesus is that the kingdom of God is established only when we strive to break down those barriers, and find ways to include even our enemies within the sphere of our love. This sort of love is not easy, and is possible only in communion with the God whose

love it imitates. It does not imply a superficial glossing over of differences or wrongs, nor does it require letting everyone take unfair advantage of us. It does mean, however, caring about the genuine good of all, including enemies; it does mean looking for the spark of divinity in every other person, especially those we find difficult, and seeing them with the eyes of God the Father.

First Reading: Leviticus 19:1-2, 17-18

The Hebrew people were challenged by the biblical law to expand their horizons concerning whom they would accept as worthy of concern. This passage from Leviticus obliges love of one's fellow countryfolk as one means of preserving the integrity of Israel as a nation. Compare this with Dt 24:17-22 which expands this love to include resident foreigners and those who have no family roots (widows and orphans). Jesus very explicitly lifts all exceptions from this command of love.

Responsorial Psalm: Psalm 103:1-2, 3-4, 8, 10, 12-13

This hymn of praise recognizes God's love and goodness as embracing all creation. We are not merely recipients but participants in God's merciful kindness. Response: "The Lord is kind and merciful."

Second Reading: 1 Corinthians 3:16-23

God builds his people into his own dwelling, and Christians in communion with one another must act in a way that this dwelling is not torn down. "Worldly wisdom" concerns itself with evaluating others according to various standards. God's wisdom — the world's foolishness — says that we must not let worldly considerations weaken the force of the love that must bind Christians together.

Questions for thought, discussion, and prayer:
1. Discuss practical ways of broadening the concept of love within your own family, group, community, church, etc.

2. What does it mean to be God's temple? ... to have God dwelling in us?

NO ONE CAN SERVE TWO MASTERS

Gospel: Matthew 6:24-34

The cycle of Sunday liturgical readings unfortunately omits Mt 6:1-23, which gives an important development of Jesus' teaching on law as a matter of the heart rather than mere external practice. Good works (vv 1-4), prayer (vv 5-15), and other religious practices (vv 16-18) have value only as expressions of inner intention. These commands of Jesus cannot be seen as simply exchanging one style of behavior for another, such as praying in your room rather than in public. They probe the heart of religious practices and emphasize that to do things for the sake of appearances or in order to buy divine or human favor is an unworthy motive.

Forgiveness in imitation of God's forgiveness (vv 15-16) is the first step to put into practice the command to love one's enemies (5:44), and is the only way that leads to true prayer. Singleness of intention before God is the greatest possible treasure and is to be preferred above all material goods (vv 19-23).

Thus the person who is confident in possessing what is truly of spiritual value can adopt an attitude of detachment toward the things of this world, even those things we often consider necessities (vv 24-34). Trust in God as Father is far removed from a "Big Daddy" approach that expects him to give us whatever we want or think we need. Nor does trust in God call us to shirk our responsibilities or think that God will rescue us from our own foolish behavior. Trust is rather an attitude that looks to his will first and all else second, and is willing to say "yes" to him even if our own needs as we see them do not seem to be filled.

The ideal of the kingdom of God as presented by Jesus is that we take one anothers' needs upon ourselves as our own. It is only by accepting and caring for one another as brothers and sisters under one Father that our own true needs can begin to be met.

First Reading: Isaiah 49:14-15

This passage is a strikingly beautiful allusion to God's motherly care for his people, and a good reminder that the reality of God is beyond whatever names or concepts we use to describe him — including the maleness of most of our images and words.

Responsorial Psalm: Psalm 62:2-3, 6-7, 8-9
     This is a song of trust by one who was being attacked by enemies. Response: "Rest in God alone, my soul."

Second Reading: 1 Corinthians 4:1-5
     The Corinthians had received instruction in the Lord Jesus from a number of teachers, but many people seemed more attached to the particular mentality of one or another of them than to their common shared faith in Jesus (see 1:10-17). This is a temptation still very much alive among us — to try to make Christianity serve lesser ideals, political attitudes, class rivalries, personal claims to superiority, etc. Paul emphasized that even he, with real claim to be an apostle, must step into the background and allow God to be the final judge, to bring forth light from darkness.
     1 Corinthians will be continued in Year B (Second through Sixth Sundays), and concluded in Year C (Second through Eighth Sundays).

Questions for thought, discussion, and prayer:
1.   What does it mean to "to give yourself to money"? . . . "to give yourself to God"?

2.   What do Paul's words about himself say about the way we should teach and serve others?

NINTH SUNDAY OF THE YEAR — YEAR A

DOING THE WORD

Gospel: Matthew 7:21-27
     Much of the teaching in the first part of this chapter (7:1-20) is also found in Luke's Gospel, and is read at Mass during Year C. Therefore it is omitted here. However, you should read it as a preparation for reflecting on this passage. The "golden rule" (v 12) summarizes the best of Jewish law, but the law of the kingdom of

God goes beyond it — to love others as we have been loved by God, and Christ is the model of this love.

The whole sermon on the mount (Mt 5-7) concludes with a warning to put Jesus' words into practice, or they will be simply worthless.

To live Jesus' words demands the solid commitment exemplified by the sturdy rock foundation of a well-built house. But the true Christian life also demands involvement in the world — doing God's will, not merely talking about it and enjoying his favor (vv 21-23). Those who only profess Christ with the voice, but do not take his words to heart as the driving force of their lives, are emphatically declared not a part of his kingdom ("I do not know you!"). They may even possess gifts of ministry (v 22), but it should be remembered that these gifts are given for mutual benefit, not just as one's own privileged possession (see 1 Cor 12-14).

First Reading: Deuteronomy 11:18, 26-28

The blessing and the curse exemplify the urgency of the covenant as well as its absolute demand: with God, blessing; without God, chaos. As much as God loves us and wants to draw us to himself as his people, he leaves the final choice up to us. God is a Lover seeking the freedom of his beloved, not a manipulator seeking slavish conformity.

Responsorial Psalm: Psalm 31:2-3, 3-4, 17, 25

This psalm expresses firm faith and trust in God even in the face of persecution and apparent hopelessness. Response: "Lord, be my rock of safety."

Second Reading: Romans 3:21-25, 28

The introduction to the letter to the Romans is read on the Fourth Sunday of Advent, Year A.

After reflecting in the first part of this letter on the failure of humankind to find God through his footprints in nature, and the inability of the law of Moses to fulfill our destiny, Paul turns to consider how we are justified by Christ.

God's justice is not merely a characteristic or a quality, but an event (v 21) — the manifestation of his fidelity to his people in Christ, and his concern that all humanity should come to be justified in him.

"Faith alone" as the way of justification does not mean some magical act that buys salvation from God. Rather, the expression emphasizes the complete giftedness of salvation. Salvation is ours in

Christ. Faith is simply opening the door to him.

This does not mean that religious practices — "law" and "works" — are in themselves bad. It does mean, however, that of themselves they have no value. No one can "buy" heaven by doing anything — whether by devotions, keeping the law, or even suffering. However, insofar as these acts are expressions of true faith — the necessary outward manifestation of what is interior — these works can be considered as having value in relation to the kingdom.

Questions for thought, discussion, and prayer:
1.   After reading this Gospel passage carefully, are you surprised or disturbed by Jesus' message? Why or why not?

2.   In what ways are we in danger of using religious practices to buy our way into heaven? How can we follow the way of salvation as indicated by St. Paul?

TENTH SUNDAY OF THE YEAR — YEAR A

COME, FOLLOW . . .

Gospel: Matthew 9:9-13
We have seen that in the sermon on the mount (Mt 5-7), Jesus gives us the "constitution" of the kingdom of God he came to establish. He outlines there the basic demands of the life of the kingdom, and makes it clear that his kingdom is built upon the foundations of the Jewish covenant and law, and at the same time fulfills them ("You have heard the commandment . . ., but I say to you . . ."").

The miracles of Mt 8-9 testify that the kingdom is already present in Christ. The restoration of order as God established it is a sign of the beginning of God's rule. This kingdom, begun and fulfilled in Christ, is to be continued and extended by his disciples, and so they are chosen and given the mission in Mt 10.

The call of Matthew is placed right in the middle of the narrative of miracles, as if to show that conversion of heart from being tied up with material things to a genuine concern for the kingdom is also miraculous. This too is a genuine healing, and is accomplished by the power of Jesus' word, "Follow me," just as the other healings.

The healing power is not restricted to Matthew alone, but extends to his friends, also sinners, at a banquet table. The early Christians had a keen awareness of the eucharist as the sacrament of pardon and reconciliation, and their recollections in the Gospels concentrate on Jesus' words and works of mercy at dinner tables.

We need to renew our appreciation of the eucharist as the sacrament instituted "for the remission of sins," as the words of Jesus that we recall say. Sharing the banquet of Christ's sacrifice overcomes sin and challenges us to break down the barriers which divide us as God's family.

This does not deny the need for the sacrament of penance, but completes and fulfills it. Confession is the gateway to restoring a broken relationship with God, and also is a source of counsel and an opportunity for reflection upon the ways to overcome obstacles to a more perfect relationship with God and others. But the privileged meeting point with Christ, who is himself our forgiveness, comes in the eucharist.

Those who allow general feelings of unworthiness to prevent them from receiving communion at every celebration of the eucharist should take heart from Jesus' words in vv 12-13. Jesus comes, not as a reward for being good, but as the savior whose love makes us truly good.

Read also the other accounts of this event, Mk 2:13-17 and Lk 5:27-32. Note how Luke interjects some elements: Levi (Matthew) leaves *everything* behind (v 28); he gives Jesus a "great reception" (v 29); and, omitting the quote from Hos 6:6, Jesus invites "to a change of heart" (v 32).

First Reading: Hosea 6:3-6

The reason for choosing this as the first reading is obvious — the last verse is quoted in the Gospel reading.

Hosea is *par excellence* the prophet of God's marriage-love for his people. His own struggles with an unfaithful wife were seen to be an image of God's continual seeking to draw his unfaithful people back to him.

Genuine love challenges the beloved to honest response — and that is the point of this reading. The people seem to be planning some sort of penance ceremony for the expiation of sin (6:1-3), and yet Hosea recognizes that their hearts are not in it. Forgiveness is not "bought" by empty rites and prayers, but only by true change of heart. If the love that God desires is present (v 6), then the sacrifices can be an expression of that love. Otherwise, they are useless.

Responsorial Psalm: Psalm 50:1, 8, 12-13, 14-15

Idolatry is not only worshiping false gods, but also worshiping the true God in a false way. God cannot be bought with sacrifices or appeased with religious practices. When we attempt to use God to satisfy our own ends we are really worshiping only our own self. Response: "To the upright I will show the saving power of God."

Second Reading: Romans 4:18-25

After pointing out that the law of Moses does not have the power to make one right before God, Paul now uses Abraham as an example of how justification by faith operates. To begin with, it is faith in the person of God that justifies — nothing else (vv 20-22). And this faith is shown in hope, even in the face of apparent impossibility (v 18). This faith and hope was the door through which God was able to work in Abraham. Similarly, faith in the person of Jesus as God's Son opens the door to allow God to work in us the same resurrection that he accomplished in Jesus.

Questions for thought, discussion, and prayer:

1. Imagine yourself as being present in the event of today's Gospel. Would your honest reaction favor Matthew or the Pharisee? How do you react when good fortune favors the people you don't approve?

2. How does faith, as described by St. Paul, open us to receive God's gift of salvation?

ELEVENTH SUNDAY OF THE YEAR — YEAR A

GO FORTH!

Gospel: Matthew 9:36-10:8

This passage is the beginning of a long discourse in Matthew on the nature of mission — being sent to proclaim the kingdom. Read also the parallels in Mk 6:7-13 and Lk 10:1-20, the latter of which speaks of the "Seventy-two" rather than the "Twelve."

The word "apostle" means "one who is sent," and their designation as the "Twelve" at this point emphasizes the missionary nature of their calling. Note that the other Gospels name them at the time of the calling (Mk 3:16-19; Lk 6:14-16), but Matthew names them when Jesus sends them forth. Being sent is the necessary "other side" of being called. No one is called merely to be a beneficiary of the kingdom, but to go forth and make the kingdom happen in the world.

Jesus mixes metaphors in speaking about the harvest (9:37-38) and sheep (9:36; 10:6) in almost the same breath (to a group who were mostly fishermen!), but these images serve to enrich the significance of the mission rather than confuse it. The picture of the harvest introduces a sense of urgency — the grain or fruit spoils and is lost if not harvested in time. Compare also Jn 4:35-38.

Jesus sees himself as a rabbi (teacher), but not one who is content to sit in a school or synagogue and allow students to come to him. His concern is to go out and encounter people where they are to be found. And he instructs his followers to do the same. Further, unlike the Pharisees (and so many "religious" people today as well), his concern is not to associate with the elite or "saved," but to gather the "lost sheep" (10:6). Jesus simply does not concern himself with calling the Gentiles (non-Jews) (10:5-6; also Mk 7:24-30); that will come later (see Lk 13:23-36; Rom 1:16). First a foundation must be laid. Those whom God has chosen first must become themselves a people with a mission.

First Reading: Exodus 19:2-6

The poetic tendereness of this passage stands in sharp contrast to the stark hardness of much of Exodus, and may have been added later (4-3 cent. BCE) by another hand. The function of priests is to be mediators between God and the people. God's promise to Israel, therefore, is not merely that they are destined to enjoy his favor, but that they are chosen to be the means by which God would make himself present to all humanity, and draw them to himself.

Responsorial Psalm: Psalm 100:1-2, 3, 5

The pilgrims approaching the Lord's temple in Jerusalem would find their hearts overwhelmed with gratitude and praise, and express it by singing this song, displaying both thanks and confidence. Response: "We are his people: the sheep of his flock."

Second Reading: Romans 5:6-11

Salvation means that God has come to us in Christ, for we are powerless to go to him on our own (v 6). The full presence of God's power and love requires death — even on God's part. In Christ, God places himself into our hands (vv 7-8)! It equally must involve dying on our part — placing ourselves into his hands.

Thus salvation is a past fact — Christ has already definitively accomplished it. But it is also an awaited reality, not yet fulfilled in us. However, the fact of reconciliation already achieved in Christ is the assurance that we who share his life now will share it for eternity (vv 9-10).

Various sections of chapter 5 are also read on Trinity Sunday and the Solemnity of the Sacred Heart, Year C; and the Third Sunday of Lent, Year A.

Questions for thought, discussion, and prayer:
1.   What does this Gospel reading tell us about Jesus' reason for calling his disciples and sending them on mission? How do you hear Jesus calling and sending you in your own life?

2.   How can we speak of death as an act of generosity in self-giving?

TWELFTH SUNDAY OF THE YEAR — YEAR A

FEAR NOT TO PROCLAIM

Gospel: Matthew 10:26-33

The whole missionary sermon of Jesus as he sends forth his disciples on a "practice run" was probably compiled by Matthew from an original brief instruction (see Mk 6:7-13), combined with sayings of Jesus from other times and places. Matthew's intent here would be to provide a more or less complete teaching on the Christian mission, just as he had compiled many sayings of Jesus into the sermon on the mount (Mt 5-7) in order to give a full picture of the moral demands of the kingdom.

Today's passage forms a commentary on Jesus' words in vv 19-20. Those who are sent to continue the message of Jesus must be prepared to face persecution, but can rely on the presence and power of God to sustain them.

Vv 26-27 are quoted as a command of Jesus, but the same saying is used elsewhere as a statement of the power which the Gospel possesses within itself (Mk 4:22; Lk 8:17; 12:2-3).

Vv 28-31 describe two motives for confidence. First, the only real adversary to be feared is Satan, the force of evil whom Christ will have already overcome. Secondly, as it is evident that God cares for all his creation, so much more does he look after those chosen and sent as his own.

Vv 32-33 emphasize that fidelity is not a one-way street. Those who are faithful to Christ can expect him to be faithful. But infidelity cuts oneself off from Christ's promise.

The exprssion, "soul," in v 28 reflects the Hebrew concept of life. The word refers to life itself, rather than the Greek-Christian concept of a soul as a distinct entity from the body. The meaning here is that "real life" or the "whole life"cannot be destroyed by persecution.

First Reading: Jeremiah 20:10-13

Jeremiah's hymn (20:7-18) gives voice to the anguish of the person who feels the relentless pursuit of God's love. This love isn't a cozy and warm feeling, but is the all-giving, all-embracing, all-demanding power of him who seeks nothing less than total submission, and who gives nothing less than his own self. Jeremiah feels within his heart both the stern yet loving call of God, and the sin and rejection of his people.

Responsorial Psalm: Psalm 69:8-10, 14-17, 33, 35

This lament can be viewed on two levels of meaning: it expresses the pain of an individual in the midst of oppression as well as the suffering of the entire people of Israel at the hands of conquering enemies. It is messianic first of all because it maintains hope in deliverance even without seeing evidence of it, a hope which is to be fulfilled in Christ. Response: "Lord, in your great love, answer me."

Second Reading: Romans 5:12-15

This is one of the most difficult passages in all the Christian Scriptures. Although Adam and Christ are shown in parallel, the basis for the comparison is Christ, not Adam. Having experienced Christ and his new life, we look backwards to the origins of human sinfulness in the act of primal disobedience in order to perceive more fully the grace of salvation. The shadow helps to define and understand the light. Paul is not trying to prove the existence of sin in the world — that is obvious. Rather, he is saying that just as all humanity experiences the bonds of sin, so the liberation from sin by Christ is universal — it extends to to all people, not just a chosen few. (See also the First Sunday of Lent, Year A, whose reading includes vv 12-19.)

Questions for thought, discussion, and prayer:
1.   What gives you a sense of your own self-worth? How can you help others understand their own worth?

2.   How does your awareness of your own sinfulness help you to understand the greatness of God's's love? How can you help others to understand it?

THIRTEENTH SUNDAY OF THE YEAR — YEAR A

WELCOME!

Gospel: Matthew 10:37-42
These words, which conclude Jesus' instruction on the mission of his followers (Mt 10:5-42), describe both the cost and the reward of discipleship. The price of sharing in the life and mission of Jesus is exactly the same as he paid: emptying oneself of self-love, and carrying the cross. And the reward of the faithful disciple is the reward of Christ: to share in his resurrection.

Most of these verses were originally sayings of Jesus belonging to different contexts, but Matthew brought them all together here because he felt they had something important to say about the mission of the disciples. It is interesting to see where the same sayings are found in other Gospels:

vv 37-38 in Lk 14:26-27
vv 38-39 in Mt 16:24-25; Mk 8:34-35; Lk 9:23-24
vv 39-40 in Jn 12:25-26
v 40 in Lk 10:16
v 42 in Mk 9:41

This passage also ties in hospitality with the Christian mission — and this is a lesson most needed today. Our world has become dehumanized, and we have become isolated and alienated from one another. It is up to the Christian to break down these barriers and to make room for one another in our hearts and homes.

First Reading: 2 Kings 4:8-11, 14-16/1

The miracle of a barren womb conceiving and giving birth is a nice reward for hospitality to a prophet, but at first glance the two facts seem to have little further connection. There is a connection, and a profound one — the prophet receives, bears, and communicates God's word. By the power of God's word life is brought forth. The attitude of hospitality — opening self to the other — is profoundly maternal. And the demonstration of hospitality in this reading is filled by God's gift of new life.

Responsorial Psalm: Psalm 89:2-3, 16-17, 18-19

This long psalm recalls the promises God made in ancient times to David (it was written in exile, four hundred years after David), and painfully calls upon God to remember his favor in the people's current distress. These verses are part of the psalm's initial praise and thanks. Response: "For ever I will sing the goodness of the Lord."

Second Reading: Romans 6:3-4, 8-11

Baptism both pledges and brings about the union of the faithful with Christ. But union with Christ cannot be a "pick-and-choose" affair — it must be union with the whole Christ. And that includes union with his death as well. The Christian is committed to die to sin and self with Christ, to become one with the sacrificed Christ in order to share his new risen life.

In these verses, Paul tells the "how" and the "why" of what had been the heart of his message from the beginning. See Acts 13:37-39; 1 Th 4:14; Gal 3:27; Phil 3:7-11; 1 Cor 15. He unfolds this doctrine even more in Colossians, which was written after Romans, especially Col 1:24; 2:9-15. The remainder of Colossians teaches the practical and moral implications of this doctrine of union with Christ. (This reading, including the omitted verses, also appears in the Easter Vigil liturgy.)

Questions for thought, discussion, and prayer:
1. How is hospitality a Christian virtue? How is hospitality connected with life and death?

2. In what ways do you die and rise with Christ in the course of your life?

FOURTEENTH SUNDAY OF THE YEAR — YEAR A

LEARN FROM ME

Gospel: Matthew 11:25-30
Chapters 11 and 12 narrate the beginnings of Jesus' rejection by his own people, foreshadowed in John the Baptist (vv 2-11), and coming to a head in the attitudes and actions of the leaders and intellectuals (chapter 12). In contrast, today's reading (vv 25-30) concentrates on the qualities of those who accept Jesus and become part of the kingdom of God.

The Hebrew background to Jesus' words helps our understanding of them. The contrast of the "children" with the "learned and clever" has its roots in Daniel 2, where the young men, in answer to their prayer, are granted greater wisdom than the sages of Babylon. Jesus compares his followers, in their gifted simplicity, with the intellectuals and legalists of his day who had made the law such a complicated affair no one could observe it. In the disciples' childlike poverty, which was really openness to God, they had the key to the wisdom that had eluded the professional "wise men."

In the Hebrew Scriptures, wisdom is always identified with full observance of the law of God, and is often referred to as a "yoke" (see Sir 51:26; Jer 2:2-9; 5:5; also Gal 5:1). Jesus cuts through the burden of legalism, and as the new Lawgiver, imposes the yoke of the new law of God's kingdom. But Jesus himself is one with the poor, a member of the poor remnant who take refuge in the Lord alone (see Zeph 3:12-13). Never forget, however, that this "easy yoke" and "light burden" is the way of the cross. Carried in union with him, the cross is indeed light because it is borne with his power. V 27 has its roots in Dn 7:13-14 — the vision of the Son of Man who receives "dominion, glory, and kingship" from the Ancient One.

First Reading: Zechariah 9:9-10
This brief passage looks forward to the restoration of the kingdom of Israel by the Messiah. The prophet, writing very shortly after the return from the Babylonian exile around 520 B.C.E., compares the anticipated Messiah to both the meekness of David (v 9) and the majesty of Solomon (v 10). Further, his rule will embrace the whole world, as did Solomon's (almost!), and it will be characterized by true and lasting peace.

Responsorial Psalm: Psalm 145:1-2, 8-9, 10-11, 13-14
This is an alphabetic psalm, in which each subsequent verse
begins with the next letter of the Hebrew alphabet. (They enjoyed
word games in those days too.) It is simply a song of praise for the
goodness of God shown in his works. Response: "I will praise your
name for ever, my king and my God."

Second Reading: Romans 8:9, 11-13
After having contrasted the impossibility of depending on observance of the law of Moses for salvation (chapter 7), with the true
salvation made possible by depending on Jesus Christ in faith, Paul
in chapter 8 contrasts the "flesh" and the "spirit." For Paul, "flesh"
stands for the way a person goes when he or she depends totally on
the self, without reference to God's gift of the Spirit. Even observance of the God-given law of Moses is of the "flesh" because the
law itself does not have the power to raise humanity out of its
natural and sinful condition, and because legalistic tendencies of
some Jewish schools of thought sought to make the law a key to
manipulate God around to their own style of salvation. "To live in
the Spirit" means to be open to God's initiative in our lives, so that
he may lead us in his way. This life in the Spirit is closely associated
with the resurrection of Christ. The Spirit brings forth new life in
the one who is dead to the "flesh" (self-centeredness), and this life
witnesses to the resurrection of Christ and the promise of our own
rising from the dead.
Vv 8-11 are read on the Fifth Sunday of Lent, Year A; and vv
14-17, which unfold the implications of the life in the Spirit, appear
on Trinity Sunday, Year B.

Questions for thought, discussion, and prayer:
1. Do you experience the burden of Jesus' cross as "easy" and
"light" or as difficult and heavy? Why?

2. Do "meekness" and "gentleness" mean passively letting
everyone walk all over you and take advantage of you? If not, what
do these qualities mean?

FIFTEENTH SUNDAY OF THE YEAR — YEAR A

PARABLES AND MYSTERIES

Gospel: Matthew 13:1-23

This set of parables in chapter 13 presents a further development of the teaching about the kingdom from that found in the sermon on the mount (Mt 5-7). The sermon gave the requirements of personal belonging; these parables reveal the inner dynamic of the kingdom itself.

In this reading, Jesus alludes to common — but not very efficient — farming practices to show the power of the seed (kingdom of God) to bring forth an abundant harvest in spite of the blindness of the learned and the worldly (v 4), the superficial enthusiasm of the crowds (vv 5-6), and the misgivings of his relatives and some disciples (v 7). The tone of the parable is optimistic — obstacles beset the sowing, but the harvest will be abundant nevertheless.

The question and answer about the purpose of the parables (vv 10-17) should be seen as emphasizing the gift of understanding given the disciples, in contrast to the indifference and incomprehension of others. Jesus' mission is not an overwhelming success in human terms, but in the light of the final judgment, those who do receive his word are blessed because they form the kingdom. The quotation from Is 6:9-10, which is associated with Isaiah's call to be a prophet, gives a word of encouragement to be strong in proclaiming the message even in the face of inevitable unpopularity. It should be understood that God does not so much cause their hearts to harden, but rather that his kingdom will be established even in spite of their rejection.

The interpretation of the parable (vv 18-23) seems to be a later addition, arising from the early experience of the Spirit-filled community of Christians. The main point of the interpretation is not the sower and the harvest, as in the parable itself, but the way the seed is received, as reflecting various motives for conversion. In the interpretation, the seed is the proclaimed word rather than the kingdom itself.

First Reading: Isaiah 55:10-11

"Second Isaiah" (chapters 40-55) is very much concerned to show the power and love of the one God, Yahweh, in contrast to the dualism (a god of good and a god of evil) and polytheism (many gods) of the other nations. Thus he shows that even setbacks and apparent evils in history have been for the good and development of his people. This brief passage sums up God's power: his word works infallibly even when human obstacles seem to frustrate it.

Responsorial Psalm: Psalm 65:10, 11, 12-13, 14

This very earthy psalm presents material abundance as a motive for praise and thanksgiving to God the Creator. Water, in all its manifestations, destructive as well as life-giving and cleansing, is a powerful symbol of God's word. Response: "The seed that falls on good ground will yield a fruitful harvest."

Second Reading: Romans 8:18-23

After speaking of the way of salvation, Paul now considers the problem of suffering: "If we have been reconciled as children of God, how can suffering and failure still affect us?" Paul's response is that we cannot do away with the limitations creation imposes on us. But ultimately, in Christ, we will rise above them. As children of God, we possess the Spirit as the beginnings, or "down payment," of this ultimate liberation, and the source of hope.

Questions for thought, discussion, and prayer:
1. How do you understand parables? What do you feel parables can teach you? How do they do this?

2. What is meant by "the Spirit as first fruits" in Romans?

SIXTEENTH SUNDAY OF THE YEAR — YEAR A

WHEAT AND WEEDS

Gospel: Matthew 13:24-43

Jesus' emphasis on the growth of his kingdom in spite of appearances to the contrary responds to the apostles' apprehensions over the enmity of the Pharisees and the defection of some disciples. Jesus rejects the temptation to make his followers into a sect of the "pure" and "enlightened," withdrawn from the hostile environment of the world and concerned only for their own welfare and salvation.

Instead, he insists that his kingdom must remain fully in the human arena, and that patient effort in imitation of God's patience will bring about its fulfillment.

The growth of the wheat and weeds together in the field addresses the obvious fact of the presence of wicked people even within God's kingdom on earth. The early Church came to recognize unfaithful members in its midst, and questioned how this could be possible in the kingdom of God. The answer, derived from these words of Jesus, is to await God's final judgment in patience.

The parable of the mustard seed alludes to the persistent growth of the kingdom, and the contrast between seemingly insignificant beginnings and the final outcome.

The image of the yeast is clear enough, portraying the growing power of the kingdom as both hidden and irresistible. Note that this passage (and its parallel, Lk 18:20-21) gives the only favorable reference to yeast in the Christian Scriptures. All other passages (Mt 16:6; 1 Cor 5:6-8; Gal 5:9) portray it as a corrupting element.

First Reading: Wisdom 12:13, 16-19

The book of Wisdom comes from one of the small colonies of Jews living in the Greek world about a hundred years before Jesus. Seeing all the immorality around them, they would naturally question why God tolerates it. The answer of this book's author is threefold: (1) God gives time as the opportunity to overcome self-centeredness and to turn to him; (2) the innocent should not perish with the guilty; and (3) the Jewish people should imitate God's tolerance. Tolerance, however, does not mean accepting evil as good and yielding to it. It means respecting the dignity of the human person and the image of God found in human freedom, and helping others to use that freedom in accord with God's plan.

Responsorial Psalm: Psalm 86:5-6, 9-10, 15-16

Even in deep distress, the psalmist recognizes that no one has greater power and mercy than the Lord, and this thought restores his confidence. Response: "Lord, you are good and forgiving."

Second Reading: Romans 8:26-27

Paul speaks of how the flesh — the way of self-centeredness — may disturb one who is of the Spirit, but cannot overcome him or her. In the midst of suffering, both the tribulations of our human condition as well as those difficulties that are the result of our following of Christ, the Spirit is with us as the pledge of the future fulfillment (vv 18-25).

Prayer, too, can be a problem in this "spirit-flesh" tension. Even the believer is tempted to pray "according to the flesh" ("we do not know how to pray as we ought") by trying to manipulate God to serve our own ends. The Spirit of Christ ensures our submission to the Father in union with Christ, and true prayer arises only out of this submission.

Questions for thought, discussion, and prayer:
1.   What place is there in the Church for bad members? Does this Gospel make you feel content or uncomfortable? Why? Which is the more appropriate feeling?

2.   How does the Spirit pray within you?

THE TREASURE OF THE KINGDOM

Gospel: Matthew 13:44-52
These three little parables about the kingdom are closely related in their message, yet each has a distinct point to contribute. In the first parable (v 44), the kingdom is a treasure, and the man is a seeker. Upon recognizing its value, he decides it is worth changing his whole life for. Note the true seeker's concern is for the treasure itself, not its monetary value. Even to sacrifice everything else is insignificant by comparison with the treasure.

The second parable (vv 45-46) seems to say the same thing, but really is just the opposite. In the first parable, the kingdom was the treasure, the object of the search. In the second, the merchant's search itself is identified with the kingdom. God finds our response to him so valuable that he is willing to give up all (divinity "humiliated" in the incarnation of his Son) to purchase the pearl of his reign in love over humanity.

The third parable (vv 47-50) contains its own interpretation (vv 49-50), and echoes the parable of the wheat and weeds. It indicates that patience is needed between the foundation of the kingdom and its fulfillment. The final outcome is to be left to God's judgment.

Note that this group of three parables begins with a sense of joy in discovery (v 44) and ends with a contrasting picture of envy on the part of those who do not bother to seek (v 50). The concluding verses (51-52) point to the unity of the Jewish law with the Gospel: Jesus has truly come to fulfill the past, not to throw it away.

First Reading: 1 Kings 3:5, 7-12

From its beginnings, Solomon's reign (961 to 922 B.C.E.) was different from that of his father, David. The period of conquest for territory and unification of one nation out of twelve tribes was over, and Solomon's task was the peaceful organization and development of a settled people. Here the young king, awed by this responsibility, seeks the Lord's wisdom, for he recognizes that the people he governs are the Lord's.

This wisdom, however, is not the divine wisdom of later writings, which seeks a part in God's wisdom as its own end. Solomon here is asking for nothing more profound than the practical judgment needed to govern the people well. He is not so much aspiring to the heights of the mystery of divinity as assuring the tools he needs to be God's good king.

Responsorial Psalm: Psalm 119:57, 72, 76-77, 127-128, 129-130

This psalm is a long alphabetic hymn (the titles before each group of verses are the letters of the Hebrew alphabet) which teaches the value of devotion to the law of God as the source of wisdom. Response: "Lord, I love your commands."

Second Reading: Romans 8:28-30

The problem of predestination ("How can a God who loves all choose some and reject others?") becomes clearer if we understand it in the sense of God's initiative. He did not create anybody for the purpose of damnation. He has given us all an eternal destiny with him. This is his initiative, not ours. Yet, we are free to choose him or to reject him. The stages of the Christian life (call, baptism, faith, death — v 30) are God's work, not ours. We simply open ourselves to his work in us.

Vv 31-34, which emphasize God's saving will, are read on the Second Sunday of Lent, Year B.

Questions for thought, discussion, and prayer:
1. Discuss what it costs you to accept God into your life.

2. How do you reconcile the word "predestined" in Romans with freedom of the will?

BREAD BLESSED, BROKEN AND SHARED

Gospel: Matthew 14:13-21

An account of Jesus' being rejected in his place of origin (13:54-58) and the death of John the Baptist (14:1-12) serve to introduce this lengthy section (chapters 14-18) in which Jesus reveals that the fullness of his role as Messiah is to be rejected and suffer death on the cross. Hand-in-hand with the revelation throughout this section of Jesus as crucified savior comes an emphasis that his disciples also must share in his cross.

The multiplication of loaves is presented not as a miracle that evokes wonder and awe, but as a sign of Jesus' true mission as Messiah. He is the successor of Moses, and so he continues to nourish his people and lead them through the desert to the banquet of promise. This feeding is an event that places the law in its proper context. Like Moses, Jesus as giver of the new law of God's kingdom does not merely enforce an external code of behavior, he nourishes and leads. The fulfillment of the law is not the court of judgment but the banquet of love and acceptance.

Two things are required in observance of Jesus' law — to let oneself be nourished by him and, in turn, to nourish one another (vv 16-17). Jesus gives both the example and the power to do this. He is the one who blesses and breaks, but the disciples distribute (v 19). The superabundance (v 20) looks forward to the overwhelming eternal banquet, but may also sadly indicate that many for whom this bread was intended had absented themselves (see the comment for the Twentieth Sunday).

This passage unmistakably alludes to the eucharist. The ritual description of Jesus' gestures (v 18) intentionally echoes the eucharistic words of institution.

First Reading: Isaiah 55:1-3

"The poor have a special place in God's heart" resounds insistently in the pages of both Jewish and Christian Scriptures. God's banquet is open only to those who hunger for it. It is rejected by those who are confident of their own resources, and therefore are not interested in what God has to offer. This is a hard lesson which a small remnant of Israelites learned only at the cost of hardship, oppression, and deprivation. We Christians must remember this every time we share in the eucharistic gift. We can assemble only as God's poor, only as those who submit themselves fully to God's initiative, as Jesus did on the cross.

Responsorial Psalm: Psalm 145:8-9, 15-16, 17-18

It is a source of never-ending wonder that the God who brought all things into being should have a personal care for his people. Response: "The hand of the Lord feeds us; he answers all our needs."

Second Reading: Romans 8:35, 37-39

Present trials are more than just something to be endured in order to get an eventual reward. Paul's faith goes beyond merely putting up with misfortune now in hopes of getting something better later. He invites every Christian to share with him a vision that God is actively at work within the contradictions and evils of this world — not to remove them but to restore order and healing in and through them.

Questions for thought, discussion, and prayer:

1. Discuss "poverty" and "nourishment" as Gospel symbols for our participation in eternal life.

2. How does the love of Christ work within the trials of life?

NINETEENTH SUNDAY OF THE YEAR — YEAR A

HOW LITTLE FAITH YOU HAVE!

Gospel: Matthew 14:22-33

In the Gospel traditions, the event of Jesus walking on the

water occurs in close connection with the multiplication of loaves and fishes (see also Mk 6:34-52 and Jn 6:1-24). This is one of the few instances where John's Gospel parallels a story also found in the other Gospels.

In understanding these miracles, it is important to see them not merely as displays of power, but as richly symbolic actions. The multiplication of loaves was done not just to satisfy human hunger, but to identify Jesus with the God who gives and sustains life, echoing God's providing manna for his people in the desert (Ex 16).

Water symbolizes the untamed forces of evil — the chaos — out of which God the Creator victoriously brought forth the universe (Gn 1:2). Thus Jesus' victory over water identifies his work as Messiah — to overcome the forces of evil and to bring creation to its fulfillment.

This event is part of Jesus' intensive training of his disciples, in which he strives to convince them of the nature of his power, and that they are called to share in it. To this end, he invites Peter to come across the water as a sign that the disciple, in union with Jesus, also possesses power over the forces of evil — and the only reason for faltering is lack of faith.

First Reading: 1 Kings 19:9, 11-13

Elijah had been concerned to purify the worship of God from false nature-worship, but now, fleeing for his life and discouraged at his apparent failure, he looks for God. In the past, God had genuinely revealed himself in the powerful forces of nature (see especially Ex 19 — see the Mass for the vigil of Pentecost). Now, however, God shows himself veiled in the gentle breeze, perceptible only to the attentive listener. His message, however, is anything but gentle (vv 15-17).

This passage is a warning for us to seek God as he is, not as we would like to make him. God is gentle, but he is also overwhelming. God is present within us, yet he is also transcendent. God's silence requires faith and solitude to be heard and understood, yet he is also found in community with others.

Responsorial Psalm: Psalm 85:9, 10, 11-12, 13-14

This psalm comes from the time the Jews had returned from exile (about 450 B.C.E.) and undertook to rebuild Jerusalem and the temple. The theme of thanksgiving for forgiveness and restoration (vv 2-4) leads to petition for help to rebuild the kingdom (vv 5-8) and confidence that God will restore his people fully (vv 9-14). Response: "Lord, let us see your kindness, and grant us your salvation."

Second Reading: Romans 9:1-5

Privilege can cause problems. Although the Israelites were privileged in the flesh so that Christ might come from them, this very privilege prevented them from receiving him — they refused to believe that their own heritage (flesh) could embody divinity. Paul's own expression of concern for his brother Jews (v 3) echoes Moses' desire to sacrifice himself for the forgiveness of the Israelites (Ex 32:32).

In these chapters (9-11), Paul struggles to find meaning in the overall resistence of the Jewish people to the message of Christ. The point here is not that Jesus was handed over to crucifixion by the Jewish leaders, but that Paul had continually experienced rejection of his own preaching of the Christian way by Jews wherever he went. Paul here reveals a deep personal hurt at the hardness of his own people against what had become the consuming passion of his life.

The major portion of these reflections in chapters 9-11 is omitted from the liturgical readings, but 10:8-13, emphasizing the unity of all peoples based on the call to faith in Christ, is read on the First Sunday of Lent, Year C.

Questions for thought, discussion, and prayer:
1. What does walking on the water say to you? How does one share in the power of Jesus to overcome the forces symbolized by water?

2. What does the first reading say about where to find God in your own life?

TWENTIETH SUNDAY OF THE YEAR — YEAR A

WOMAN, YOU HAVE GREAT FAITH!

Gospel: Matthew 15:21-28

The first part of Mt. 15 is omitted from the lectionary, but the parallel in Mk 7:1-23 will be read on the Twenty-Second Sunday of

Year B. In that section, Jesus confronts the traditional interpretations of the law by the Pharisees. He condemns the narrowness of Pharisaic practices (vv 1-20), but in the very next incident (vv 21-28), he appears to equal their narrowness by excluding a non-Jewish woman from the benefit of his ministry.

These two sections may be taken as a follow-up to the multiplication of the loaves. Why were there twelve baskets of fragments left after Jesus had multiplied enough for all to eat their fill (14:20)? It may be significant that Jesus had intended just enough with no surplus, but that the Pharisees in the crowd refused to eat with unwashed hands (15:2), and no one would share the bread with the non-Jews present. Chapter 15 addresses both these situations: the refusal and the deprivation of the bread which symbolizes the fullness of God's Word.

The spirited dialog between Jesus and the woman betrays something of the mentality of the time and place. More significant, however, than Jesus' first refusal — which may have been something of a word game — is the reason why Jesus finally does share his bread (the asked-for healing) with her. Her faith was what the faith of the Jewish people ought to have been. She did not merely approach him as a wonder worker or a healer who might cure her daughter. She came to him as Messiah (v 22 "Son of David") and persisted in her belief even in the face of initial refusal. By faith she became what she could not be by ancestral heritage.

First Reading: Isaiah 56:1, 6-7

This passage begins "Third Isaiah," which was written by an anonymous author in the tradition of Isaiah after the return from the Babylonian exile (538 B.C.E.). The Jewish people never succeeded in restoring Jerusalem and the kingdom to its former glory. Their dream was to subjugate all other nations of the world under their rule, and the hoped-for Messiah would lead them to military victory to accomplish this. The vision of the prophets, however, was more realistic and it better reflected God's destiny for all peoples. They proclaimed a moral mission for the Israelites to call all humanity into the fold of God's worshipers rather than to dominate them. Thus the temple was not to be merely for the Israelites, but for all (v 7) — and this temple was to be the Messiah himself.

Responsorial Psalm: Psalm 67:2-3, 5, 6, 8

This psalm expresses the hope that, through the chosen people of God, all peoples might recognize God's lordship and accept him.

Response: "O God, let all the nations praise you!"

First Reading: Romans 11:13-15, 29-32

Paul faces the problem of God's apparent rejection of the Jewish people, and he answers it by showing that God remains faithful — it is his people who have turned away from him (v 29). Because human free will has the last word, the conversion of Paul's brother Jews can be no more than a hope (v 14). But it was Israel's rejection of the apostles' preaching that drove them to begin proclaiming the Gospel to the Gentiles. And so their sin became the doorway for the salvation of the world. Unknowingly, by their disobedience they fulfilled their prophetic destiny expressed in the Jewish Scriptures.

Questions for thought, discussion, and prayer:

1. Do you find outstanding examples of faith in people who would otherwise be considered "unbelievers"?

2. How do these readings speak of God's will to save all people?

TWENTY-FIRST SUNDAY OF THE YEAR — YEAR A

THE KEYS OF THE KINGDOM

Gospel: Matthew 16:13-20

This Gospel passage has been traditionally understood as a proof of Peter's primacy over the apostolic Church, and therefore of the legitimacy of the pope's claim, as Peter's successor, to be the head of the Church throughout all ages. True as this may be, there is also a deeper meaning in the event related in this Gospel.

The title which Peter gives to Jesus (v 16) is that he is the Messiah, the fulfillment of God's revelation and promise, not someone less (v 14). The phrase "Son of the Living God" by itself does not assert Jesus' divinity because it is used often in the Jewish Scriptures to describe angels (Gn 6:1-4; Job 1:6), judges (Ps 82:6-7), and the king (2 Sam 7:14; Ps 89:27-28). In itself, this phrase affirms no more than that Jesus' messiahship is from God rather than from some other source. This need not disturb us, however, because the whole context of the Gospels and the rest of the Christian Scriptures amply confirm the truth of Jesus' divinity.

Jesus continues his intensive instruction of his disciples by sharing his messiahship with them as soon as they recognize it. He shares with Peter the prerogatives of the messianic mission: he is the firm invulnerable rock (see Is 28:16), and is given the keys to David's house (see Is 22:22; Rev 3:7). The extremes of "binding and loosing" express all possible power, which Jesus as Messiah would have, and which he shares with Peter and his Church.

First Reading: Isaiah 22:15, 19-23

This passage gives a detailed description of the investiture of a royal court official. The robe, the sash, and the keys are insignia of his office. The fullness of his power is symbolized by the key, which both opens and closes definitively — a phrase which foreshadows the power of binding and loosing proclaimed in the Gospel.

Responsorial Psalm: Psalm 138:1-2, 2-3, 6, 8

In this psalm, David thanks God for having raised him from lowly origins and shared his power with him as king over the people of Israel, God's own people. Response: "Lord, your love is eternal; do not forsake the work of your hands."

Second Reading: Romans 11:33-36

Paul here gives what must be the bottom line and last word of any prayer or petition which we make before God: he is Lord, the transcendent One before whom we must bow. Our place is to give him glory, not to try to mold him after our own desires. Paul quotes extensively from the Jewish Scriptures in this brief acclamation of God's greatness. See Ps 139:6,17,18; Is 40:13; and Job 41:3.

Questions for thought, discussion, and prayer:
1.   What do Jesus' words about Peter and the Church mean to you in your personal spiritual life?

2.   In the light of Romans, would "mystery" best be described as "the unknowable" or "the overwhelming"?

TWENTY-SECOND SUNDAY OF THE YEAR — YEAR A

FOLLOW IN MY FOOTSTEPS

Gospel: Matthew 16:21-27

The event of this Gospel marks a turning point in Jesus' training of his disciples. Having elicited from them a profession of faith in himself specifically as the Messiah — the awaited Savior sent from God — he begins to teach them how he will fulfill his mission.

There can be very little doubt that Jesus did foresee his own death, but his predictions do not necessarily indicate a detailed knowledge of the exact time and manner. Undoubtedly crucifixion as a method of execution was on his mind, but perhaps stoning was too (see Mt 23:37). We can reasonably expect that the early community and the authors of the Gospels would remember, proclaim, and record Jesus' words in the light of their fulfillment in subsequent events. Thus, the important part of Jesus' message here is the fact that his mission would lead inevitably to death (and to resurrection), and that this is in fulfillment of the Scriptures. (The force of "must" in v 21 is "destined as foretold.")

The parallels and contrasts of this section lead us to understand the connections between Jesus' mission and the call of his disciples (and us) to mission. Just as previously Peter was the spokesman for the rest of the disciples in professing faith in Jesus as the Messiah (v 16), so he also demonstrates the weakness and imperfection of that faith in v 22. As Jesus replied with a blessing in v 17, so he replies with a curse in v 23. Finally, just as Jesus followed the profession of faith with a declaration that his followers would share in his mission as Messiah, so he follows his revelation of the implications of that mission with the teaching that all his followers must share in his sufferings (vv 24-27).

First Reading: Jeremiah 20:7-9

Jeremiah seems to have been of rather downcast temperament, wounded deeply by the rejection which his prophecy entailed (see chapters 15, 16, 20 and 26). Many of those called to serve the Lord, however, have similar complaints, for example, Moses in Ex 32, Elijah in 1 Kgs 19, and Jonah in Jon 4. The witness of spiritual values is always unwelcome among people devoted to materialistic and self-centered values.

The marriage covenant is a strong image in Scripture, and the element of seduction (v 7) corresponds to that image. The mystery of God binds and demands unconditional surrender. Real encounter with God produces an agony and tension within the human heart that will not be experienced if God remains merely an intellectual idea or a religious moral code. Jeremiah is foreshadowing the mystery of the total self-giving of the sacrifice of the cross.

Responsorial Psalm: Psalm 63:2, 3-4, 5-6, 8-9
This is the prayer of one who feels away from what is held most dear, the treasure of the heart. Response: "My soul is thirsting for you, O Lord my God."

Second Reading: Romans 12:1-2
Paul has concluded the doctrinal section of this letter, and these two verses introduce his moral exhortation regarding the relations of Christians with each other (12:3-13); with others not of the Christian community, especially their enemies (12:14-13:14); and the strong with the weak (14:1-15:13). The words "sacrifice" and "spiritual worship" are significant here, for they tell what the value of freedom from sin and life in the spirit (chapters 6-8) really is. What we do is both the sign and the reinforcement of what we are. Life itself — the totality of our being — is what is offered in the new sacrifice, made in union with Christ's sacrifice.

The next section contains a brief summary of Paul's teaching that we are truly members of one body in Christ, therefore our diverse gifts and ministries must be put to one anothers' service out of love (vv 3-21). 1 Cor 12-14 expands greatly upon this passage.

Questions for thought, discussion, and prayer:
1. How do we, like Peter, impose our own ideas of what Jesus should be, and blind ourselves to what he is?

2. What is "spiritual worship" in Romans?

TWENTY-THIRD SUNDAY OF THE YEAR — YEAR A

JOIN YOUR VOICES TO PRAY

Gospel: Matthew 18:15-20

The account of the transfiguration of Jesus (17:1-9) is read on the Second Sunday of Lent each year. This event provides a glimpse of divine confirmation of Jesus' messiahship to help give solid foundation to his self-revelation as crucified servant of God. The remainder of the chapter focuses on the mystery of the cross and Jesus' relation to the forces of evil (vv 14-21) and the to the powers of the world (vv 24-27).

Chapter 18 concerns the attitude of Christ's followers toward one another, particularly as regards the area of sin and weakness. Vv 1-3 set the tone by commanding humility; 5-11 emphasize that sin itself is to have no place in our lives, and must be rooted out ruthlessly. However, our attitude toward sinners themselves must be characterized only by pardon. The sinner should not be left in the cold, but actively sought out with love and brought back (vv 12-14).

Vv 15-18 give the practical method for doing this. The community of Christ's people has the power to pardon (v 18 — the same words given to Peter in 16:19), and this power comes through prayer in common (vv 19-20). The only acceptable attitude of the injured party in a conflict is a desire to pardon without limit (vv 21-22), and the motive for pardoning looks to our own final judgment: we can expect to be forgiven only to the extent we are willing to forgive (vv 23-35).

Thus the Church's power of judgment and the way it is carried out, the subject of today's reading, must be aimed only at securing the acceptance of pardon. The only truly unforgivable sin is the refusal to be forgiven.

First Reading: Ezekiel 33:7-9

God doesn't give his word to the prophet just for his own edification. God's gift brings with it a responsibility to look after the welfare of others. This passage shows the extent of this responsibility.

The prophet in each of us must have the courage to challenge the evil around us — our own salvation, as well as the salvation of the world, depends on our response to this prophetic call more than on any outward signs of success.

Responsorial Psalm: Psalm 95:1-2, 6-7, 8-9

This psalm begins with an invitation to praise, but warns in strong terms derived from history that we must be open to God fully. Response: "If today you hear his voice, harden not your hearts."

Second Reading: Romans 13:8-10

Paul has just advised his readers that they must obey laws and legitimate authority, not merely out of fear of punishment but because that is what is right (v 5). The way of love does not replace law, but rather fulfills it. The motive is genuine love of the other person whose rights the law is intended to protect, rather than any fear of punishment. Vv 11-14, which continue this reading, are found on the First Sunday of Advent, Year A.

Questions for thought, discussion, and prayer:

1. What does the power of "binding and loosing" have to do with your personal obligation to forgive those who have offended you?

2. "Love and do whatever you will." Do you agree or disagree? Why?

TWENTY-FOURTH SUNDAY OF THE YEAR — YEAR A

FORGIVE!

Gospel: Matthew 18:21-35

The duty of forgiving the offenses of others was a part of Jewish doctrine and life, but the rabbinic schools debated over how often one was required to pardon. The number usually varied for different types of people: one must forgive a wife so many times, children so many times, brothers so many times, etc. Seven, as symbolic of fullness, seems to have been the maximum number of times required by most schools of thought. In this sense, seven really means an indefinite number, but it also gives parsimonious nit-pickers a way out — after a symbolic seven (carefully counted), one could say enough to forgiveness, and refuse further pardon.

Jesus' answer (v 22) does not literally mean 490 times. Leading into the parable about the king and his official, Jesus proclaims that the number of times to forgive is not even a worthy question for his followers to ask. They are to forgive as they have been forgiven. Pardon is not a matter of moral obligation that can be classified, graded, enumerated, and analyzed — as the rabbinical schools had done. It is rather the necessary result of realizing one's own sinfulness, and the immensity of God's forgiveness.

Notice that the question of strict justice does not even enter into the parable. The unforgiving servant could make a good legal case for his position. Just because his own debt was canceled, he wasn't thereby obliged in justice to remit his debtors. But God's kingdom is not a business proposition or a court of law. God's kingdom is totally his gift, and only those who recognize the giftedness of his pardon and mercy, and seek to imitate it and share in it, can be participants.

It is a sobering thought that our own judgment will be based more on how well we forgive others than on how well we keep the rules.

First Reading: Sirach 27:30-28:7

The book of Sirach was written about two centuries before the time of Jesus by a learned rabbi in Jerusalem named Jesus ben (son of) Eleazar ben Sirach. It gives a summary of Jewish history and religious traditions and proverbs for the people of his day. As a deutero-canonical (apocryphal) work, it is not included in the Hebrew Bible nor in Protestant Bibles, but it has been accepted as inspired and canonical by the Catholic Church from the earliest times.

This passage expresses the summit of Jewish thinking about the obligation and reason for mutual pardon. The law of retribution ("an eye for an eye") still underlies much of Sirach's teaching. We should abstain from vengeance because we fear God's vengeance (vv 1-3). We should pardon others because we hope that God will pardon us (vv 2, 4-5). Jesus' teaching brings forgiveness into a whole new dimension. We do not forgive merely because we hope to be forgiven; we forgive because we are aware that God has already immeasurably forgiven us. We love even enemies not in a self-righteous and condescending way, but because we realize that we too have been just as unfaithful to God, and have received his mercy.

Responsorial Psalm: Psalm 103:1-2, 3-4, 9-10

Although God is the Creator and Lord of all, his loving care is seen as the greatest of all his works. Response: "The Lord is kind and merciful; slow to anger, and rich in compassion."

Second Reading: Romans 14:7-9

Paul had to face a situation in which diversity of practice characterized the Christian community, similar in many respects to the diversity within the Church today. Unless they attack the essentials of faith or stand in the way of the spread of the Gospel, these differences should not only be tolerated but encouraged among those who share the same faith. The same Lord of life and death, in whom all are equal, is being honored. Rather than be a source of conflict and dissension, these differences should be a source of enrichment and strengthening. Genuine mutual appreciation is the obligation of all Christians united in the love of the same Lord.

Two further excerpts from the concluding section of Romans are found in the Sunday lectionary: 15:4-9 on the Second Sunday of Advent, Year A; and 16:25-27 on the Fourth Sunday of Advent, Year B.

Questions for thought, discussion, and prayer:
1.   What happens if you don't feel that you have been forgiven, or don't feel you need forgiveness?

2.   Read all of Romans 14:1-11. What does the passage about life and death have to do with the rest?

TWENTY-FIFTH SUNDAY OF THE YEAR — YEAR A

ENVY AND GENEROSITY

Gospel: Matthew 20:1-16

Chapter 19, omitted from the cycle of Sunday readings, continues the theme of God's transcendence over human ways, and the challenge to adopt God's mentality as the realization of his kingdom. The cross in the Christian life is not an abstract ideal, but shows itself in the difficult decisions concerning committed relationships and our attitudes toward justice and the use of the world's goods.

The parable about the laborers in the vineyard is sandwiched between two repetitions of the same saying of Jesus, "the last shall be first and the first last" (19:30; 20:16). The verse itself does not correspond perfectly to the parable. There is no question in the parable that the last ones hired were given any real priority over the first. The problem arises because they were given equal treatment. The complaint against the owner (v 12) is that he is unjust — the same complaint of the elder son in Lk 15:29-30, the legalistic Jews in Ez 18:25, and Jonah in Jon 4:2. The point of the parable has nothing to do with God's first and last choices, but rather exemplifies the overwhelming goodness of God surpassing our limited concept of justice. God's covenant with his people is not a business contract, but a completely free gift on God's part, seeking only our acceptance and response.

The "first-last" saying seems to refer specifically to the Jewish-Gentile situation — the Jews (the "first" to receive God's covenant) rejected Christ and became the last; the Gentile (i.e., non-Jews) were not included in the first covenant, but shared its fulfillment in Christ.

First Reading: Isaiah 55:6-9
An awareness of the total giftedness of God's love runs through all the prophets. The Lord can be found only because he has made himself near (v 6). Even the worst of us have no reason to despair of his mercy, but every reason to turn to him confidently seeking forgiveness, because God is not limited by our narrow ideas of justice and retribution. It should be noted that God is often proclaimed as a God of love, mercy and tenderness in the Jewish Scriptures. The Christian Gospel adds a radical new dimension to this love of God by seeing his people not merely as recipients of his love but as participants in his very act of loving. We are challenged to duplicate his love and forgiveness in our relations with others.

Responsorial Psalm: Psalm 145:2-3, 8-9, 17-18
The words of this psalm echo those of Isaiah in the first reading. Even though the Lord created the universe in all its splendor, the greatest of his works is his compassion. Response: "The Lord is near to all who call him."

Second Reading: Philippians 1:20-24, 27
After an introduction in which he expresses his deep affection for the Christian community at Philippi (see the Second Sunday of Advent, Year C), Paul points to his own example of how to hear the voice of the Lord speaking in the circumstances that face us. He is writing from prison, uncertain of the outcome. He may be released

or he may face death. The meaning of living in the spirit takes on a new and more urgent perspective. The power to choose what will happen is out of his hands, yet he remains perfectly free. If he is to die, death would fulfill his wish to be with Christ. If he is to remain alive, release from prison would fulfill his desire to strengthen the Lord's people by his presence with them. (For more background on this letter, see the Second Sunday of Advent and the Fifth Sunday of Lent, both in Year C.)

Questions for thought, discussion, and prayer:
1.   Discuss the Gospel in relation to envy in your own life.

2.   How do the Gospel and the first reading speak to the meaning of conversion of heart?

TWENTY-SIXTH SUNDAY OF THE YEAR — YEAR A

FAIRNESS AND OBEDIENCE

Gospel: Matthew 21:28-32
    The entry of Jesus into Jerusalem (21:1-11 — see Palm Sunday, Gospel for the Procession) marks the beginning of the fulfillment of the kingdom. The symbolic gestures of cleansing the temple and cursing the fig tree establish a clear set of priorities: materialistic greed and empty show have no place in the kingdom because they produce no genuine fruit.
    The parable in the liturgical reading (vv 28-32) is addressed to the "professional holy men" — the chief priests and elders (v 23) — as a response to their questioning of Jesus' authority. He had addressed similar parables to Pharisees, who were not religious officials, but a "super-saved" lay sect (Lk 7:40; 15:2; 18:9).
    It should be clear that Jesus does not prefer sin to virtue. But he emphasizes that many of those classified as sinners are actually closer to salvation through repentance than those who profess themselves just but are blind to the real demands of God's love.
    The parable originally shed light on the Jewish rejection of Jesus and the Gentile acceptance of him. God did not decide at a particular moment to reject the Jews and choose Gentiles. He consistently wills all people to share in his love. But, for the ones who re-

jected Jesus, their "yes" to their own sense of being favored by God stood in the way of their saying "yes" to the very fulfillment of that favor in the Gospel of Jesus.

For us Christians, there is an important moral. A professional "yes" or a loudly proclaimed "yes' to God may contain so much "system" or so much ego that a real "no" is lurking behind the facade. On the other hand, one who begins by saying "no" outwardly, may really be searching for a genuine image of God to say "yes" to.

First Reading: Ezekiel 18:25-28

Ezekiel emphasized personal responsibility to the Lord for one's own actions in an age when it was held that descendants inherited the punishment for their fathers' sins. (See Ex 20:5-6; Dt 5:9-10; 29:18-21.) It is quite true that a child may inherit the consequences of a parent's sin. If a father squanders a fortune, his son enters the world poor through no fault of his own. Also, an innocent individual may suffer the consequences of collective guilt. Everyone in Germany suffered in the Nazi defeat. However, Ezekiel is fighting against a fatalism that says, "If we must pay for the sins of our fathers, what point is there in changing or being good ourselves?" Here personal responsibility has the last word. In the final analysis, each person can be held accountable only for his or her own deeds.

Responsorial Psalm: Psalm 25:4-5, 6-7, 8-9

This psalm is the prayer of a sinner who understands the consequences of his sin, yet trusts in god's mercy. Response: "Remember your mercies, O Lord."

Second Reading: Philippians 2:1-11

Philippi was one of Paul's favorite communities. Relations were affectionate, and little of the dissension that occasioned many of Paul's other letters is found here. Paul writes to them in a positive vein, seeking to lead them to greater perfection in the love of one another based on Christ.

The core of Christian perfection is humility (v 3),which is based on the humility of Christ (vv 5-11). The humble person does not have to look at himself or herself as dirt, but must be motivated by a healthy appreciation of the other person's value. Humility is not an invitation to unhealthy insecurity or paranoia. In fact, only the whole and secure person can really forget titles, privileges,and self-praise, and concentrate on the good and worth of others. Christ's attitude is an invitation to health. Holiness is wholeness.

Vv 6-11, the great hymn of Jesus' lordship through self-emptying, is also read each year on Passion/Palm Sunday. In chapter 3, Paul reflects on the place of Christ in his own life as a model for his hearers. The stern yet hopeful tone of this chapter makes it appropriate for Lent, and two sections appear on Lenten Sundays in Year C — 3:8-14 on the Fifth Sunday of Lent and 3:17-4:1 on the Second Sunday of Lent.

Questions for thought, discussion, and prayer:
1. Do you find the Gospel passage comforting or disturbing? Why?

2. How, in a practical sense, can Christ's attitude be yours?

TWENTY-SEVENTH SUNDAY OF THE YEAR — YEAR A

THE LORD'S VINTAGE

Gospel: Matthew 21:33-43
Foreign absentee landlords controlled much of the land in Judea and Galilee in the time of Jesus. The tenant farmers, who rented these lands, naturally held considerable resentment towards these rich and powerful (and often foreign and pagan) landowners. The Zealot party, a band of guerillas who fought to overthrow foreign domination, stirred up opposition that occasionally became violent, just as the action of the tenants in the parable. Killing the heir of the property might be a way of getting possession of it. By law, in the absence of an heir, ownership would fall to the first occupant. In the parable, the workers made the mistake of forgetting that the owner, upon his return, could give his land to others.
Jesus may have originally addressed this parable to the leaders of the Zealot party, to emphasize that their goals and methods were alien to the true kingdom of God. Injustice in human affairs there might be, and we cannot be indifferent in our efforts to bring about justice. But the justice of God's kingdom cannot come about through partisan violence and hatred. The leaders of the Zealots, then, would have been identified with the vineyard workers, and because of their infidelity to the true purposes of God's kingdom, their responsibility would be given to others.

In the course of the first few decades of the Church, the Zealot question was no longer a burning issue, but the Jewish-Gentile problem remained. By the time the Gospel was written, the emphasis of the parable seems to have changed. The workers were now seen to represent the Jews who had rejected Christ, and therefore were unfaithful to their "chosen" status. And so the kingdom itself was taken from them and given to the Gentiles. It also became an explanation of the reasons for Christ's death, and its consequences — he was rejected and put to death because he was a threat to the personal security of Jewish leaders as God's favored people.

First Reading: Isaiah 5:1-7
At first glance this allegory seems very similar to the Gospel parable, but it is likely that Jesus did not have this in mind at all. Notice that the subject is vastly different: in Isaiah, the grapes do not ripen; in Matthew, the tenants revolt. The outcome is different: in Isaiah, unredeemed ruin predicted; in Matthew , Jesus foretells transfer of possession. The point of this allegory in Isaiah is to contrast the tender care which God lavishes upon his people with their ingratitude and unresponsiveness.

Responsorial Psalm: Psalm 80:9, 12, 113-14, 15-16, 19-20
This psalm extends the allegory of the vine as representing God's people, and asks him to care for it once again. Response: "The vineyard of the Lord is the house of Israel."

Second Reading: Philippians 4:6-9
Paul's final words to his beloved Philippians are not just a pious bit of farewell advice. There is a sense of urgency in his parting exhortations. The catalogue of virtues that should underlie a good life are not merely intended for the community's own self-perfection. The missionary dimension of the Christian life is never far from Paul's mind. Christians are to behave well so that their lives maybe a sign of the love of God to others. Note that vv 4-7 are read on the Third Sunday of Advent, Year C.

Questions for thought, discussion, and prayer:
1. How can the Gospel parable apply to your life today?

2. How do you understand the meaning of "God's peace" in Phil 4:7?

THE WEDDING BANQUET

Gospel: Matthew 22:1-14

This parable of the wedding feast and the invited guests presents us with several difficulties as Matthew tells it. A much simpler version is given by Luke (14:16-24). Luke's telling of it speaks of the original guests refusing the invitation and the poor being brought in, clearly referring to the rejection of the kingdom by the Jewish leaders and its acceptance by the Gentiles.

Matthew adds a number of elements to the telling. This is a wedding banquet given by a king for his son (v 2). In Jewish prophecy, God is often presented as the husband of his people (see Is 54:4-10; 62:1-5; Jer 2-3; Ez 16 & 23' Hosea 1-3). The Christian Scriptures continue this image, seeing Christ as the bridegroom (see Mk 2:19; Jn 3:29; Mt 25:1-13; 2 Cor 11:2; Eph 5:22-27) and his final coming as the consummation of his marriage with his people (Rev 19:6-9; 21:2; 22:7). The wedding banquet indicates that this parable refers to the kingdom both now and in its future fulfillment.

The hostility of some of the invited guests (vv 6-7) should be seen in the light of the increasing hostility of the chief priests and pharisees (21:45-46), and reflects very strongly the preceding parable of the vineyard workers (21:33-43). But it is a somewhat awkward addition to the parable by Matthew, because no appropriate reason for such a reaction is given.

V 10 emphasizes that both bad and good come into the banquet. This refers to the time of the Church, and, in connection with the expulsion of the man without the proper garment (vv 11-13), indicates that mere external membership in the Church does not guarantee true justice or final salvation. A garment is an outward expression of what a person is inwardly. These words relate to Paul's about putting on Christ (Gal 3:27: Eph 4:24; col 3:9-10). V 14 simply emphasizes the extensive generosity of God in calling all to his banquet, and laments that few respond. It does not indicate any form of predetermined salvation or predestination.

First Reading: Isaiah 25:6-10

Read all of Is 24-28 which sets the salvation of a remnant within the context of the general destruction of the wicked. This section depicts the enthronement banquet of God when he victoriously establishes his kingdom. A banquet on the occasion of the enthronement of a king was a public manifestation of his power as well as a sign of his generosity and friendship with the people over whom he rules.

Responsorial Psalm: Psalm 23:1-3, 3-4, 5, 6
  Sharing and providing food is one of the strongest signs of love and care for another person; here it describes God's care for his people. Response: "I shall live in the house of the Lord all the days of my life."

Second Reading: Philippians 4:12-14, 19-20
  Having or not having material possessions is not so important. What is important is looking beyond merely having or getting so that we see Christ at the heart of what we have or need. Detachment from material things, therefore, must also go hand in hand with generosity.

Questions for thought, discussion, and prayer:
1. What are the characteristics of a meal that make it a good image of God's kingdom?

2. What can you do to make your meals a better image of God's kingdom? How about your participation in the Lord's Supper, the eucharist?

TWENTY-NINTH SUNDAY OF THE YEAR — YEAR A

GOD AND GOVERNMENT

Gospel: Matthew 22:15-21
  Read all of chapter 22. Matthew gives us here three "temptations" of Jesus by different groups of people, all of which serve to illustrate the types of refusal to the feast of the kingdom at the beginning of the chapter.

The Herodians were partisans of king Herod, and characterize those who are so attached to a particular earthly kingdom that they have no time for submission to God's authority. The Sadducees (v 23) represent those who cannot (or will not) see beyond the here and now. The Pharisees (v 34) are those who cannot see the forest for the trees — they are so meticulously concerned with details that they lose sight of the whole picture.

The simple message of Jesus' reply is that there is no opposition between genuine civil obligations and responsibilities, and the obligations of God's kingdom. Concern for God's kingdom cannot be used as an excuse to neglect the realities of the world in which we live, any more than earthly concerns can be allowed to cloud over our response to God's invitation to his kingdom.

First Reading: Isaiah 45:1, 4-6

Cyrus, the pagan king of Persia who conquered Babylon in 539 B.C.E. and liberated the captive people, including the Hebrews, is here described in terms that reflect an intimate relationship with God — anointed (v 1) and shepherd (44:28). The one God is seen as master of all events, and therefore even a foreign pagan king can be the instrument of his will.

Responsorial Psalm: Psalm 96:1, 3, 4-5, 7-8, 9-10

This psalm praises God for his lordship over all creation and over all peoples. Response: "Give the Lord glory and honor."

Second Reading: 1 Thessalonians 1:1-5

Paul wrote this letter from Corinth not long after he had established the Christian community in Thessalonica. He is encouraged by their progress in faith. He emphasizes that the preaching of the word is the first step of the Christian life, but the completion rests solely on the power of God, the Holy Spirit. Faith is deepened and strengthened in hope — through the patient endurance of trials we grow.

Questions for thought, discussion, and prayer:
1. Should a Christian in government behave differently from a non-Christian? What sort of issues should he or she approach differently?

2. Abortion, capital punishment and prison reform, education, rights and opportunities of minorities, the "Third World" nations, nuclear armament — does the relationship between God and Caesar spoken of by Jesus have any bearing on these issues?

THE FOUNDATION OF THE KINGDOM

Gospel: Matthew 22:34-40

There are three accounts of this great commandment in the Gospels, each having its own characteristics. In Mk 12:28-24, a scribe comes to Jesus with good intentions, seeking to be enlightened, and reacts favorably to Jesus' response. In Lk 10:25-28, the lawyer, not Jesus, states the commandment, and Jesus expands its meaning with the parable of the Good Samaritan. Here in Matthew, the question is put to Jesus in bad faith as a test.

The two great commandments as Jesus gives them are from Dt 6:4-5 and Lv 19:18. The concluding verse (v 40) is found only in Matthew. "The law and the prophets" refers to the entire structure of Jewish faith and life (see also Mt 5:17; 7:12). Thus, these two commandments support the whole structure, which crumbles if either one is neglected. This is a pointed allusion to the Pharisees who preferred discussion of the finer points of the law to the basic obligation to love God and others.

First Reading: Exodus 22:20-26

If society is to maintain peace and justice, laws must often have a certain degree of harshness. Effective punishments are necessary to insure observance. Yet — and this is equally true of all legal systems — justice must be tempered with compassion. Included in all judgments must be an awareness of extenuating circumstances. A society without justice is chaotic, but a society without compassion is inhuman.

But law must go beyond the mere preservation of order in society. If true justice is to be done, lawmakers must have a special concern for the rights of those who are powerless and have no one else to speak for them. The rich and the powerful have the resources to take care of themselves; the poor and the unseen and oppressed do not. They have God's special favor. Do they have ours as a Christian community?

Banquet of the Word

Responsorial Psalm: Psalm 18:2-3, 3-4, 47, 51

This psalm praises God for his compassion shown in victory and deliverance. Response: "I love you, Lord, my strength."

Second Reading: 1 Thessalonians 1:5-10

The power by which the Church grows is not of human origins but the Holy Spirit. However, the pattern of growth is by imitation. Imitation of God is fundamental to both the Hebrew and the Christian Scriptures (Lv 19:2; Mt5:48; Lk 6:36). We can imitate one another, as well, insofar as we are signs of God to one another. Imitation of Jesus is basic to Christianity, but here Paul speaks of the Thessalonians imitating himself, and in turn becoming models for others.

This tells us the direction that the Christian mission of evangelization should take. The Gospel is not proclaimed by propaganda, coercion, or argumentation. Only when Christians live their faith singleheartedly and visibly will non-Christians be able to perceive something that has the power to touch the depths of their own spirit.

Questions for thought, discussion, and prayer:
1.   "I love mankind, it's people I can't stand," says Linus in an old "Peanuts" cartoon. What "hidden restrictions" do we put on our concept of neighbor, and how does this limit our love?

2.   "It's OK, as long as it doesn't hurt anybody," is often used to justify things that are considered wrong. Could there be hidden hurts that this statement tries to cover up? Discuss what they might be.

THIRTY-FIRST SUNDAY OF THE YEAR — YEAR A

ONLY ONE TEACHER

Gospel: Matthew 23:1-12

The point of Jesus' condemnation of the Pharisees in this chapter is their hypocrisy — a basic rejection of the meaning of God's law which masquerades as acceptance, and even the self-righteous enforcement of external observances on others. For faith in God, they had substituted argumentation; for fundamental, loving obedience, they had substituted meticulous rule-making.

In vv 7-10, Jesus obviously does not disapprove the use of titles, like rabbi, teacher, or father, as terms of identification. Instead he condemns avaricious grasping of empty marks of respect. He objects to a religion of outward professionalism without inner spirit. Those who would use these verses to build a case against the Church simply because those titles happen to be used are guilty of the same sort of nit-picking legalism that Jesus condemns in the Pharisees. (In a spirit of loving criticism, one could certainly find many more areas of needed improvement in the Church than merely its use of titles!)

First Reading: Malachi 1:14-2:2, 8-10
Malachi was an anonymous prophetic voice (the name means "my messenger" and is evidently a pseudonym) in the fifth century B.C.E., after the return from exile, but before the religious and civil reforms of Ezra and Nehemiah. It seems that, upon their return to Jerusalem, the people quickly returned to old habits. Taking God's presence for granted, they substituted outward forms of worship for the inner spirit of true dedication. God was to be appeased and bought by ritual acts, rather than loved in justice, truth, and compassion. Malachi preached against this civil and moral decadence, and paved the way for eventual reform.

Responsorial Psalm: Psalm 131:1, 2, 3
This brief song presents a homey and attractive image of confidence in the Lord. Response: "In you, Lord, I have found my peace."

Second Reading: 1 Thessalonians 2:7-9, 13
Paul speaks to the Thessalonians as a loving father, as one who had brought forth life and nurtured it in them. The warmth and tenderness of this relationship is true to the reality of paternity, and is the exact opposite of the appropriation of empty titles (even "father") that Jesus condemned in the Gospel. There is a difference between paternity and paternalism! A portion of Paul's fatherly exhortation to holiness (3:12-4:2) is read on the First Sunday of Advent, Year C.

Questions for thought, discussion, and prayer:
1. What is a father? What is the title "father" based on? What responsibilities does it carry? How many different ways can we use (and abuse) the word?

2.   What sort of respect is proper toward Church authority? How should we behave toward authorities when we disagree with them?

WISE AND FOOLISH

Gospel: Matthew 25:1-13

Chapter 24, with allusions both to the destruction of the Jerusalem temple (vv 1-36), which happened in 70 C.E. (about twenty years before the Gospel was written), and to the end of the world (vv 37-51), was primarily intended to encourage Christians who were suffering rejection and persecution for the kingdom to be strong and persevering in faith. No matter what the present calamities may be, God's justice will have the last word. We must be watchful, not so much for a future coming, as to capture the opportunities for making the justice of God's kingdom a reality now in spite of obstacles, so that the present moment may give birth to the future and final fulfillment.

The parable of the liturgical reading (25:1-13) concentrates not so much on watchfulness as on the need for preparation, and must be understood in the light of the wedding customs of Jesus' day. The marriage celebration was a long and festive ritual, centering on a solemn procession in which the groom led the bride from her family home into his own house, signifying the acceptance of one another as husband and wife. Lengthy discussion and negotiation between the groom and the bride's parents would precede the procession, and often lasted well into the night. Thus the attendants would need torches to light the way, and could never be sure just when the whole affair would begin. A banquet lasting for days would be held in the groom's house after the bridal party arrived.

Locking the doors at such a celebration (v 10) guarded against uninvited intruders — freeloaders, pickpockets, etc. — that might be attracted to such a feast. Securing the heavy doors of a wealthy person's house was not an easy task, and nobody would want to open them agains except for an emergency (or perhaps a very important guest). Any ordinary guest who neglected to arrive on time could not expect to be admitted.

The attendants in the bridal procession represent the Church on pilgrimage to the fulfillment of God's kingdom. Mere membership in the Church does not insure salvation. Faith must be kept alive, nourished, and growing — it cannot be allowed to drift or be taken for granted. The wise keep their goal ever in mind, and plan their actions accordingly.

First Reading: Wisdom 6:12-16

The book of Wisdom is a summary of late Jewish religious thought, written in Greek about a hundred years before Christ by an anonymous author who enhanced his words by attributing them to Solomon, the ancient king (970-930 B.C.E.) who was characterized by wisdom (see 1 Kg 3). This passage beautifully emphasizes the goodness of God in sharing his own wisdom with all who seek it. Wisdom is depicted not as the goal of a difficult search, but as actually going out to seek those who will open their hearts to her. Wisdom, which means seeing and judging all things as they really are, brings true freedom (v 15).

Responsorial Psalm: Psalm 63:2, 3-4, 5-6, 7-8

Wisdom awakens a deep hunger for God. The wise seek the Giver, rather than rest in possessing the gifts. Response: "My soul is thirsting for you, O Lord my God."

Second Reading: 1 Thessalonians 4:13-18

Paul wrote this letter so soon after the time of Jesus (51-52 C.E.) that it was still possible for all Christian converts to look forward to the second coming of Christ in their own lifetimes. Jesus was expected to appear at any moment and gather his faithful to be with him. Paul had exhorted (as had Jesus) to daily vigilance and preparation. But the question arose, how could the dead who were no longer here be gathered with Christ? Paul's answer was that the living would have no advantage over the dead because the resurrection of Christ is the pledge and the pattern of the resurrection of the dead Christians. However, his thinking is not so refined about the details as it will be later (see 1 Cor 15, written about five years afterward). The "scenario" (vv 16-17) should not be taken too literally because it reflects an overly materialistic popular concept of Christ's coming. The important element of this teaching is the implication of "being with Christ" — it involves sharing not only his company, but his very life.

Questions for thought, discussion, and prayer:
1.   What is wisdom? Think about it long and hard — don't be con-

tent with just a dictionary definition or a "pat" answer.

2.   In the same way, play with the meaning of prudence. Start with the dictionary, but don't end there.

TRUSTWORTHY SERVANT

Gospel: Matthew 25:14-30

Delay is very significant in Matthew's account of these parables about the kingdom. When Paul wrote to the Thessalonians, the second coming of Christ was expected just around the corner. After the destruction of Jerusalem and the temple (70 C.E.), when Matthew was composed (85-100 C.E.), it was obvious that the time of the fulfillment was completely uncertain. Not only vigilance (24:45-51) and preparation (25:1-13) were needed, but also diligent and productive activity, as emphasized in this parable.

Investment of resources always involves a risk. Those who take the risk of putting what they have on the line, who see their gifts not as personal possessions but as opportunities for service, will be part of the kingdom's fulfillment. Those who hoard what they have cut themselves off from the kingdom, and so will lose even what they try to save. Again, note that during the time of waiting, the good and the bad, the productive and the unproductive coexist in the Church, and are more or less indistinguishable from each other. Another theme repeated here is that mere membership in the Church (receiving the "silver pieces") does not in itself insure salvation.

First Reading: Proverbs 31:10-13, 19-20, 30-31

In late Jewish society, when this hymn of the prized wife was composed, women still had an inferior status, but not nearly so lowly as in most cultures of that time. The woman pictured here contrasts with the adulterous, troublesome wife that is often given as the image of unfaithful Israel (Hos 1-3; Jer 2-3; Ez 16 and 23). She is industrious in wifely duties, and these encompass every area of the life of both her and her husband. In her work she is seen not as the servant but as the true partner of her husband, and this responsible fulfillment is the source of her prestige. A fitting lesson for the Church as the bride of Christ.

Responsorial Psalm: Psalm 128:1-2, 3, 4-5
The ideal family life is seen as the result of fidelity to the Lord in this psalm which prays for blessings upon the faithful. Response: "Happy are those who fear the Lord."

Second Reading: 1 Thessalonians 5:1-6
Although Paul's teaching in this letter was colored by the expectation of an imminent return of Christ, his message is no less valid, and is even more urgent today when we tend to grow complacent. Not knowing the "when" of the final moment gives greater importance to each passing moment as a unique opportunity of grace, never to be repeated. The ever-present challenge is to live and act in accord with what we are — NOW! Our own salvation and the salvation of the world depends on it.
The conclusion of the letter, an exhortation to rejoice in gratitude, is read on the Third Sunday of Advent, Year B.

Questions for thought, discussion, and prayer:
1. What do you feel is God's greatest gift to you? Why? Think about your answer. What does it tell you about you?

2. What do these readings say about how the Church (parish, diocese and/or universal Church) should use its resources?

THE SOLEMNITY OF CHRIST THE KING — YEAR A
(THIRTY-FOURTH OR LAST SUNDAY OF THE YEAR)

THE POOR AND NEEDY KING

Pope Pius XI established this feast in 1925 to counteract secularism and atheism in modern society. Although the concept of king as a symbol does not speak to our world with the impact it had hundreds of years ago, the reconciliation of all people under the lordship of the crucified and risen Jesus and his vision of the kingdom of God remains the goal of this feast. The interdependence of Church and State in modern society, as well as their functional separation, needs to be continually recognized and maintained.

Gospel: Matthew 25:31-46

This parable concludes the teaching on the Church in the light of the final fulfillment, which was begun in chapter 24. After exhorting his followers to vigilance, preparation, and attentive ministry during the period of uncertain delay before his second coming, Jesus now speaks of judgment in terms derived from the daily life of a shepherd — the separation of sheep and goats into their own pens after a day of grazing together.

Notice that the final condition for entry into the kingdom does not involve any special ethnic or even religious requirement. The Jewish concept of the final judgment was the triumph of the Jewish people over all other nations. The early Church was tempted to think in a similar way; membership in the Church, or mere profession of faith in Christ, as insuring a favorable judgment. According to Jesus' words, however, the basic standard by which we will be judged is our recognition of one another as brothers and sisters in a genuine and active sense — what we do or fail to do for them springs from our attitude toward them, and ultimately, our attitude toward Christ.

The Christian who is called to profess faith explicitly in Christ must fulfill that faith by accepting even the most unacceptable ("my least brothers") as he or she would accept Christ. But this passage assures us that even those who are incapable of believing in Christ — and there may be many causes of this incapacity — are nevertheless really receiving him to the extent that they receive those in need. Jesus showed great care for the "little ones" (Mt 10:42; 18:1-14). Whoever does the same is sharing the spirit of Christ; even if unawares, their action is truly of God. Christians have the gift of faith, then, not for their own glory, but to witness that God is present in the patterns of human relationships. Every genuine attempt at human solidarity already has the seed of divinity within it. The Christian task is to bring this seed to fruition.

First Reading: Ezekiel 34:11-12, 15-17

Ezekiel is writing after the return from exile in Babylon, and it is apparent that neither the people nor their leaders had learned their lesson. As they became prosperous again, they also became corrupt and less concerned with such "unprofitable" things as justice and mercy. Through the voice of the prophet, the Lord promises that he will lead his faithful himself. Jesus in the Gospel reading appropriates to himself this image of God as shepherd of his people.

Responsorial Psalm: Psalm 23:1-2, 2-3, 5-6
    Pray the words of this familiar psalm as though for the first time. Response: "The Lord is my shepherd; there is nothing I shall want."

Second Reading: 1 Corinthians 15:20-26, 28
    The effect of the resurrection is the restoration of all things in the order that God intended. The doctrine of this passage is far more developed and complex than what we saw in 1 Thessalonians. Christ himself has already accomplished this restoration, but it is brought to completion only on the battleground of the human will of each person.

Questions for thought, discussion, and prayer:
1. "You are judged by what you do." Is that a fair statement? What are some different ways to consider "judgment"?

2. Why bother being a Christian if you can get to heaven just by following your conscience? Is this question put in proper terms?

YEAR B

ADVENT-CHRISTMAS SEASON
AND RELATED FEASTS

AWAKE AND WATCHFUL

Gospel: Mark 13:33-37

Advent begins with a call to watchfulness. This Gospel passage concludes Jesus' teaching on the signs that would characterize the last days — indeed, those very signs have been a part of every age. Jesus is not giving a schedule to predict his final coming, but rather he is telling what sort of watchfulness is demanded of his followers. We cannot wait passively or occupy ourselves with our own interests, even if they are spiritual interests, but must work diligently for the advancement of his kingdom as his servants — each of us with our own gifts, abilities, and particular tasks (v 34). On the one hand, we are told to open our eyes to read the signs of the times (v 28), but on the other hand, even the vigilant will be surprised at the suddenness of the fulfillment (vv 36-37).

We can catch glimpses of the suddenness and surprise of the Lord's presence in our day-to-day lives, if we but look with eyes of faith.

First Reading: Isaiah 63:16-17, 19; 64:2-7

These words give voice to the cry of a people who are broken and in need of restoration. They call upon the Lord to return to them and to show again the favor of his presence. Yet they realize that he has not walked out on them, rather it is they who have been unfaithful to him. God is addressed as Father and Redeemer because human attempts at salvation have failed. The sought-for solution is a manifestation of God's power from on high (63:19), yet this hope stands in contrast to the real fulfillment of God's power we have experienced — it comes not in awesome splendor but incarnate in humble human flesh: Jesus, Son of Mary.

Note that the entire prayer (63:7-64:11) recalls God's past favors as motive for confidence in seeking his saving work in the present. This gives us an example of the type of ancient Jewish prayer from which the Christian eucharistic prayer developed.

Responsorial Psalm: Psalm 80:2-3, 15-16, 18-19

This prayer depicts God as the caretaker of his people, and it

utilizes the imagery of a vineyard. Read the whole psalm carefully —
it reflects both fear of destruction and danger, as well as confidence
in God's protection and restoration. Response: "Lord, make us turn
to you, let us see your face and we shall be saved."

Second Reading: 1 Corinthians 1:3-9
    Paul's first letter to the church at Corinth tackles problems of
an early, small Christian community — they are newborn infants living in a hostile atmosphere. This passage is from the greeting, but
the apostle already gives the key to his teaching: unity in Christ is
both the means and the goal of the Christian life (v 9). Salvation
comes from God's power, not from human wisdom (v 7), but this
salvation is not a once-and-for-all gift; it is a growing, ever-
expanding reality (v 8).

Questions for thought, discussion, and prayer:
1. What sort of signs of the Lord's presence or of his coming
should we be watchful for?

2. How is (or should be) the church itself, your family, or yourself a
sign of Christ's coming?

SECOND SUNDAY OF ADVENT — YEAR B

PREPARE THE WAY

Gospel: Mark 1:1-8
    Mark's Gospel presents the most human and, in many ways,
the least polished account of Jesus, yet it begins by clearly affirming
that Jesus is the Son of God. The quotation from Isaiah 40:3 aptly
describes the role of John the Baptist, who not only points to Jesus
by his preaching, but also emphasizes his uniqueness by the contrast
of his lifestyle. John imposed on himself a most austere existence to
be sure that nothing would distract from his mission to preach the
coming of the kingdom of God. His own limited role was high-
lighted by his rugged simplicity. Jesus — the more powerful one to
come after — lived in much more ordinary poverty (see Mt
11:18-19) to show that God dwells where we are. We may have to go

out into the desert (literally or metaphorically) to prepare ourselves to receive God into our lives, but we do not find him there. Rather, he finds us in the commonplace happenings of day-to-day life.

The word "baptism" means a bath, a full immersion into water. John immersed repentant sinners as a sign of their sincere change of heart. This baptism powerfully expressed death to an old way of life and a rebirth into a new course, a new intention guiding the direction of one's life. But this change of heart in itself could not forgive sins and restore God's life, it could only prepare oneself to receive the gift of forgiveness and new life. Thus, Christian baptism is everything that John's was, and more: it conveys God's response to the change of heart, which is really the result of God's initiative, and signifies the immersion of the repentant sinner into the Holy Spirit who overwhelms him and assures God's mercy, forgiveness, and gift of new life.

First Reading: Isaiah 40:1-5, 9-11
The "book of consolation" or "Second Isaiah," chapters 40-55, was written about two hundred years after chapters 1-39 (about 540 B.C.E.). The anonymous author followed the tradition of the original Isaiah in order to strengthen the faith and patience of the Jews held in exile in Babylon that their deliverance and return to Jerusalem was at hand. This promised event was seen as a new exodus — God leading his people from slavery through the desert into the promised land of freedom. A "sacred highway" had been built in Babylon for processions honoring the god Mardok. The prophet alludes to the same sort of highway built for the Lord to lead his people back home (vv 3-4). The Lord's glory is manifested in the free praise of his people (v 5). Finally, the Lord in freeing his people is both powerful (v 10) and gentle (v 11). (Note that v 3 is changed when quoted in the Gospels. Isaiah reads "a voice cries: 'In the desert prepare the way of the Lord!'" The Gospels, "a voice crying in the desert: 'Prepare the way of the Lord!'" — see Mk 1:3; Mt 3:3; Lk 3:4; Jn 1:23.)

Responsorial Psalm: Psalm 85:9-10, 11-12, 13-14
This psalm emphasizes that salvation is not from any human agency, but from the Lord alone. Response: "Lord, let us see your kindness and grant us your salvation."

Second Reading: 2 Peter 3:8-14
The author of this letter had to face a spirit of discouragement among many Christians at the delay of Christ's coming. He em-

phasizes that this apparent delay actually manifests God's patience
— to allow greater numbers to come to repentance. The Christians
are advised to hasten the coming of Christ by the goodness of their
lives. The end of the present age and the dawning of "new heavens
and a new earth" are emphatically seen not as a punishment for
wickedness but as the fulfillment of goodness.

Questions for thought, discussion, and prayer:
1.   "Baptism" means both a total immersion in something and a
passing through. What does this say of your own life? What are you
"immersed in"? What do you "pass through"?

2.   Deep down, do you want to hasten or delay Christ's coming?
Why?

THIRD SUNDAY OF ADVENT — YEAR B

TESTIMONY TO THE LIGHT

Gospel: John 1:6-8, 19-20
John's Gospel is very much concerned with the question,
"Who?" This Gospel, which probes most intently "Who is Jesus?",
depicts John the Baptist professing adamantly, "I am he who is
not!" (vv 19-23, 27). Thus, the negation of John as a personality of
importance throws the importance of Jesus into sharp relief. John's
purpose is to point to Jesus, not to be a figure having his own meaning.
The institution of prophecy had been dead for several centuries
in Judaism at this time, yet the hope was alive that it would be re-
vived as a preparation for the Messiah (see Ez 7:26; Lam 2:9; and
then Dt 18:15-18 and Is 2:1-3). Yet John, although he truly fulfilled
this function, denied that he had any importance. A tradition, based
on Mal 3:23, that Elijah would return to herald the Messiah, was
current. John also denied any relevance of this to himself, even
though Jesus expressly affirmed that John was the fulfillment of
that expectation (see Mt 11:14; 17:10-13; also Lk 1:17). It is typical
of the Gospel of John to lead from an incident and a dialogue into a
deeper understanding of the meaning of Jesus. The identity and personality of Jesus, not John, is at issue here.

Note that John's Gospel here opposes the baptism of water with the baptism of the Spirit (as do the synoptic Gospels: Mk 1:8; Mt 3:11; Lk 3:16), but elsewhere he united water and the Spirit as one (see Jn 3:5).

First Reading: Isaiah 61:1-2, 10-11
In chapter 61, the prophet contemplates his mission (vv 1-3), the effect of his message (vv 4-9), and the joy of all people in the fulfillment of God's word (vv 10-11). The description of the prophet's role in the opening verses — to proclaim God's word, which has power to heal and set free in the Spirit — Jesus appropriates to himself in Lk 4:14-21. The word "prophet" means one who speaks for another. The work of the prophet is to make God's word a living reality among his people. This Jesus did in perfect fullness (see Jn 1:14).
The enveloping and adorning garments of v 10 speak of a joy which is based on the inner reality of salvation — clothes may not "make the man," but they are always chosen to express what one is.

Responsorial Psalm: Luke 1:46-48, 49-50, 53-54
Mary's canticle, a hymn of praise at the awareness of God's overwhelming favor toward his "little ones," picks up and continues the theme of the last verses of the first reading. Response: "My soul rejoices in my God."

Second Reading: 1 Thessalonians 5:16-24
Christian rejoicing, based on a sense of trust in God (v 24) is not to be merely an empty and superficial hilarity, but a deep and enduring quality of a Christian life in community and in love. Joy both derives from thankful prayer and gives rise to it (vv 17-18). The work of the Spirit needs to be accepted freely (vv 19-20), yet his manifestation must not be accepted uncritically, but tested (v 21), lest they lead to the evil of division and dissension (v 22). Paul will develop this teaching more fully later in 1 Cor 14. V 23 is not speaking merely of individual wholeness, but the unity and health of the Christian community (the Church) as the Body of Christ (see 1 Cor 12).

Questions for thought, discussion, and prayer:
1.　What are the parallels between the roles of John the Baptist and ourselves as Christians?

2.　What is praise? What does it mean to praise?

FOURTH SUNDAY OF ADVENT — YEAR B

LET IT BE DONE

Gospel: Luke 1:26-38

The Sundays of Advent give us a step-by-step preparation for the incarnation, the mystery of God-become-flesh. Today we approach the heart of the mystery in the story of the annunciation.

Luke's telling of this event has many important roots in the Jewish Scriptures, each pointing to Jesus as the fullness and completion of God's salvation begun in the history of the Jewish people. The archangel Gabriel is the herald of the final kingdom of God (Dan 9), and its fulfillment takes place exactly seventy weeks (Dan 9:24) from the time the angel first appears to Zechariah until the presentation of Jesus in the temple. The angel's greeting to Mary recalls Zeph 3:14-16, and so the favors of the redeemed Jerusalem are found in Mary. The expression "favored" (full of grace) has the significance of a woman who is pleasing to her husband (see Prov 5:18-19; 18:22; 31:10-11). Israel proved unfaithful as God's bride (see Hos 1-3), but Mary was found perfectly faithful.

The titles of the son to be born of her (v 32) come from the vision of the prophet Nathan is 2 Sam 7:12-16. His name, Yeshua (Jesus is the latinized form), means "Yahweh (God) our Savior," and recalls two key figures in Jewish history: Joshua, who led the Israelites into the promised land (see the book of Joshua and Sir 46:1-7); and Joshua, the priest at the return from exile (see Zec 3:1-10; Hag 2:1-9).

The virginity of Mary (v 34) is a sign of God's power. In the Jewish Scriptures, virginity stands for desolation or rejection (see Is 60:15; 62:4; 47:1-5; Jer 14:17; Lam 2:13; Joel 1:8; Amos 5:2; also Jdgs 11:37). Mary, in taking on freely this status of unfruitfulness, through her spousal relationship with God, becomes fruitful beyond measure in giving life to the Messiah, and through him, new life to the world. V 35 recalls the cloud which manifested God's presence in the ark of the covenant (Ex 40:34-38), but, perhaps more pointedly, the Spirit (breath or wind) here echoes the very act of creation in Gn 1:2 and 2:7.

First Reading: 2 Samuel 7:1-5, 8-11, 16

David's concern to build a permanent temple — a house for the

Lord — reflects the need for a center of worship if the people are to
remain united as God's people. God rejects this thought at least for
the moment, and counters it with the promise that he will be with
David and his dynasty. His true temple will not be stones and mor-
tar, but the people themselves with whom he dwells.

Responsorial Psalm: Psalm 89:2-3, 4-5, 27, 29
   This psalm speaks of God's promises to David to be fulfilled in
Christ. Response: "Forever I will sing the goodness of the Lord."

Second Reading: Romans 16:25-27
   The "mystery" which Paul refers to is the entry of the Gentiles
on the way of salvation that formerly had been promised only to the
Jews. This is the theme of the entire letter to the Romans. And this is
the secret (mystery) of the world to come: that all humankind —
even all creation (see Rom 8:20-22) — is to be drawn together and renewed in Christ.

Questions for thought, discussion, and prayer:
1.   How is Mary's role in the coming of Jesus a model for us?

2.   How do you conceive of God's presence with his people and its
implications for your own life?

SOLEMNITY OF CHRISTMAS — DECEMBER 25

VIGIL MASS
MIDNIGHT MASS
MASS AT DAWN
MASS DURING THE DAY

See YEAR A for all the readings, pages 28-34.

FEAST OF THE HOLY FAMILY, SUNDAY AFTER CHRISTMAS — YEAR B

WISDOM, AGE, AND GRACE

Gospel: Luke 2:22-40/1

God has immersed himself fully in his people. Salvation is not some distant gift to be hoped for in an uncertain future, but the real presence of God with us in the flesh. Luke, writing for non-Jewish readers, records these incidents to show Jesus as both rooted in the Jewish history and tradition, and yet transcending it as its fulfillment.

We can take it for granted that any pious Jewish family would fulfill the laws regarding childbirth (Lv 12) and the consecration of the first-born (Ex 13:1-16), and so Jesus' identity as fully a Jew was made evident.

But Simeon and Anna carry this identification of Jesus into another dimension. Simeon looks backward and sees Jesus as the fulfillment of Israel's prophetic hopes. Anna bursts forth with the good news of deliverance. Together, they bear witness to the full reality of Jesus as Savior.

Simeon has the credentials of a prophet — open to the work of God in his life and speaking by the Spirit's power (vv 25-26). His words echo the whole prophetic tradition, especially Isaiah (42:6-9; 46:13; 49:6) and Micah (ch 3). The prediction of vv 34-35 is not merely directed at Mary personally, but insofar as she symbolizes all Israel: out of the painful wound of Israel's destruction, salvation is born for all humankind. In another sense, the piercing sword of God's presence puts one face to face with one's own sinfulness. This self-revelation in full light can lead either to conversion and acceptance or to despair and destruction.

Anna follows in a line of Jewish women who witnessed to God by holiness of life. In those times especially, a faithful widow — without a family and never remarried — typified poverty because she was totally without any support she could claim by right and was dependent upon the generosity of others to live. Recognizing God's Gift, she turns around and proclaims it for all to hear.

The simple words of v 40 testify that Jesus accepted fully the limitations of human nature — he developed and matured just as one of us.

See YEAR A for the first and second readings, pages 34-35.

SOLEMNITY OF MARY, MOTHER OF GOD — JANUARY 1, YEAR B

See YEAR A for all the readings, pages 35-36.

SOLEMNITY OF THE EPIPHANY — YEAR B

See YEAR A for all the readings, pages 36-38.

SECOND SUNDAY AFTER CHRISTMAS — YEAR B

See YEAR A for all the readings, pages 38-39.

FEAST OF THE BAPTISM OF THE LORD — YEAR B

MY BELOVED SON

Gospel: Mark 1:7-11

John the Baptist sums up his mission as one of preparation. His baptism signifies everything humanly possible to turn to God, but lacks the power to bring the new life that only God's Spirit can provide.

Mark's account of the baptism of Jesus is the earliest and

simplest version of the story. Jesus is depicted as making the pilgrimage from his home town to the place where John was baptizing (near the Dead Sea — a distance of about fifty to sixty miles). He arrives and is baptized like any other pilgrim, and at that point receives the Spirit of his mission.

As Mark describes it, Jesus alone saw the vision. The violent opening of the heavens alludes to Is 64:1, and is a sign of the coming of the new age. The dove was a symbol of love, and also of the people of Israel as God's beloved (see Hos 11:11; Ps 74:19). The dove attests to Jesus' becoming the representative of God's new people in the Spirit. The voice from the heavens echoes Is:42:1 (in the first reading), and affirms that Jesus is truly the Lord's chosen servant.

See YEAR A for the first and second readings, pages 39-40.

YEAR B
LENT-EASTER SEASON

See readings for YEAR A, pages 42-43.

FIRST SUNDAY OF LENT — YEAR B

THE TIME OF FULFILLMENT

Gospel: Mark 1:12-15

Mark's is the Gospel that begins to consider Jesus as the Messiah with the baptism in the Jordan (1:1-11). Being the first Gospel set to writing, it reflects the earliest preaching of the apostles, which was concerned only with Jesus' ministry, not his pre-history (see Acts 10:38). Later Gospels searched for his roots in earlier events. The baptism is a sign of Jesus' full immersion into the human condition (v 9), and he emerges as the open channel between God and humanity, signified by the image of the parting heavens (vv 10-11).

The temptation in the desert (vv 12-13), covered very briefly in Mark (see the fuller accounts, showing later developments, in Mt 4:1-11 and Lk 4:1-13 — they are commented upon in the First Sunday of Lent, Years A and C), forms the pivot between the baptism and the beginning of his ministry. Aware of his power as Messiah, being fully divine as well as human, the very human temptations to misuse or shortcut his mission would provide the material for a major struggle. Would he fully accept the human condition — and thus allow God to become fully one with us — or would he use God's power for selfish ends: to satisfy purely material needs, to evade death, or to attract a huge following? Our salvation hangs upon his freely willed fidelity as man to the Word-of-God-made-flesh that he is. He emerges from the struggle victorious in new strength, proclaiming the coming of the kingdom — the new and full relationship between God and humankind — and its requirements: a change of heart and faith (vv 14-15).

First Reading: Genesis 9:8-15

Christian tradition has always seen the flood as an image of the "waters of baptism that make an end of sin and a new beginning of goodness" (Rite of Baptism, Blessing of the Water). Both aspects of destruction and new life are conveyed in the flood story. As sin is destroyed, so new life comes forth, borne up on the same water. The flood is not simply a chance event or the amusement of a capricious god; it is the result of humanity's sinfulness. But in the midst of this catastrophe, the saving will of God is at work, and the basic goodness of creation and of humankind is reaffirmed in the covenant God makes with Noah.

Responsorial Psalm: Psalm 25:4-5, 6-7, 8-9

Of all God's works, the greatest are forgiveness and mercy, for in this way he brings his creation to fulfillment. Response: "Your ways, O Lord, are love and truth, to those who keep your covenant."

Second Reading: 1 Peter 3:18-22

Most commentators consider 1 Peter an early baptismal instruction in which the Christian life is described for new converts as to its meaning and obligations. This passage quotes a simple formula of faith in Christ: "Jesus died to flesh and rose to the spirit (v 18); he descended to the realm of the dead (v 19), and went to heaven at God's right hand in power (v 22)." The author adds a footnote comparing the baptism that the new Christians now experience with the flood of Noah's time (vv 20-21). The descent into hell (that is, the realm of the dead) seems to signify Christ's lordship over all creation without exception — even the underworld — and allows the good news of salvation to be proclaimed to those who had gone before.

Questions for thought, discussion, and prayer:
1. Lent originated as the time of preparation for the celebration of baptism, and the restored Rite of Christian Initiation of Adults has brought this significance back into the forefront of the Church's celebration of this season. How can this influence your understanding and practice of Lent now?

2. Discuss the role of temptation in the Christian life. What is it, and what purpose does it serve?

LISTEN TO HIM

Gospel: Mark 9:2-10

This event shows several striking similarities to the baptism of Jesus (Mk 1:9-11). In the one, Jesus is immersed in water as a sign of his solidarity with sinful humanity; in the other, he is enveloped in glory as a sign of his divinity. In both, a voice speaks from the heavens proclaiming Jesus as God's Son. In the transfiguration comes the added command, "Listen to him." In all the Gospels, the baptism marks the beginning of Jesus' ministry, while the transfiguration marks the beginning of the disciples' awareness of the true nature of his mission. Note that the transfiguration is presented in very close connection with Jesus' teaching about his death and resurrection (see Mk 8:27-28; 9:9-13, 30-32).

Elijah features in the narrative because the suffering and death of John the Baptist (the new Elijah) foreshadowed that of Jesus (9:9-13). Moses, in leading the chosen people out of slavery, through the sea, into the freedom of the promised land, prefigured the suffering-death-resurrection passage of Jesus, which his followers must also share (8:34-38).

The six days, the mountain and cloud, and the booths or tents are all a clear reference to the yearly Jewish feast of tabernacles, which celebrated the anticipation of the Messiah and his enthronement. In his transfiguration, Jesus proclaims that he is the awaited Messiah, but that his glory would be fulfilled through suffering.

First Reading: Genesis 22:1-2, 9a, 10-13, 15-18

This story of the sacrifice of Isaac displays many levels of meaning as a part of the Jewish scriptural tradition. It consecrates the mount of the temple (Moriah) as a place fitting for sacrifice. It condemns the practice of infant sacrifice, which was prevalent in the eighth and seventh centuries B.C.E., by demonstrating a substitute sacrifice to redeem the first-born, who belong to God. Moreover, it emphasizes that true sacrifice lies in faith and obedience rather than in actual slaughter. Finally, it demonstrates that the fulfillment of God's promise of descendants to Abraham does not depend on physical procreation through Isaac alone, but on the power of God. This event looks forward to the death and resurrection of Jesus, in which the giving up of life into God's hands brings forth new life in abundance.

Responsorial Psalm: Psalm 116:10, 15, 16-17, 18-19
This psalm is the prayer of thanksgiving of one who was faithful to God even in the midst of darkness and affliction. Response: "I will walk in the presence of the Lord, in the land of the living" (v 9).

Second Reading: Romans 8:31-34
At the heart of faith is the confidence that, if God wills to save us, he does not will to accuse and condemn us. His saving will is shown in his raising Jesus up to be our savior, not merely by his death, but by his continued presence with the Father, commending us to his love and mercy.

Questions for thought, discussion, and prayer:
1. How do you understand the idea of suffering and death in relation to glory?

2. What is the meaning of sacrifice in your life?

THIRD SUNDAY OF LENT — YEAR B

DESTROY THIS TEMPLE

Gospel: John 2:13-25
John places the incident of cleansing the temple at the very beginning of Jesus' ministry, while the other Gospels show it as part of the events immediately preceding the passion (Mk 11:15-18; Mt 21:12-13; Lk 19:45-48). In the structure of John's Gospel, the events of these days echo the work of creation and salvation in the Jewish Scriptures. The first words of the Gospel recall the beginning of Genesis: the enumeration of days (Jn 1:29, 35, 43; 2:1) leading up to the wedding feast at Cana recall the six days of creation and the seventh day of rest (or fullness) in which the events of God's salvation are set in motion. Now this cleansing of the temple, explicitly connected to the passover, gives the theme of God's salvation in Christ. Just as the passover event was the destruction of the bonds of slavery in Egypt and the passage to a new life as God's people in

the promised land, so in Christ the sinful stranglehold of materialism would be broken, and the new life of God's true temple would be built up. In John's pattern, we see Jesus as the fulfillment of creation (in the wedding feast) leading creation into the new dimension of the resurrection (vv 21-22). The rest of the Gospel of John continues to explore what is already contained in this passage as a seed.

First Reading: Exodus 20:1-17

The decalogue or ten commandments is found both here and in Dt 5:6-21 in almost the same form. It appears as a brief, easily memorized summary of the entire law of God, and indeed has been traditionally used as such in religious education. The first commandment (vv 2-6) sets the rest of the commandments within the context of the covenant. The law is seen as the means of being faithful to the alliance God has made with his people.

Although the commandments are in accord with what we may perceive as natural law and with any reasonable ethical system, they also rise above nature. They are expressions of the personal will of God as the way to live in union with him. In the commandments, we have an example of God elevating nature to be an expression of his love. For the Christian, the commandments of the Jewish Scriptures are the first word, not the last word — the beginning of the Christian life, not its totality. Keeping the commandments is the foundation upon which a life of Christian love, which goes beyond mere laws, is to be built. (See also the Ninth Sunday of Year B for a commentary on the third commandment — the sabbath rest — as found in Dt 5:12-15.)

Responsorial Psalm: Psalm 19:8, 9, 10, 11

This psalm sees the harmony of the universe, expressed in God's law, as a powerful sign of his love. Response: "Lord, you have the words of everlasting life" (Jn 6:69).

Second Reading: 1 Corinthians 1:22-25

The root problem in the Christian community at Corinth was a division into factions based on personalities (1:12; 3:4) and rivalries over the value of various "spiritual gifts" (ch 12). These divisions show themselves even at the very heart of the community's life, the Lord's supper (11:18-22), and give rise to other problems of immorality (5:6-6:20). In this passage, Paul diagnoses the problem as caused by a search for worldly wisdom — using reason to argue one's own way as more "perfect" than that of others. Paul's remedy is simply to disregard the pretensions of philosophical arguments, and to call for a patterning of one's life after the cross — self-giving unto the total emptiness of death. This is foolishness in the eyes of those whose motto is "Look out for Number One," but is the only true wisdom in the eyes of God.

Questions for thought, discussion, and prayer:
1. What more is asked of us as Christians than to keep the ten commandments?

2. Is there a real opposition between faith and reason, between revelation and science?

FOURTH SUNDAY OF LENT — YEAR B

GOD SO LOVED THE WORLD

Gospel: John 3:14-21
Nicodemus had all the credentials of a very proper Jewish gentleman and leader, and so, because of the beginning opposition to Jesus among his own associates, he would have to approach him secretly by night. But this whole event signifies far more than a nocturnal lesson in doctrine — it is an experience of the birth of faith. Nicodemus, who represents all that is best in Judaism, comes to Jesus out of a darkness that even the past revelation of God in the Jewish Scriptures could not dispel. He is a teacher (v 9), and he comes to Jesus, the Teacher, for enlightenment. But actually he encounters the Light of the World, who alone can dispel darkness. He knows the Scriptures, he has seen Jesus' signs, and now he hears his words. But that is not enough. The rebirth (vv 3-8) that so puzzles Nicodemus (vv 4 and 9) is nothing other than entering a personal relationship with Jesus as the Christ. Faith is not merely accepting a doctrine or the understanding of a certain teaching, it is the intimate contact with Jesus the Christ, in whom we touch God.

The coming of Jesus Christ, God's Word-made-flesh, is itself judgment: acceptance of Jesus in faith is itself rebirth to eternal life, rejection in disbelief is itself condemnation. In the presence of the light, it is possible to prefer darkness, and therefore to hate truth (vv 19-20). But those who do the truth (v 21) are not merely engaged in abstract and disinterested intellectual speculation. They accept truth as the guiding principle of life and living. Note that "light" is not merely something we see; it is that by which we see everything else. Faith in Jesus transforms all reality by first of all transforming the way we look at reality.

First Reading: 2 Chronicles 36:14-17, 19-23

The books of Chronicles recount basically the same history as Samuel and Kings, but with more of a theological than political emphasis. The author makes it clear that the greatness of the kingdom under David was due to his fidelity to proper worship of God, and the decline under subsequent kings was caused by their abandonment of the traditions of temple worship and their failure to listen to God's word.

This reading recounts the destruction of Jerusalem, and the exile in Babylon (537 B.C.E.), and the reason for it, as well as the beginning of the restoration (538 B.C.E.). The books of Ezra and Nehemiah were written by the same author, and detail the reconstruction after exile. (See the Third Sunday of Year C.) V 21 alludes to Jer 25:11-12, and focuses on the disregard of the Sabbath as the summation of the peoples' infidelity, and therefore the reason for destruction and exile.

Responsorial Psalm: Psalm 137:1-2, 3, 4-5, 6

This psalm was composed after the return from exile, and recalls the sadness of that time — together with an all-too-human desire for vengeance (vv 8-9). Response: "Let my tongue be silenced if I ever forget you!"

Second Reading: Ephesians 2:4-10

Just as our creation is not our own doing, so the restoration of this creation is not our own doing. It is accomplished in Christ. Yet that faith by which we receive God's gift (v 8) is an active doing the truth, not merely a passive, non-involved acceptance. We cannot earn God's gift, but we can and must respond to it by living in accord with it.

Questions for thought, discussion, and prayer:
1.   How does the season of Lent help you to "act in truth"?

2.   What does the word "judgment" mean? How does it apply to your relationship with God?

FATHER, GLORIFY YOUR NAME

Gospel: John 12:20-33

The appearance of the Greeks (i.e. non-Jews, perhaps converts to Judaism) flows logically from the remark of the Pharisees in v 19 — which, of course, was more true than they suspected. Jesus does not seem to grant their request to see him, yet he more than fulfills it in v 32. When he is glorified, salvation (represented by "seeing him") will be available to all peoples.

The true meaning of glory is not empty fame or even well-deserved praise. Glory is inner value. Suffering and death itself is the glory of Jesus because he thus manifests his true self in loving obedience to the Father (v 27), and this glory is shared with his followers in their joining with his sufferings (v 26). The resurrection is not merely a reward for undergoing suffering and death, it is the result of the gracious and loving acceptance of Jesus' self-gift by the Father. The act of yielding (dying) gives birth to new life (v 29).

The judgment of v 31 is the same as we saw last week: men and women judge themselves by their acceptance or rejection of the crucified (glorified) Jesus.

First Reading: Jeremiah 31:31-34

The imperfection of the Jewish covenant was not God's fault. He cared for his people as his own, yet they broke faith repeatedly. But because the covenant was essentially external ("I took them by the hand," v 32; they needed to teach others, v 34), it could not be fully kept. The new covenant hoped for in this passage would be eternal and unbreakable because it is already adhered to perfectly in the person of Jesus Christ, and would extend to all who cling to him in faith. Forgiveness of sin (and forgetting it!) is the reverse side of the covenant — the binding relationship itself heals alienation.

Responsorial Psalm: Psalm 51:3-4, 12-13, 14-15

These words of David's psalm of repentance express the confidence in God's forgiveness that should be ours through Christ. Response: "Create a clean heart in me, O God."

Second Reading: Hebrews 5:7-9

Jesus carried out the ideal of inner sacrifice — obedience — spoken of by the prophets (1 Sam 15:22-23; Ps 40:7-9; Is 1:10-20; Amos 5:21-24; Micah 6:6-8). He is the perfect high priest because only he, as God-the-Son, can make God's very self present and active, and as man-in-the-flesh, can fully respond in obedience. Only he can perfectly represent God to us and us to God!

Questions for thought, discussion, and prayer:

1. What is obedience? Why was it important in Jesus' life? Why is it important in your life?

2. Even if sin is forgiven and forgotten, why and in what ways is it still necessary to "make up for" sin?

PASSION/PALM SUNDAY — YEAR B

HOSANNA!

Gospel for Procession: Mark 11:1-10 or John 12:12-16

Either Gospel passage may be read in conjunction with the blessing and procession of palms. Both tell of the same event, Jesus' majestic entry into Jerusalem the week before his crucifixion, but they approach the story from different angles. Mark shows the authority of Jesus in the details. John bypasses details and emphasizes the meaning: Jesus is entering to glory through the approaching suffering (v 15, quoting Zech 9:9). Ps 118:26 is quoted in both readings, and the entire psalm was chanted in ritual processions to the temple in Jewish worship. "Hosanna" was a liturgical acclamation meaning "save us, we pray," and here was used to show recognition of Jesus as Messiah.

Gospel of the Mass: Mark 14:1-15:47

The Passion according to Mark. Mark's account of Jesus' passion shows many of the characteristics of the rest of his Gospel. It is a lively narrative in "spoken" rather than "literary" style. It concentrates on facts and details, and does not hide nor downplay elements that might seem offensive. Jesus is presented as not so much in control of events as freely relinquishing control. The crucified

Messiah, who allows himself to be handed over to a shameful death — this is a mystery and a scandal which is presented in Mark without explanation or apology, and simply demands acceptance and submission.

The story line may be divided into four sections:

(1)   The Lord's supper and prayer in the garden (14:1-42);

(2)   the arrest, the religious trial, and Peter's denial (14:43-72);

(3)   the civil trial, sentencing, and mockery (15:1-20);

(4)   the way of the cross, death, and burial (15:21-47).

See YEAR A for the first and second readings, pages 53-54.

THE SACRED TRIDUUM

HOLY THURSDAY — MASS OF THE LORD'S SUPPER

See YEAR A for all the readings, pages 54-55.

GOOD FRIDAY, CELEBRATION OF THE LORD'S PASSION

See YEAR A for all the readings, pages 55-56.

EASTER VIGIL

See YEAR A for all the readings, pages 56-58, except:

Gospel: Mark 16:1-8

Mark's emphasis in describing the discovery of the resurrection is witness. The early Church was faced with a need to express these events clearly in order to give an account of their faith in the risen

Jesus. It could not merely be an invention of the apostles, because the empty tomb was discovered by the women whose only purpose was to care for the corpse. The words of the formula of faith, "he has been raised up," are spoken by a mysterious, heavenly being. Witness of this is carried to the apostles by the women, and the apostles in turn carry it to the world. Peter is mentioned specifically in virtue of his call to be the "rock" upon which the Church is to be built.

EASTER SUNDAY— YEAR B

See Year A for all the readings, pages 58-60.

SECOND SUNDAY OF EASTER — YEAR B

ONE HEART AND ONE MIND

Gospel: See Year A, page 60.

First Reading: Acts of the Apostles 2:32-35
This reading gives us a glimpse of the spirit of the early Christian community in Jerusalem. The unity of worship (see 2:42-47) and unity of faith (v 32) cannot be separated from unity of genuine selfless love. The common bond manifested here is in itself the most powerful witness to the presence of the risen Jesus.

Responsorial Psalm: Psalm 118:2-4, 13-15, 22-24
This hymn of praise recounts God's deliverance of his faithful servant from death, and is a song of God's glory. Vv 22-24, while referring to the oppressed nation of Israel directly, is also a beautiful summary of God's power raising Jesus to life, and establishing him as Lord of all creation. Response: "Give thanks to the Lord for he is good, his love is everlasting."

Second Reading: 1 John 5:1-6
The most effective sign that can lead one to faith is the experience of the power of faith as found in the Christian community.

Personal faith in Jesus as Messiah overcomes the worldly spirit that can drag us down. A child of God lives as a child of God — and that life cannot help but be visible, and make present the love of God in an outward, noticeable fashion. In terms of witness (or evangelization, or making present the good news of God's kingdom) the way we as Church live what we believe is far more important than anything we say about it. This letter will continue to be read through Easter season this year.

Questions for thought, discussion, and prayer:
1. How have you seen Christ in the Christian lives of others?

2. Can we recapture something of the spirit that characterized the early community as depicted in the Acts of the Apostles? What can be done in your own life, your family, your parish, your diocese?

THIRD SUNDAY OF EASTER — YEAR B

WE ARE HIS WITNESSES

Gospel: Luke 24:35-48

This appearance of Jesus to the apostles builds upon his self-revelation to the two disciples at Emmaus (vv 13-35 — see the Third Sunday of Easter, Year A). First he appeared to them bodily, but they did not recognize him. Then he explained the Scriptures to them (v 27). Finally, they recognized him in the breaking of the bread (v 30), and only then did they begin to understand what they had experienced (v 32) and rush to share it with the others (vv 33-35).

When Jesus appears to this assembled body of apostles, they are at first incredulous about the fact of the resurrection (a "ghost," v 37). He proves the bodily nature of his presence by touch and by eating food (vv 39-43), but that is only the beginning. He opens their minds to an understanding of the meaning of the resurrection through the Jewish Scriptures (vv 45-46), and then sends them forth to preach and witness to this new life ("forgiveness of sins," vv 47-49).

The prophecies of the Jewish Scriptures are not merely predictions of future events, but events themselves which point to their completion in Christ. Understanding the Scriptures does not mean looking to them for a detailed plan of future happenings, but instead allowing them to give the light in which the event they look forward to can be understood. In Jewish history as embodied in the Scriptures, God reveals a pattern of the way he works. He perfected that pattern and gave it a new and universal dimension in Christ — and his work in and through us now follows that same pattern. The pattern is one of passage through freely accepted death (death to the old life, to sin, to darkness, to the slavery of selfishness and unconcern) to new life (free, loving, self-giving, divine, eternal).

First Reading: Acts of the Apostles 3:13-15; 17-19

This reading gives us an example of Peter preaching according to the pattern given in the final verses of the Gospel: he explains the events of the Jewish Scriptures in the light of their fulfillment in Jesus (vv 13-15, 17-18), and then calls on the people to reform their lives in order to be able to accept God's forgiveness (v 19).

V 16 focuses the whole meaning of Christ on the present event — the cure of the crippled beggar (vv 1-10). Thus the message is this: (1) look what God has just done (cure this man); (2) look what God has done in the past (save his people, raise Christ from the dead — we are witnesses of this); (3) look what God can do for you (forgive your sins).

Responsorial Psalm: Psalm 4:2, 4, 7-8, 9

This psalm is a confident prayer that God will make himself and his saving power known to us. Response: "Lord, let your face shine on us."

Second Reading: 1 John 2:1-5

A right attitude toward sin is important. We must realize that sin cuts us off from union with God. But religious systems or purifying rites in themselves cannot restore that contact. Nor can we take refuge in a denial of sinfulness. Our only salvation is to recognize our completely helpless sinfulness, but also to accept the fact that God pardons us and receives us into his grace. Confession of sin must in some way be outward and public — an acknowledgment that communion with God the Father means also communion with our brothers and sisters in Christ. Observing the commandments shows that our love is genuine, but also enables God's love to enter freely and without hindrance into our hearts.

Questions for thought, discussion, and prayer:
1.   What would you consider the most convincing evidence that Jesus was raised from the dead?

2.   "Jesus has been raised from the dead, and is enthroned as Lord for ever!" What does this acclamation mean to you?

FOURTH SUNDAY OF EASTER — YEAR B

THE GOOD SHEPHERD

Gospel: John 10:11-18
        Words can paint pictures. Modifying an old adage, a picture painted with a few words speaks more than thousands of words of explanation. We don't merely hear the words, we see the image in our mind's eye, we spend time with the teller, with whom we explore and contemplate. Today we are invited to see God in shepherd's clothing. This vision can also be a mirror for us — are we sheep or wolves?
        God is frequently depicted as a shepherd throughout the Hebrew Scriptures, beginning with Gn 49:24. Psalm 23 is most familiar, but see also psalms 74 and 80. The great king David had been a shepherd (see 1 Sam 16:11-13), and is referred to as shepherd of the people in Ps 78:70-72. Later leaders were often corrupt and called unfaithful shepherds by by the prophets who gave voice to God's promise that he would shepherd his people himself (see Jer 23 and Ez 34).
        Sheep can graze on land that is almost barren, but they need to be led to pasture, to water, to shelter. They are hardy animals, but have little sense of finding their own way. If separated from the flock, they must be sought out — they will never look for or find a way back themselves. Shepherds established a striking rapport with the sheep in their care. Even when flocks mingled together in shelters, each sheep would recognize its own shepherd, and would follow him wherever he led. It was not unknown for a shepherd to be killed in defending his flock against thieves and wolves. On the other hand, many shepherds were dishonest and would steal from the sheep's owners.
        Jesus simply takes the Hebrew Scriptures' imagery of God as

shepherd and shows himself to be the fulfillment of its prophetic promise.

First Reading: Acts of the Apostles 4:8-12
Read all of chapters three and four. Peter and John were arrested on the pretense of bringing a sick person into the temple in violation of the law (3:8; 4:7; see Lev 21:18), but the real reason was that the Sadducees rejected the resurrection of the body. While Peter's discourse to the people after the cure (3:12-20) emphasized the historical roots of Christ whose power was revealed in this event, his address to the priests in today's reading is more direct: the healing of this man is proof that Jesus is risen from the dead, and is the source of salvation for all.

Responsorial Psalm: Psalm 118:1, 8-9, 21-23, 26, 27, 29
This whole psalm refers to the Israelite nation, oppressed by other nations and yet favored by God. Early Christians, as in the first reading, saw these words as typifying the Jewish reaction to Jesus as the fulfillment of God's saving work. Response: "The stone rejected by the builders has become the cornerstone."

Second Reading: 1 John 3:1-2
This is a good opportunity to read all 1 John at one sitting. These verses are a pivot between the first part, concerned with knowledge and love of God and its obligations, and the second part, which reflects on our new life as God's children. We are called to recognize the full dignity of what we are now, and live accordingly, for that is the seed of what we will become.

Questions for thought, discussion, and prayer:
1. Does the image of a shepherd still speak to us technologized twentieth-century Americans? If not, can you suggest other images that might convey the same deeper reality faithfully and more clearly?

2. How would you understand "resurrection of the body" as compared with "salvation of the soul"? Which expression is more important in Scripture? Which is more important in your life? Why?

BEAR FRUIT IN ME

Gospel: John 15:1-8

The Hebrew Scriptures frequently speak of the people of Israel as a vine or as God's vineyard — often producing sour grapes because of their infidelity (see Ps 80; Is 5; Jer 2:21; 12:10-11; Ez 15: 17; 19). When Jesus applies this image in this passage, he first of all is affirming that he is faithful in bearing the fruit of God's work, in contrast to the infidelity of the Israelites. God, at last, finds true fidelity in Jesus, the true vine, a fidelity shown by obedience even up to the cross.

True followers of Jesus are attached to him just as branches to the vine — they share his life and they accomplish his work (bearing fruit). Both elements of the Christian life are essential: work depends on life, and life must overflow into action. Inactivity is a sign that there is no life, and that branch is cut away (v 6).

But even fruitful branches need to be trimmed in order to increase their yield (v 2). The suffering of the Christian life and mission is a loving act of the Father to purify those who are in Christ from the traces of sin and from deadly egotism, so that they may bear better and more abundant fruit.

The vine also recalls the eucharist, for the ultimate result is the good wine of fidelity, the fruit of "living in Jesus" (v 7), which is the intimate contact with Jesus brought about and expressed in the eucharistic sharing of communion.

First Reading: Acts of the Apostles 9:26-31

This passage tells of Saul's acceptance by the early Jerusalem community of Christians after his conversion. It also gives us a taste of the internal problems that were beginning to beset the infant Church. Fearful protectionism (v 26) would eventually lead to factions — especially between Jewish and Gentile Christians — and create serious problems for Paul later. However these rumblings do not yet seriously threaten the inner spirit of unity and the growth in faith of the Jerusalem community (v 31).

Responsorial Psalm: Psalm 22:26-27, 28, 30, 31-32

The first part of this psalm is a cry for help from the Lord's faithful servant in deep distress — an image of Jesus on the cross. The second part, which is quoted here, praises God the deliverer. One who has experienced God's saving works cannot keep silent, but is impelled to proclaim his praises to all. Response: "I will praise you, Lord, in the assembly of your people."

Second Reading: 1 John 3:18-24
How can we be sure that our faith is true? How can we tell if we are really pleasing God and living in his presence? All the ways of discernment boil down to one: keeping the commandment to love one another. Conscience is not merely a good feeling or an opinion about what is right. Conscience is the measure of our own attitudes and acts against the criterion of mutual love. Faith in God and love of one another are inseparable. Claiming one without living the other is phony.

Questions for thought, discussion, and prayer:
1.   Vatican II stated that the eucharist is the "summit" and the "source" of the Christian life. What does this mean to you?

2.   What are the problems that harm our Christian communities today? What solutions does the Gospel message direct us to seek?

SIXTH SUNDAY OF EASTER — YEAR B

LOVE AS I LOVE

Gospel: John 15:9-17
This section continues the theme of union with Christ begun in last week's Gospel. Here Jesus draws out the implications of "living in him" (vv 4-7).
The most profound spiritual activity is love, which seeks full union with the beloved. And if love is true, the lover becomes transformed into the beloved in a way that it is true in some sense to say they are no longer two but one. The test of love is obedience. Love leads a person to sacrifice a personal point of view and put oneself confidently into the will of the other — not in fear or abject submission, nor to calculate a certain benefit, but simply to adapt oneself to the contour of the other. Jesus himself has done this, conforming

himself as the Son of God to us by becoming a man, and as a human being, conforming himself to the will of the Father. He now commands that we do this with one another.

Love brings forth joy. In the midst of pain and obstacles, love rises above self-love and self-pity. Love can be joyful only when it is fully free. A forced sacrifice or submission is no sacrifice or gift at all.

First Reading: Acts of the Apostles 10:25-26, 34-35, 44-48

This passage is a brief condensation of what is told in the whole of chapter 10 — read it all. This incident of Cornelius' conversion marks a turning point in the attitude of the early Christian community. God himself demonstrates that he is not partial to any "chosen few." By his gift of the Spirit independent of the decision of the apostles, he forces them to recognize in act (rather than merely in theory) the basic equality of all peoples in the face of God's love and call.

Responsorial Psalm: Psalm 98:1, 2-3, 3-4

The best of Jewish scriptural tradition, reflected in these psalm verses, recognized that God's love is universal, and that he chose a particular people in order to make possible his salvation for all peoples. Response: "The Lord has revealed to the nations his saving power."

Second Reading: 1 John 4:7-10

God's love is not something we can earn or deserve. God's love is ours as the starting point: he has loved us first overwhelmingly. Thus our motive for loving one another is not to hope to gain God's favor. We love because he has already loved us without our meriting it and without preconditions.

Questions for thought, discussion, and prayer:

1. Christians are challenged to tear down walls of division and build bridges of understanding. How in practice can we do this without compromising our principles? What principles?

2. What do the ways of building and maintaining human friendships tell us about living our friendship with Christ?

GO INTO THE WHOLE WORLD

Gospel: Mark 16:15-20

Faith is born in witness of signs. This ending of Mark's Gospel, which in all probability was not part of the original writing, shows how Jesus remains present with his Church. By his power, the disciples will manifest the same signs of the presence of God's kingdom that he showed. The important thing here is not the sign itself — different signs may be appropriate for different times — but the faith that is God's gift. When the Church proclaims and lives the Gospel, and bears witness to the presence of Christ, the Lord himself is at work.

See YEAR A for the first and second readings, pages 69-70.

GOD DWELLS IN US

Gospel: John 17:11-19

Today's Mass ponders the meaning of Jesus' enthronement as Lord and his sending of the church to continue his mission, which we celebrated in the Ascension; it also anticipates his gift of the Holy Spirit.

Jesus concludes his farewell discourse to his disciples (ch 14-17) with a prayer for them (17:9-19) and for all believers (17:20-26). In this prayer, he confidently places his concern for his followers in the Father's hands. Until now, his presence has assured their unity and growth in faith. Now that he is leaving, this unity is endangered, and must take on a new and more complete dimension to survive and be fruitful.

This new dimension is "holiness" or "consecration," which in a limited sense may mean removal or separation from the world (v 5). Yet mere protection from the world is not the answer, for this cannot redeem the world. "Consecration in truth" (v 19) does not consist in isolation but in immersion into the fullness of reality (truth), of which the world itself is a part (not, however, the "spirit of the world" which is self-centered blindness to the beyond). True holiness is characterized by a vision and a way of acting that regards the world as a sacrament of God — revealing as well as hiding him, and open to being transformed by his love.

First Reading: Acts of the Apostles 1:15-17, 20-26
The disciples in the upper room have become aware of Jesus' enthronement as Lord and Messiah, and are now awaiting his return as he had promised (v 11). They do not know what form this return will take, and so they wait in confidence and prayer. (Jesus' return was begun on Pentecost, when the Holy Spirit renewed the disciples in his life and impelled them to continue his mission. His return will be fulfilled at the end of time.) Meanwhile, the Twelve consider it important to restore their full number, after the desertion of Judas. This number looks backward to the twelve tribes of Israel (whom the apostles would judge, i.e., lead; see Lk 22:30; for the idea of judge as leader, see Jdgs 2:16-18) and forward to symbolize leadership of the Church in its fullness (the number "twelve" represents completion).

Responsorial Psalm: Psalm 103:1-2, 11-12, 19-20
This is an enthronement psalm which emphasizes the fatherly love of God and his justice towards the poor. Response: "The Lord has set his throne in heaven."

Second Reading: 1 John 4:11-16
Faith rests on a precarious foundation — no one has seen God (v 12). Knowledge of him is based on testimony (v 14), a testimony of action. One who truly believes in Jesus Christ lives accordingly, and the love of God shines through his life and bears witness to that love for all to see.

Questions for thought, discussion, and prayer:
1. What is a sacrament? How and in what sense can the world be called a sacrament?

2. What is the relationship between what you believe and what you do? How do actions speak?

VIGIL and MASS OF THE DAY

See Year A for all the readings, pages 72-75.

SOLEMNITIES OF THE LORD FOLLOWING EASTER SEASON

SOLEMNITIES OF THE HOLY TRINITY — YEAR B
(SUNDAY AFTER PENTECOST)

WE ARE CHILDREN OF GOD

Gospel: Matthew 28:16-20

Jesus as risen Lord, the focal point of the renewal of all creation (v 18) sends his disciples forth on the mission that sums up the entire purpose of the Church: to make disciples of all nations. "Baptism in the name of" someone signifies belonging — immersion of one's own reality into that person's reality. Thus the Christian belongs to the Trinity, united to the Son as a child of the Father, a union accomplished and vivified by the Holy Spirit. The new covenant of Jesus is not merely a new set of laws, but a totally new way of life, founded on his continued presence. The life and activity of the Church continues (or should continue) to display the living Jesus to the world. (See also the commentary on the Gospel of the Solemnity of the Ascension, Year A.)

First Reading: Deuteronomy 4:32-34, 39-40

Moses' exhortation here serves as a preamble to the Jewish covenant-law. The law was not simply a set of rules to be obeyed for good order, nor, as later tradition distorted it, a necessary condition for pleasing God. The law was the constitution of the people God had chosen as his own. Observance of the law was the way of life that corresponded to the covenant. Thus Jesus, by establishing the new covenant, did not so much replace the law as fulfill it.

Responsorial Psalm: Psalm 33:4-5, 6, 9, 18-19, 20, 22

This psalm praises God's past works and acknowledges that he still works to save his people. Response: "Happy the people the Lord has chosen to be his own."

Second Reading: Romans 8:14-17
This passages sums up the meaning of the Trinity for us. V 15 alludes to our right to make the prayer of Jesus our own. But union with the Trinity does not happen automatically. Our active participation means joining with Christ as he is — in the suffering of the cross — rather than as we might wish him to be.

Questions for thought, discussion, and prayer:
1. Describe your understanding of the distinctive personalities of the Three Divine Persons.

2. What difference does your belief in God as Three Persons make in your life?

SOLEMNITY OF CORPUS CHRISTI — YEAR B
(IN U.S.A., SUNDAY AFTER TRINITY)

THE BLOOD OF THE LAMB

Gospel: Mark 14:12-16, 22-26
In omitting vv 17-21 about Judas the betrayer, the liturgical reading clearly shows the connection between the passover and the eucharist. Originally the feast of unleavened bread (mazzoth) and the passover ritual slaughtering and eating of a yearling lamb were two distinct celebrations. They were combined later in Jewish history to commemorate the deliverance from Egypt and so recall the most significant of God's saving deeds for his people. See Ex 12 for the Jewish Scriptures' summary of the meaning of these rituals.
Unleavened bread symbolized both getting rid of the encumbrances of household living to prepare for a journey, and ritual purity as well — leavening being a rather foul ("sour-dough") substance that well signified corruption. The blood of the lamb symbolized the offering of life in exchange for life (the first-born) to assure continuity of the race, and eating its meat brought about a symbolic union with God, through sharing in the flesh of an animal that was God's consecrated property.
In the eucharist, Jesus fulfilled and gave new meaning to this ritual. He is the passover lamb par excellence. He purifies us of the unnecessary things of life that stand in the way of union with God, and he is the effective sign which both expresses and brings about

that union in its fullness (see Is 53:7; Jn 1:29, 36; Acts 8:32; 1 Pet 1:19).

Just as the occasion of the passover makes present the entirety of God's saving acts of the past in the particular moment of celebration, so the future fulfillment of the kingdom is also contained in this ritual (v 25). Thus in the eucharist, the whole of salvation is focused in this moment of contact with Christ. The eucharist is not merely a passive reception of Christ, but an intensely active sharing in everything that he is.

First Reading: Exodus 24:3-8
Life's blood is holy because it is the source of life, and reflects the life-giving power of God. The blood of young bulls — sacred animals because they symbolize strength and the male element of the transmission of life — in this ritual becomes the sign of contact with God. In the act of sprinkling the same blood on both God's altar and his people, the covenant-union between God and the people is symbolically brought about.

Responsorial Psalm: Psalm 116:12-13, 15-16, 17-18
God has shown his goodness to his people; their proper return is a sacrifice of the heart. Response: "I will take the cup of salvation and call on the name of the Lord."

Second Reading: Hebrews 9:11-15
The letter to the Hebrews is concerned with relating the Jewish religious spirit and practice with who Jesus Christ was and what he did, and exploring the implications of a life of faith in him. The revelation and ritual of Judaism before Christ is seen to be good but imperfect, incapable of fully accomplishing what it signified, and so pointed towards the fullness of Christ. Jesus Christ, however, is the perfect sign, accomplishing fully the union of God and humanity that his sacrifice symbolized.

Questions for thought, discussion, and prayer:
1. Reflect upon your experience of blood — even though it maybe unpleasant. What about blood makes it an appropriate symbol of life?

2. How would you describe the meaning of the eucharist in your own life from a biblical point of view? In the life of the Church?

BLOOD AND WATER

Gospel: John 19:31-37

On the preparation day the paschal lamb was customarily killed and prepared according to the passover ritual (see Ex 12, especially v 46). Jesus is presented by John as the Lamb whose blood liberates his people from death and brings about their release from captivity (Ex 12:13). The yearly slaughter of the paschal lamb and the ritual meal (seder) continued to make present sacramentally the exodus liberation to the Jewish people. The blood and water from the side of Jesus allude to the continuing sacramental presence of Jesus' redemption in his Church. Blood speaks of sacrifice, and water in John's Gospel plays an important role as symbol of the Spirit (see Jn 4:14; 7:37-39). A few moments earlier, Jesus had cried out in thirst (19:28). Having experienced the depth of human need, Jesus is now able to fill that need with his Spirit.

First Reading: Hosea 11:1, 3-4, 8-9

Why does God still love, pursue, and forgive his unfaithful people? The prophet Hosea not only pondered but actually lived this question. His unfaithful wife, whom he continued to love and bring back repeatedly to himself, became the symbol of Israel who had forsaken God for idols, yet whom God continued to cherish. God calls us as his people for no other reason than his love; and God continues to pardon only for the same reason. As his people, we are called also to love as he loves.

Responsorial Psalm: Isaiah 12:2-3, 4, 5-6

The prophet Isaiah quotes a song as an appropriate expression of thanksgiving for God's promised day of salvation. Response: "You will draw water joyfully from the springs of salvation."

Second Reading: Ephesians 3:8-12, 14-19

Paul's mission is to make known the mystery of redemption. In Christ all peoples are made one under the fatherhood of God. The work of the Spirit accomplishes this unity, and we open ourselves to this work through faith and express it in love. The goal of redemption is that we together "attain the fullness of God himself."

Questions for thought, discussion, and prayer:
1.   What do the sacraments do in your life to continue the redemptive sacrifice of Jesus?

2.   Think about and discuss the power of love as displayed in these readings.

YEAR B
SEASON OF THE YEAR

COME AND SEE

Gospel: John 1:35-42

John the Gospel-writer takes pains to make explicit the link between John the Baptist (and therefore the whole of Jewish scripture and history) and the beginnings of Jesus' ministry. Yet this link is not presented as an automatic transition from one to the other: the Baptist's followers do not just suddenly start to follow Jesus. They first hear John's word, and they begin to inquire. Jesus responds to their inquiry, and invites them to "Come and see" (vv 38-39). Through them, other relatives and friends hear the call to follow Jesus (vv 40-42).

Vocation — the calling of every Christian — has several elements which are outlined in this reading. The natural interest which prompts one to seek is part of God's gift, but only the first step. Inquiry has no place to go without God's response, the invitation to "Come." This beckoning, however, is not a "Come and get it," but a "Come and see" — God does not merely dole out goodies to those who want them, he opens himself for our inspection. This culminates in the invitation "Dwell with me." This sharing in God's life transforms our own lives entirely, signified both by the readiness of the disciples to leave their former lives, and by the name-change from Simon to Cephas (Rock, or Peter). (John's Gospel did not feel the need to defend the primacy of Peter, so he summarized Mt 16:13-19 into one simple verse, 42.)

The final element of vocation is not explicit here, but comes later — yet it is inseparable from the first elements: "Go forth. You are sent to proclaim the new creation you have become."

First Reading: 1 Samuel 3:3-10, 19

This account of the prophetic call of Samuel prefigures the call by Christ to discipleship. God's word in itself does not confer privilege or power. it simply calls and invites. The prophet is endowed with insight and spirit only through the self-binding of obedient listening (v 10). The further experience of Samuel puts before us the prophet's mission. Samuel did not merely recite a prepared text. He was a man caught between two conflicting worlds — between the faction of Israelites that wanted to remain tribal nomads with a loose political organization and the faction that wanted a centralized urban monarchy. He struggled to discern God's will, and lead the people accordingly. Although his heart was in the nomadic way of life, he had to bear the burden in his old age of instituting the kingly rule, together with all the strife that entailed (see 1 Sam 8-12).

Responsorial Psalm: Psalm 40:2, 7-8, 8-9, 10

Public thanksgiving is the proper response to personal favor from God. The psalmist, a sick person restored to health, realizes that God's purpose is not limited to satisfying individual desire for happiness, and so acknowledges God's goodness before others. Response: "Here am I, Lord; I come to do your will."

Second Reading: 1 Corinthians 6:13-15, 17-20

This passage is part of the conclusion to the first part of 1 Corinthians in which Paul points to the signs of spiritual immaturity of the Christians at Corinth — the existence of factions, pride in their wisdom, and, here, a distorted sense of sexual morality. Influenced both by Greek philosophy and the prevailing immorality of a prosperous port city, some members of the community seemed to think that if they were spiritually enlightened, behavior did not matter. It even appears that one of Paul's central points in his preaching had been misunderstood and backfired. The doctrine that in Christ we are freed from slavery to the flesh and to law (see especially Rom 6-8) seems to have given some of them a good excuse for immoral behavior (v 12), which Paul points out is a reversion to enslavement.

Paul sought to bring their way of acting into line with their commitment to Christ. Morality is not empty rules, but the necessary result of a life in union with Christ. It is a matter of reality, not law. Immorality is wrong, not because of any laws but because it enslaves one to a way of life that is incompatible with the following of Christ.

Questions for thought, discussion, and prayer:
1. What does "vocation" mean? How is God calling you to your vocation? What does he give you to fulfill it? What does he expect from you?

2. Why are morality and rules a necessary part of the Christian life?

COME, FOLLOW ME

Gospel: Mark 1:14-20

Mark's version of the call of the first disciples repeats the essentials of last week's reading, but carries a very different emphasis than John's version that was read last week. Jesus' continuity with John the Baptist is portrayed by his preaching the same message. The first disciples in Mark's account are engaged in their worldly occupation; they are not seen as already disciples of the Baptist. John's Gospel gives us a hint of the process of inquiry and call, whereas in Mark the call of Jesus comes suddenly and without preparation. It is obviously a call charged with power: they will share power as "fishers of men" and they respond without hesitation. Divine power is emphasized in Mark's telling; John's Gospel emphasizes God at work in the human process of seeking and drawing close to Jesus as the source of life.

Jesus is recognized as a rabbi (i.e. teacher or master, see vv 21-22), but his style is not that of the seated learned man with a crowd of students at his feet. He wanders from place to place, pointing out the reality of life and the signs of his new life to his disciples who keep up with him, and to the crowds that gather around him.

First Reading: Jonah 3:1-5, 10

God's power surpasses our expectations in unexpected — and sometimes unwelcome — ways. Jonah went to Ninevah to proclaim God's vengeance and destruction upon a sinful pagan people. He suspected that God would be merciful, so he tried to run away. But God had some rather striking ways of getting him back to business. When the suspected but unwanted results actually do occur — the repentance and saving of the people — Jonah becomes disgruntled. But God gives him a lesson in humility and mercy. Read the whole story.

Please note that this is a rather humorous — do we need to be told? — and purely fictional story intended to broaden the Israelites' concept of God's love. It was written around the fifth century B.C.E., when the remnant who returned from exile in Babylon were struggling to make sense of their identity as God's people in the face of defeat and oppression. Searching for remains of a fish that could transport Jonah without digesting him, or trying to justify it as a miracle, would be a useless exercise in religious trivia and would only distract from the deeper meaning.

Responsorial Psalm: Psalm 25:4-5, 6-7, 8-9

This psalm is a somewhat rambling meditation on God's goodness, which he shows by mercy and forgiveness, and well as by leading us to an every-deepening understanding of his ways. Response: "Teach me your ways, O Lord."

Second Reading: 1 Corinthians 7:29-31

Beginning with chapter 7, Paul responds to specific questions that were brought to him by messengers from the community. His lengthy advice on marriage in this chapter is largely a plea for moderation in the face of wildly diverse attitudes toward marriage, virginity, and sexuality. Some members of the Corinthian Church apparently tolerated extreme licentiousness while others held very strict views on celibacy and disdained marriage altogether.

Paul's specific advice in this passage centers on the use of time. Time is always short, and we must order our activities in view of the eternal kingdom of God. Paul's words are rooted in the expectation that Christ would return soon, but they apply equally today when we are conscious of the urgency of realizing Christ's presence and fulfilling his will.

Questions for thought, discussion, and prayer:
1. God wills the conversion of sinners, not their death. How do you feel about people who sin against you?

2. Can even "religious activities" be a sort of "worldly occupation" that Christ might call us away from?

FOURTH SUNDAY OF THE YEAR — YEAR B

SPELLBINDING AUTHORITY

Gospel: Mark 1:21-28

This passage contains a nutshell summary of the whole mission of Jesus: to free humankind from enslavement to the forces of evil, which he does by the power of his word — his is God's Word-made-flesh (Jn 1:14). To use this passage to argue the pros and cons of personal demons and diabolical possession risks missing the point: all humanity is in the grip of the power of evil without Christ.

This first miracle of Jesus in Mark's account climaxes the introduction to his Gospel. Read from the beginning of the gospel up to this point. V 1 gives the title, an unmistakable identification of Jesus. John the Baptist, as herald, preaches repentance and preparation (vv 2-8). Jesus embarks on his ministry in the power of the Holy Spirit (vv 9-11), struggles with the forces that would distort his ministry and run it off true course (vv 12-13), and sets off to continue and fulfill what John had begun (vv 14-15). He gathers disciples (vv 16-20), and he teaches (vv 21-22).

Notice that Jesus does not seek out the possessed man. The demon is threatened by the very presence of Jesus and his word, and confronts him. In its fearful rejection of Jesus, the force of evil itself witnesses to him (v 24). Jesus is not asked by anybody to cure the man, he simply orders the demon to release him. V 27 relates his word of teaching with his word of power — it is one and the same word. Those who hear his word experience his power. His teaching cannot be separated from his person. He is what he teaches.

First Reading: Deuteronomy 18:15-22

Although these words are put into the mouth of Moses as law-giver, they actually date from much later in Jewish history. The entire book of Deuteronomy is a compilation of laws and traditions formulated during the monarchy (tenth to sixth centuries, B.C.E.) and finally codified around the end of that period.

The description of the four major offices of Israelite society (judges, 17:8-13; kings, 17:14-20; priests, 18:1-8; and prophets, 18:9-22) presents an ideal of social order that seldom occurred in reality, so there was always hope for a better future. The prophet is depicted as being God's true representative, as opposed to the falsity of pagan oracles. The prophet was seen to have the power to proclaim God's will in a way that would bring about the deeds that the words signified. Thus Jesus is the fulfillment of the true meaning of prophet.

Responsorial Psalm: Psalm 95:1-2, 6-7, 7-9

A sound with no one to hear it is no sound at all. Even the voice of God, spoken through the prophets, through his Son, through his Church, has no power unless freely received — heard and understood, taken to heart and acted upon. And so we must pray that we will hear his voice when he speaks. Response: "If today you hear his voice, harden not your hearts."

Second Reading: 1 Corinthians 7:32-35

Paul's purpose here is not to advise whether or not to marry. He was obviously unmarried himself — as a traveling missionary, he had no fixed home, and so marriage and family would have been impossible (see v 8). However he regarded marriage very highly, calling it a sign of the union between Christ and his Church (see Eph 5:21-33). Here Paul holds up an ideal of detachment from the things and ways of the world, using virginity as a sign of this detachment, not as its only means of fulfillment. No matter what our state in life, the important thing is to keep our eyes firmly fixed on what is beyond, and not let ourselves become helplessly entangled in the passing concerns of the here and now.

Questions for thought, discussion, and prayer:
1.   How do words have power? What does this say about the power of God's word in your life?

2.   How and where do you see the power evil at work in your own life? How can the power of Jesus counter it?

FIFTH SUNDAY OF THE YEAR — YEAR B

WE MUST MOVE ON . . .

Gospel: Mark 1:29-39

The expulsion of the demon in last week's Gospel reading demonstrates the power of Jesus' word: his teaching drives out the demon of unbelief. On the other hand, the cure of Simon's mother-in-law (vv 29-31) focuses on the compassion of Jesus. It was a Sabbath (v 21), and so people would not be able to journey very far until after sunset (see Acts 1:12 — about three thousand feet). The whole town heard about Jesus, and gathered in front of Simon's home.

Imagine yourself a part of the crowd, and it is very easy to see why Jesus commanded the demons to silence (v 34, see also vv 44-45): his mission was to go about announcing the establishment of God's kingdom, but you would prefer that he stay in your town and become the village doctor! Miracles loudly broadcasted often become ends in themselves rather than signs of something deeper. Thus Jesus counters the enthusiasm of his disciples at his success (v 37) with a rather stern and urgent declaration that they cannot stay in one place (vv 38-39).

Jesus' prayer — a totally absorbing communication with his Father (v 35) — is seen to be the source of his power: as the enfleshed Word of God Jesus accomplishes his work. Note the connection between preaching and doing in v 39.

First Reading: Job 7:1-4, 6-7

The book of Job is a long dramatic poem in which worldly wisdom struggles with the wisdom of God on the battlefield of suffering and deprivation. In this passage, Job reflects on his condition — and the entire human condition as well — in sad and hopeless terms. An awareness of the inevitable passing of time, in which good moments pass quickly, and labor and pain continue, opens the door either to empty despair or to deepened trust in God.

Responsorial Psalm: Psalm 147:1-2, 3-4, 5-6

This psalm is the prayer of the Israelite nation upon return from exile. The same wisdom that made the universe now heals our wounds and restores our hearts. Response: "Praise the Lord who heals the brokenhearted."

Second Reading: 1 Corinthians 9:16-19, 22-23

Every treasure exacts its price. The cost of true discipleship of Christ is to proclaim the Gospel in word and in life in spite of the difficult and terrifying obstacles one encounters. An awareness of being freely gifted by God's word cannot fail to lead to a compulsion to share this great gift with others (v 16). To refuse or neglect ministry of the Gospel means to lose it, for that involves a denial of what we are. Yet proclaiming the Gospel does not depend on human words or our own abilities. It demands only that we be fully what we are in Christ, and live accordingly wherever we are and whatever we do (v 22).

The original question of chapter 9 concerns Paul's position and rights as an apostle. Apparently he did not demand certain rights or privileges that they expected of apostles, such as being supported by the community, and they thought less of him for it. Paul emphasizes that it is true freedom to be able to give up your claim to rights for a higher ideal.

Questions for thought, discussion, and prayer:
1. What does it mean to imitate Jesus? What elements of his behavior as seen in the Gospel can you take as a pattern for your own life?

2. What can you say to someone who is facing great suffering and questions God? Put yourself in that person's place. Would your answer satisfy you?

SIXTH SUNDAY OF THE YEAR — YEAR B

BE CURED!

Gospel: Mark 1:40-45

Leprosy, as found in the Bible, is a generic term for a variety of skin diseases; it did not refer only to what we now call leprosy, or Hansen's disease. Lv 13-14 describes various forms of skin disease, and prescribes the precautions of isolation outside the city for those afflicted, and examination by the priests to verify healing. Thus leprosy and its consequences signified uncleanness and alienation from society, and therefore became a symbol of sin and condemnation. The Hebrew mentality made little distinction between physical and moral evil, seeing them both in terms of sin and God's disfavor.

In these early miracles, Jesus appears to act quite spontaneously, motivated by compassion alone. Later (2:5) he associates healing with forgiveness, and still later, with faith (5:34, 36). Now, at the beginning of his ministry, Jesus emphasizes that his human love for others is the channel of God's love for them. He is also anxious that the man not omit the legal investigation, and so he also seeks official recognition of his power as Messiah (v 44). At the same time, he tries to avoid the misunderstanding that premature popular acclaim would bring. Of course, just the opposite happens: word of his wonders spreads, and crowds gather — often out of curiosity and self-seeking — and the officials of the established religion remain unconvinced, begin to be threatened by his presence, and eventually reject him totally.

First Reading: Leviticus 13:1-2, 44-46

These four verses fail to do justice to the complexity of the

Levitical law on skin diseases. Lv 13-14 gives detailed procedures for the evaluation and quarantine of those so afflicted, but shows little concern for suffering or interest in healing. The laws must naturally look to the common good — protecting society from infection — rather than the welfare of the individual. The priest was not intended to be a physician but a judge. Undoubtedly there were also various forms of medicinal remedies, but it was not the purpose of a book of laws to discuss them.

Responsorial Psalm: Psalm 32:1-2, 5, 11
This psalm speaks of sin (especially David's sin, 2 Sm 11-12) in terms very similar to those used in describing leprosy. Response: "I turn to you, Lord, in time of trouble, and you will fill me with the joy of salvation."

Second Reading: 1 Corinthians 10:31-11:1
Read all of chapters 10 and 11, for these few verses cannot be understood properly apart from their context. 10:1-13 is an introduction (see the Third Sunday of Lent, Year C). 10:16-17 gives the key teaching: the eucharist is the one body of Christ so that we may become one with the body of Christ (see the Solemnity of Corpus Christi, Year A). 11:2-16 is a sort of footnote, and does not carry the same weight as 11:17-34 which tells how to put the key teaching of 10:16-17 into practice.

If we are united to Christ, we form an organic unity — one body — with all who share the eucharist. In addition to being a sign and source of our unity as Church (i.e. the community that believes and worships together), the eucharist also calls all humankind to this unity. Therefore we must celebrate the eucharist so that our unity in Christ's love is evident. If we truly celebrate the unity we profess, then we must also live what we celebrate. God's glory (v 31) is that all humanity be united together in Christ. The faith-filled life of a true disciple is a source of of inspiration and example to all (vv 33-34).

Questions for thought, discussion, and prayer:
1.   What is healing? In what ways do we need to be healed? How does the eucharist have to power to heal us — and all humanity? Why do we observe so little effect of it?

2.   What are the positive values of laws, as well as their limitations, in relation to balancing the welfare of a society with the good of individuals?

HOLINESS IS WHOLENESS

Gospel: Mark 2:1-12

The previous healings of Jesus recorded by Mark emphasized the compassion of Jesus and the power of his word. In each of them, some obstacle to participation in the society (and the kingdom of God) is overcome — demonic control, illness, legal defilement. Now the stage is set to focus on the primary barrier — sin. The power of Jesus' word is here shown by the multitudes attracted to him. Yet, the very effect of his teaching — in this case the gathered crowds — can be an obstacle or a challenge to the faith of those who see him. Jesus perceives the inventiveness of the companions of the paralyzed man as a sign of faith, and it is noteworthy that their faith influences Jesus' response to their friend's need (v 5). Here physical healing is presented as a sign of the forgiveness of sins, but this pardon depends not only on the sinner's own faith, but also on the faith of the community around him.

Those in the crowd who hear Jesus' teaching (v 3) marvel at his miracle (v 12). But those close by who hear his words of forgiveness harden their hearts against him (vv 6-7). At this point begins the trial ("he blasphemes" see Mk 14:64) that will lead to his death. A wandering preacher and wonderworker they could tolerate. A Messiah who came in might and judgment (against their enemies, of course!) they would welcome. But the forgiving and merciful presence of God they could not abide. And this Son of God would not only speak a word of pardon, but would die for the truth of his word.

First Reading: Isaiah 43:18-19, 21-22, 24b-25

One of the biggest obstacles we place in God's way is the poverty of our expectations. We seem so often like small children crying for candy when given nourishing food, content with trinkets when offered treasure. Our problem is not that we are unworthy of God's gifts; it's that we simply don't want them! This is nothing new. Isaiah complained that the Israelites rebelled for the same reason. The Jewish leaders rejected Jesus because he wasn't their kind of Messiah. Our biggest need as Christians today is to educate our values and desires to want what God has to offer us.

Responsorial Psalm: Psalm 41:2-3, 4-5, 13-14

This psalm of thanksgiving for restoration to health expresses the first step on the road to life with God. The attitudes of thanks for "what God has done for me" must lead to praise of God for "who he is in himself." Response: "Lord, heal my soul, for I have sinned against you."

Second Reading: 2 Corinthians 1:18-22

The first part of this reading concerns Paul's reasons for not visiting Corinth as he had planned. It appears that he had to reassure them of his love and concern for them. But he concludes with a statement that sums up the role of the Trinity in the Christian life. God the Father has fulfilled his promises to us in Christ, the Son of God, and through him we worship the Father by joining our wills (our "Amen") to his (v 20). This unity of will with Christ is accomplished by the Holy Spirit, who is the "down-payment" of the promised eternal union with God already present among us (vv 21-22).

Questions for thought, discussion, and prayer:
1. Can your faith — or lack of it — have any bearing on the well-being of others? How?

2. How can we "educate our desires" to seek what God has to give rather than expect him to be guided by our wants?

EIGHTH SUNDAY OF THE YEAR — YEAR B

NEW BEGINNINGS

Gospel: Mark 2:18-22

The account of the call of Levi (Matthew), vv 13-17, has parallels in Mt 9:9-13 (read on the Tenth Sunday of Year A) and Lk 5:27-32. Here Jesus' relationship with those outside the law begins to antagonize the religious elite. This leads into the following sections in which Jesus gives a more human (and therefore divine) perspective to law.

Jesus and his disciples showed an independence from the traditional practices of Jewish law that was not merely carelessness or disregard. Rather, they recognized the law as important, but they also subordinated it to more important concerns. Jesus came to those in need of salvation (2:13-17), and laws, such as the Sabbath observance (2:23-28), exist in order to serve our relationship with God, not hinder it. Fasting had traditionally been a sign of waiting for the Messiah, and so by their failure to observe the customary fasts, Jesus and his disciples gave the impression that they were not interested in the messianic hope (v 18). On the contrary, Jesus affirmed that there was no longer any need to give signs of waiting — the awaited Messiah had come (v 19). However, with the next breath Jesus emphasized that fasting — and the entire attitude of discipline and self-denial — would be a necessary part of life for his followers, awaiting his final return in glory (v 20).

The proverbs about the cloth and the wine skins unfold this teaching by emphasizing that the new order Jesus had come to establish is incompatible with the old mentality. The person who tries to compromise by living according to the old standards of judgment, yet professing to follow Christ's way of love, will be ripped apart. The proverbs themselves do not say whether the old or the new is better (however, Lk 5:39 notes that human nature inclines toward the old and familiar), but rather simply state that a choice must be made which involves the person's whole being — to receive the "new wine" of Christ's presence requires a new heart.

First Reading: Hosea 2:16-17, 21-22
Hosea lived in the northern kingdom of Israel around the eighth century B.C.E., when religious decline, through the worship of the gods of nature and of the neighboring peoples, was going hand in hand with political instability resulting from unwise alliances. Both the prophet's life and words present the ideal of marital fidelity as an image of fidelity to the covenant. Idolatry is adultery of the people against God. Hosea's repeated attempts to win back his unfaithful wife embody in sign God's faithfulness to his people even though they have deserted him. This image of God as husband of his people is strong in the Hebrew Scriptures, and gives rise to the image of the Messiah as bridegroom in the Christian Scriptures.

Responsorial Psalm: Psalm 103:1-2, 3-4, 8, 10, 12-13
This beautifully phrased psalm simply rejoices in the love that

God has shown his people. Response: "The Lord is kind and merciful."

Second Reading: 2 Corinthians 3:1-6

In this passage, Paul gives the reason for the assurance and firmness with which he speaks — his words do not come from human abilities, but are based on the power of God's covenant (v 3). The Corinthian community, as we have seen, was divided into cliques, each following the personality of a different missionary (see 1 Cor 3:5). Apparently, even after his previous letter (1 Corinthians), some continued to question his authenticity as an apostle. In both letters, Paul emphasizes again and again that the word of faith comes from God through Christ, and Christ is the source of unity. The ministry of Paul himself and of others comes from God alone, and cannot be allowed to degenerate into divisive factions.

Questions for thought, discussion, and prayer:
1.   What is the value of observing the laws and practices of the Church, such as fasting and Sunday worship? for you personally? for the Church as a community?

2.   Is idolatry a danger within the Church today? What reasons or examples can you give for your answer.

NINTH SUNDAY OF THE YEAR — YEAR B

THE LORD OF THE SABBATH

Gospel: Mark 2:23-3:6

The Biblical law governing the Sabbath was not violated either by the disciples picking grain or by Jesus' acts of healing. However, they did run counter to a rabbinical interpretation of the Sabbath law that not all Jews agreed with anyway. Jesus here attempts to raise his challengers above nit-picking interpretations, and see the basic import of the law, which is to support true human values in relation to one's life before God in community. Jesus points out that there is scriptural precedent for putting laws second to need (v 25; see 1 Sm 21:2-7; Lv 24:5-9). Jesus' healing on the Sabbath raises the law to a new plane. In Deuteronomy (see first reading, Dt 5:15), the command of Sabbath rest was connected to the deliverance from the slavery of Egypt. By freeing the man of his affliction, Jesus not only did not violate the Sabbath, but fulfilled its true meaning.

The Pharisees with their narrow and closed minds (v 5) failed to see and appreciate the values that are obvious to the person who is in tune with God. A mind and heart closed in upon itself will tend to give laws and procedures absolute value rather than subordinate them to a greater end. Law cannot be disregarded; it is properly a manifestation of God's will. But law must be seen in relation to the whole working of the Spirit.

First Reading: Deuteronomy 5:12-15
The sabbath rest is basic to the Jewish religious spirit. It is not only found at the center of both listings of the ten commandments (Ex 20:2-17; Dt 5:6-21), it is also repeated in Ex 23:12 and 34:21. The reason for the Sabbath rest is to maintain human dignity in accord with the order of God's creation. God himself is shown to set the example (Ex 20:11) by resting on the seventh day of creation. This law was directed primarily towards employers and slaveholders to insure that their workers would be treated humanly and not be driven like animals.

The sabbath laws as found in the Bible indicate that the sabbath was made holy by leisure from labor. Later traditions turned it around: the sabbath was the holy day, therefore all must observe it by avoiding work. It is important to understand "leisure" not merely as empty time for meaningless activity (or inactivity), but as time that is free of the cares of ordinary living in which one can pursue higher and lasting goals. (See also the Third Sunday of Lent, Year B, for a commentary on the ten commandments as found in Ex 20:2-17.)

Responsorial Psalm: Psalm 81:3-4, 5-6, 6-8, 10-11
This psalm of thanksgiving expresses joy in fidelity to God's law. Response: "Sing with joy to God our help."

Second Reading: 2 Corinthians 4:6-11
Paul often faced the criticism that he was not a true apostle. Sometimes this was because he was not one of the Twelve, but more often because of his failings and shortcomings. Here he turns this argument around and uses it as evidence for his authenticity. Through his weakness, God's power is more clearly in evidence. He not only defends himself, but underscores a basic principle of the Christian life: in our failures, we share in the dying of Jesus so that

in the new life brought about by God's power, the resurrection of Jesus is also accomplished in us.

Questions for thought, discussion, and prayer:
1.   What does the Lord's day mean to you? What do you do that makes it different from the rest of the week, and why?

2.   How can your failures and weaknesses reveal God's glory?

TENTH SUNDAY OF THE YEAR — YEAR B

SIN AND HOPE

Gospel: Mark 3:20-35

After laying the foundations of his ministry by proclaiming the presence of God's kingdom as a call to repentance, and performing the works of the kingdom by freeing men and women from captivity to demons, disease, and legalism, Jesus shares this power with chosen disciples. The Twelve represent the original chosen twelve tribes of Israel, and so they are symbolic of the new people of God. Mark immediately contrasts their acceptance of Jesus with rejection by those who should have been the first to accept him — the religious leaders and his own family.

The Scribes were respected professional experts in the Jewish law, but their diagnosis of Jesus (v 22) is a good example of twisting the obvious to conform with a prejudgment. The kingdom that Jesus proclaimed and lived had no resemblance to their expectations; therefore, if Satan obeyed him it must be because he was in league with Satan. Jesus easily shows the lack of logic in this reasoning (vv 23-27), but then strikes forcefully at the heart of their attitude: they were closed to the working of the Spirit, and had made themselves incapable of salvation (vv 29-30). From God's side, no sin is unforgivable; but we can render ourselves incapable of receiving forgiveness through hardness of heart.

Mark's Gospel portrays Jesus' mother and his family as among those who misunderstood him and did not accept his kingdom (v 21). They were unable to rise above natural ties, and sought to limit him: "Why don't you come home like a good boy, and stop making all this fuss? It's embarrassing to us and dangerous for you!" Jesus, in answer, uses this rejection to put the relationship of his followers with himself on a higher level of faith and acceptance (vv 33-35).

First Reading: Genesis 3:9-15

Sin always involves blindness, for sin is always a refusal to see and acknowledge God's order. The basic temptation is for the human to want to become God (Gn 3:5). Once the attempt fails and the consequences must be faced, the flight from responsibility for sin is again a refusal to acknowledge light (vv 9-13). For eyes that feel comfortable and secure in the darkness, light is painful — yet healing can come only through letting the light in and facing up to one's responsibility in sinning. The real tragedy of sin here is not the act of disobedience itself, but the refusal to acknowledge it and repent. Adam, in the name of all humanity, locks himself in sinful refusal of God's forgiveness. Nowhere in the whole story is there any hint of sorrow for the sin. There is only shame and denial. But even in human weakness and hardness of heart, God promises that evil forces will be overcome (v 15). Jesus the new Adam would open himself to reconciliation, in the name of all humanity, by submission to the Father. (See also the commentary for the Solemnity of the Immaculate Conception.)

Responsorial Psalm: Psalm 130:1-2, 3-4, 5-6, 7-8

This psalm of sorrow expresses dep trust in God even when the sinner must suffer the consequences of sin. Response: "With the Lord there is mercy and fullness of redemption."

First Reading: 2 Corinthians 4:13-5:1

Hope is a very human virtue. We are carried through bad times by the hope of good times. Yet this virtue, so necessary for human survival, is not yet a God-centered hope. In fact, according to Paul in this passage, for our hope to have God truly as our goal, we must give up our human hopes and attachments (v 18). Paul had to struggle with his own set of inner forces (see 2 Cor 12:7-9) as well as outward opposition to come to this conclusion, and so he expresses it here with deep conviction. There is a temptation to put our real hopes in lesser things, like prosperity, health, and success; and use God as a last resort. To claim Christian hope, we have to place God first and put lesser hopes and goals aside for him.

Questions for thought, discussion, and prayer:

1. Is confession important for forgiveness? Why? Is it necessary to confess outwardly, as in the sacrament of reconciliation, or is it

enough just to God alone? Why or why not?

2.   What is faith? What is hope? How are they related to each other? What do these virtues mean in your life?

THE SEED OF GOD'S REIGN

Gospel: Mark 4:26-34
      The parables of Mk 4 concern the establishment and growth of God's kingdom. The first lengthy parable of the sower and seed, and its explanation, is read in Year A, Fifteenth Sunday, in the somewhat more developed version found in Mt 13:1-23. Vv 21-25 explain how these parables are to be heard — they must be received and pondered with an open heart in a way that allows them to illumine the course of our lives. Only when we have made them our own can we begin to share their insights with others.
      The two parables of the liturgical reading run counter to our desires for instant results. The seed when planted is gone from sight, but that does not mean nothing is happening. Similarly, the work of Jesus, as well as our ministry as his followers in God's kingdom, cannot be measured by immediate and observable results. Christians have to resist the temptation to apply cost-efficient standards to ministry; we cannot let our share in the work of Christ be measured by outward evidence of success. Seeds that we plant will bear fruit in the Lord's time by his work. Our task is to plant the seeds, and to plant them well. Neither can we use God's power to accomplish his work as an excuse for lazy ministry or shoddy work either.
      The use of parables in itself is a lot like planting seeds. A parable is not a lesson like "Today I learned that the kingdom of God grows slowly." Instead, a parable is a story that draws the learner into it, and invites exploration of its meaning. Parables bear repeated telling and hearing, and each time new insight can be discovered.

First Reading: Ezekiel 17:22-24
      This poem is also a parable. The figure of a tree is strong and often used in the Hebrew Scriptures. Here, the old cedar is the old

Israel, nearly destroyed by its enemies. But God himself will save a remnant — a tiny twig — and transplant it so that it might become a tree that will spread its branches over the whole earth. The little twig, however, is fragile and will grow only under the power and protection of God. The new Israel — the Church — is born in weakness and insignificance, yet spreads throughout the earth under God's care.

Responsorial Psalm: Psalm 92:2-3, 13-14, 15-16
    This song of praise recounts the response of both the wicked (vv 6-12) and the just (vv 13-16) to God's goodness. Response: "Lord, it is good to give thanks to you."

Second Reading: 2 Corinthians 5:6-10
    The strength of Christian hope puts the rest of the world in perspective. On the one hand, the Christian cultivates a certain indifference toward his or her own position in the world. On the other hand, the world becomes extremely precious as the scene in which salvation is accomplished and God's order restored.

Questions for thought, discussion, and prayer:
1.   In what way could we say that patience is one of the most important requirements for Christian ministry?

2.   Does storytelling have a place in your life as a follower of Jesus? Why or why not?

TWELFTH SUNDAY OF THE YEAR — YEAR B

PEACE . . . BE STILL!

Gospel: Mark 4:35-41
    This story of Jesus calming the storm in the Sea of Galilee was undoubtedly very popular in the preaching of the early Church, for it is recorded in all three synoptic Gospels (see also Mt 8:23-27 and Lk 8:22-25). It serves as a prelude to the expulsion of the demons from the Gerasene man (see 5:1-20) and shows that Jesus has power over the forces of evil in nature as well as in the human heart. We see also a contrast between the disciples' lack of faith (4:40) and the

strong and active faith of the man healed of his demonic affliction (5:18-20).

The sea recalls creation (Gn 1:1-2) but was more often seen as the dwelling place of the forces of evil, and so control of the sea was a sign of divine power (see Ps 89:8-9; 93:3-4; 106:8-9; Is 51:9-10). Jesus' sleep in the midst of danger echoes a recurring theme in the Jewish Scriptures: when God did not intervene to save his people and appeared to lose interest, he was said to be "asleep" and had to be wakened — see Ps 35:23; 44:23-24; 59:5; Is 51:9.

Jesus' words to the storm recall Ps 104:7, and are the same that Jesus used in Mk 1:25 the first time he cast out a demon. They appear to be a standard Jewish formula of exorcism, and emphasize that Jesus is binding the powers of evil to render them harmless. Thus, this event is symbolic of the cosmic struggle between good and evil, and assures that God's power will triumph.

First Reading: Job 38:1, 8-11

The book of Job raises more questions than it answers concerning the problem of evil in the world. The innocent afflicted man, although accused of guilt by his "friends," must remain content with unseeing trust in God. In chapter 38, God is depicted as affirming his superiority over the seas, symbolizing evil. God implies that the final victory is his, therefore Job has no reason to doubt.

Responsorial Psalm: Psalm 107:23-24, 25-26, 28-29, 30-31

This psalm depicts God's dominance over the forces of nature, and his protection of those who are afflicted by superior forces, if they place their faith in him. Response: "Give thanks to the Lord, his love is everlasting."

Second Reading: 2 Corinthians 5:14-17

Paul's motive in all he does is the overwhelming love which Christ has for him and for all people. This love overcomes all contrary forces, and therefore we can become a totally new creation, no longer defeated by our human hesitations and limitations.

Questions for thought, discussion, and prayer:
1.   Think about the water of the sea — and discuss the feelings and emotions you have about it.

2.   What do the readings today have to say about baptism?

THIRTEENTH SUNDAY OF THE YEAR — YEAR B

ARISE ...

Gospel: Mark 5:21-43

This Gospel reading presents two models of faith — both imperfect but open to growth. The father and the woman come to Jesus as a last resort. Their hearts are not centered on God but on their own need. They approach Jesus to get something from him rather than to become his disciples. Jesus does not condemn or scorn their self-centered and superstitious attitude that sees him as wonder-worker and healer rather than as revealer of divine love. Instead, Jesus responds to their overwhelming sense of need as they present it to him, thereby removing this obstacle to their growth in faith. In both instances, Jesus explicitly turns their sense of need into faith (vv 34, and 36), and both miracles free those affected not only from the bonds of evil, but for fullness of life (vv 34, 42).

Our own understanding of Jesus may be limited and our awareness of our needs may be self-centered. Yet that should not hinder us as long as we are open to be led by Jesus as he wills, not merely as we want. In faith we can ask for whatever we wish, but we must remember that God's power will always lead us beyond our needs to self-abandonment in him.

Read this passage carefully, and pay attention to the many little details and nuances that Mark gives us. This Jesus who is aware that he is God's Son is also very human and not afraid to show emotion. He is clearly in possession of himself and his divine powers, yet he seems also to be growing in his understanding of how best to use them to fulfill his mission. Compare parallel accounts (Mt 9:18-26; Lk 8:41-56) which are more concise, but also modified to show a more refined view of faith (see especially Mt 9:18, 22, 24).

First Reading: Wisdom 1:13-15; 2:23-24

The book of Wisdom is one of the deutero-canonical (second list) or apocryphal (hidden) books. It was never in the Hebrew canon of Scriptures, and is omitted from most Protestant versions of the Bible (or put in an appendix). It was written in Greek less than a hundred years before the birth of Jesus. The author, living outside Israel (probably Alexandria in Egypt) during religious persecution, sought to encourage his fellow Jews to remain faithful to the traditions of their ancestors. The words are attributed to Solomon in order to emphasize their continuity with the best of traditional Jewish wisdom, represented by Solomon (see 1 Kgs 3). Wisdom is presented as the only real response to the adversity and poverty that the readers had to face in their daily lives.

The point of this passage is that death cannot be part of God's plan because God does not act only to see his work end in corruption. Death therefore comes through human sin. Those who bind themselves to evil strangle the life that is God's gift in them.

Responsorial Psalm: Psalm 30:2, 4, 5-6, 11, 12, 13

This song is the thanksgiving of a person who has recovered from a serious illness. Note the contrasting emotions of sadness giving rise to pleading, and the overwhelming joy spontaneously bringing forth praise. Response: "I will praise you, Lord, for you have rescued me."

Second Reading: 2 Corinthians 8:7, 9, 13-15

Chapters 6 and 7 have been omitted from the liturgical readings. There is little of doctrinal significance in them that is not found elsewhere, but since Paul speaks about his relationship with the Corinthians in a very personal and heartfelt way, they give us a valuable insight into his character.

In chapters 8 and 9, Paul encourages the Corinthians to be generous in a collection for the impoverished Jerusalem church. The motivation he gives is twofold: (1) imitation of the generosity of Christ (v 9) and (2) a demonstration of equality between Greek and Jewish Christians. Sharing one's possessions with another in need is a concrete gesture of receiving the other as an equal.

In chapters 10 and 11, he returns to an impassioned defense of his own ministry as an apostle.

Questions for thought, discussion, and prayer:
1.   How can faith overcome sickness and death?

2.   "We need the poor more than they need us." True? False? Why?

POWER IN WEAKNESS

Gospel: Mark 6:1-6

Like last week's Gospel reading, this focuses upon faith as the condition for Jesus' work to be manifest. Apparently his own townsfolk were interested in him — they turned out in large numbers (v 2) — but very skeptical. They had no problem accepting him as an ordinary rabbi — there were many who laid claim to the title of teacher, and widely diverse opinions have always been acceptable in Judaism. But they were not open to anything beyond his repeating the traditional (and non-threatening) styles of speculation they were accustomed to hearing. They would listen respectfully to what they wanted, and would even enjoy spirited intellectual debate, but when he challenged them to deeper faith in God and a type of understanding that would mean a change in their lives (repent!), which is the true function of a prophet, they refused to follow. They found their excuse in recalling his humble origins. Note again the human emotions of Jesus coming to the fore (v 5) — he was upset and depressed by this rejection, and he just could not work there. Yet rejection at Nazareth became the stimulus for him to broaden his mission (v 6).

The words used for "brothers" and "sisters" in v 3 mean just that. But the same words can also be used in a broader sense, to include those having any sort of affinity. This verse cannot be interpreted as saying anything to affirm or deny the perpetual virginity of Mary. The principal evidence that Mary remained a virgin her whole life is from early Christian tradition rather than Scripture.

First Reading: Ezekiel 2:2-5

In this account of Ezekiel's call to be a prophet, an impossible task is given him: to make God's word alive to a people who had been hardened over a long period of time. The expression "son of man" emphasizes that he is no mighty super-hero, but very human and very weak. Yet in this frailty God's word becomes effective.

Responsorial Psalm: Psalm 123:1-2, 2, 3-4

This song comes from a soul pushed to the limit of endurance. There is still confidence, but just barely: a spirit of resignation is being sought, but not quite achieved. Response: "Our eyes are fixed on the Lord, pleading for his mercy."

Second Reading: 2 Corinthians 12:7-10
     We have seen that many people in Corinth took their spiritual
gifts too seriously: "I have this or that charism or ability, therefore
I'm better than you." In 1 Cor 12-14, Paul emphasized that these
gifts were nothing without love. Here Paul tries to match their arrogant boasting by pointing to his own weakness as manifesting
God's power. Nobody really knows what the "thorn in the flesh"
really was, but that doesn't stop our overeager imaginations from
dreaming up all sorts of things, from concupiscence to stigmata.
     Paul concludes the letter by again assuring them of the
authenticity of his mission in their regard and of his concern and
love for them, manifested in his promise to visit them again soon.

Questions for thought, discussion, and prayer:
1.   "In weakness power reaches perfection." How can we see this
in Jesus and Ezekiel? In your own life or someone you know?

2.   Do you feel that the traditional doctrine of Mary's perpetual
virginity has anything important to say to your life as a Catholic
Christian today? Why (and what) or why not?

FIFTEENTH SUNDAY OF THE YEAR — YEAR B

TRAVEL LIGHT

Gospel: Mark 6:7-13
     Jesus, having been rejected by his own townspeople and rela-
tives, now devotes himself to instructing and preparing his disciples.
This formation does not consist merely of instruction or even practical experience, but is based on an intimate and ever-deepening relationship with Jesus himself. The sending of the disciples displays a
real sharing in the total mission of Jesus — the beginning of what
was to be continued and brought to perfection in the mission of the
Church (see Mk 16:15 and Jn 20:21).
     Jesus' instructions to the disciples (vv 9-11) concentrate on
freedom from unnecessary things in order to be able to give full
energy to the mission. Their preaching of repentance and works of

healing are seen as extensions of Jesus' own mission (see Mk 1:15; 2:17; also 6:5-6). Anointing the sick with oil probably follows a popular custom — a home remedy for healing and comfort. The Church has seen this gesture as prefiguring the sacrament of anointing of the sick.

First Reading: Amos 7:12-15

In ancient Israel, prophets held somewhat the same place in society as today's think tanks and institutes of higher learning. They formed professional groups who were often tools of the established monarchy. But many of them exhibited a fierce independence, and protested the status quo by taking dangerously unpopular stands. Amos, as a prophet, disassociated himself from these professional groups and the politics and intrigues they involved. He emphasized that he was directly responsible to God. Originally a shepherd and a farmworker, he was not dependent on professional prophecy to make a living, and therefore he could be independent of both the will of the monarch and popular opinion.

He prophesied disaster in a time of prosperity. He put tomorrow's price for today's goods before the eyes of the leaders. He emphasized that a wealth extracted by injustice and greed would be paid for by ruinous domination by foreign forces. In short, he spoke the hard truth that so effectively calls forth the antagonism of the prosperous, the powerful, and the privileged.

Responsorial Psalm: Psalm 85:9-10, 11-12, 13-14

To become a prophet requires first of all a listening ear. God can give his life only to those who are open to him. Response: "Lord, let us see your kindness, and grant us your salvation."

Second Reading: Ephesians 1:3-14

The letter to the Ephesians is a meditative discourse on the plan of God fulfilled in Christ and continued in the Church, focusing on the reconciliation of Jew and Gentile, and therefore on the restoration of all humanity.

This passage is an extended blessing-prayer of praise, which details the principal aspects of God's work. His choice does not restrict salvation to a single "chosen people" (vv 3-6). Paul's idea of predestination does not seek to limit the saved to a select few, but to stand in awe at the awareness that God has chosen us, so that "all might praise." Redemption and wisdom (vv 7-10) overcome the limitations that sinful nature imposes on us. Restoration of all in Christ has already begun, but is not complete until the whole of creation is one with him.

Questions for thought, discussion, and prayer:
1. What sort of excess baggage does the modern world impose on us (personally and as a Church) that can hinder us from fulfilling the mission of Christ?

2. How does your personal union with Christ relate to the restoration of all creation in him? What role does the Church play in this?

SIXTEENTH SUNDAY OF THE YEAR — YEAR B

COME AWAY AND REST

Gospel: Mark 6:30-34
    This passage logically follows last week's. The story of the beheading of John the Baptist (6:14-29) is an interlude which helps to emphasize the new phase of Jesus' mission, independent now of the Baptist's preparatory work.
    Jesus recognizes the necessity of reflection upon the experience of mission for the disciples' growth, and makes plans to take them aside for a time of quiet. However, the best-laid plans of even the God-man cannot always be fulfilled, and try as they might, they cannot escape the ravenous crowds (v 33). Although Jesus responds completely to their emptiness (vv 34-44), he could not survive without "getting away" — and he makes certain arrangements to do so (vv 45-46). The disciples, however, still are caught up in the turmoil of events and emotions (v 52), and are hindered from reflection and prayer as much by inner darkness as by force of circumstances.

First Reading: Jeremiah 23:1-6
    The last of the kings of Davidic ancestry, Zedekiah, was reigning and proving himself as false as his predecessors (v 30). He had sacrificed the good of the people for a nationalistic foreign policy based on a compromising alliance with Egypt against the stronger Babylonian power. It was a sticky political situation, and Jeremiah realized it was a no-win struggle no matter which way the political leaders went. While he saw no earthly possibility other than yielding to superior forces, he also maintained a vision of God's rule

transcending nationalistic political ambitions. This image of God's Messiah as the true shepherd of his people, promising justice for the faithful remnant rather than victory for the nation, provides a healthy lesson for us when we are tempted to try to put God on "our side" in the arena of politics and international relations.

Responsorial Psalm: Psalm 23:1-3, 3-4, 5, 6
This familiar psalm expresses affirmation and acceptance of God's personal lordship, placing confidence in his rule rather than in one's own means. Response: "The Lord is my shepherd; there is nothing I shall want."

Second Reading: Ephesians 2:13-18
Christ fulfilled God's reign spoken of in the reading from Jeremiah. Only because of the perfect union between God and humanity accomplished in himself can the inner resources come forth for us to overcome deep-seated political, social, racial, and personal divisions. Thus the peace that all seek can be found only in him, not as if by magic or as an automatic result, but simply by living the mystery of the cross in the power of the Spirit.

Questions for thought, discussion, and prayer:
1. Why are times of quiet reflection and creative leisure important? How is this different from the type of rest that is an exhausted collapse into numbness? How can you achieve true leisure?

2. What is the individual Christian's, and the Church's, role in politics and the quest for the world peace and justice?

SEVENTEENTH SUNDAY OF THE YEAR — YEAR B

THE SIGN OF BREAD

Gospel: John 6:1-15
The lectionary now turns from Mark's Gospel to John's account of the feeding of the large crowd with a few loaves and fish. The next five Sundays' readings will be devoted to Jn 6, which unfolds the meaning of this event in the light of the eucharist.
This is one of the most frequently recorded events in the

Gospels. In addition to this passage in John, it occurs twice in Matthew (14:13-21; 15:32-38) and Mark (6:34-44; 8:1-9), and once in Luke (9:10-17). Whether there were two separate occurrences or different tellings of the same happening is uncertain — and doesn't matter. Several incidents in the Jewish Scriptures are strikingly similar, and the similarity is both intended and meaningful. Jesus' giving of bread fulfills the giving of manna (Ex 16:1-36), which is already seen in the Jewish Scriptures as a sign of God's nourishing word (see Dt 8:2-3; Wis 16:20-21) and an invitation to faith. 2 Kgs 4 (see first reading below) relates several works of Elisha that also pre-image Jesus' work.

In John, the feeding of the multitude and walking on the sea are signs that lead to Jesus' teaching concerning himself as bread of life. The crowds had already been attracted to him by signs of healing (v 2), and so, as a prelude to his teaching them (v 5), he gives them a more profound sign, one of nourishment. Mention of the passover (v 4) ties this event in with both God's salvation of the past and Jesus' death and resurrection, the fulfillment of God's life-giving work. Barley bread was cheaper and more plentiful than wheat, therefore it was the food of the poor. The quantity of food brought up was a little more than enough for one meal, but not enough for two — it would constitute a very meager shared meal. It is significant that God's power works for the poor in freely giving and sharing what one has, however little it may be (see Is 55:1-4).

In giving this sign (v 14), Jesus reveals himself as the new Moses, the prophet of Dt 18:15-18. The crowds misunderstand the meaning of this sign (v 15), and so it is reinforced in the following event. Details in vv 16-21 are problematic, and in the Greek original v 19 could be understood as "walking along the shore" as well as upon the water. Little matter, because the point of the story is not the miracle so much as Jesus' revelation to his disciples of his identity as more than prophet — as the divine person. "It is I" in v 20 is so phrased as to reflect the divine name, Yahweh, revealed to Moses (Ex 3:13-15).

First Reading: 2 Kings 4:42-44

2 Kings 4 and 5 are a collection of miracle stories to show that Elisha truly possessed prophetic powers as the successor to Elijah. More significant than the deeds themselves is the evidence of Elisha's concern for the poor, the helpless, and the outcast. For commentaries on the miracle stories of Elijah, see the Thirty-Second Sunday of Year B and the Tenth Sunday of Year C; of Elisha, see the Thirteenth Sunday of Year A and the Twenty-Eighth Sunday of

Year C.

Responsorial Psalm: Psalm 145:10-11, 15-16, 17-18
This psalm praises the glory of God shown in the generosity of his sustaining and nourishing his people. Response: "The hand of the Lord feeds us; he answers all our needs."

Second Reading: Ephesians 4:1-6
The major portions of chapter 3 are read on the Solemnity of the Epiphany and the Solemnity of the Sacred Heart, Year B.

The unity of the followers of Christ as one body, given life by his one Spirit, and challenged to act with one accord (one heart), forms the core of all Paul's teaching (see also Rom 12 and 1 Cor 12). This insight was born and brought to maturity in suffering — the almost constant struggle against life-threatening divisions and factions in the infant Christian communities — and cost him humiliation, rejection, and even imprisonment and torture to maintain. From prison he now pleads with followers of Christ simply to live what they are.

Questions for thought, discussion, and prayer:
1. What is a "sign" as John uses the term? What do signs do? How do they do it?

2. Discuss what the overabundance of this food (Jn 6:12-13) might mean.

EIGHTEENTH SUNDAY OF THE YEAR — YEAR B

HIMSELF OUR NOURISHMENT

Gospel: John 6:24-35
The crowds fail to rise above the material level. They do not see Jesus' work as a sign leading beyond itself, but merely as a satisfaction of the physical needs of the moment (vv 26-27). When he attempts to deepen their understanding, they get argumentative (vv 30-31) in order to justify their refusal to look beyond their immediate desires. The search for the reality behind the sign is the beginning of faith. What Jesus does leads to who he is — he is

himself the ultimate sign of God's self-revelation: the Word of God become human. Echoing the manna of Israel's desert sojourn, the multiplication of loaves is the sign that in Christ the fullness of God's love is extended to the world.

The expression "bread of life" has no precedent in Jewish Scriptures. Jesus means something completely new by it: his importance is not what he does but what he is. He does not merely give nourishment, which is by nature limited and temporary. He is himself unlimited and unending nourishment. Coming to him in faith does satisfy our hunger because he restores the right order of creation with God. Our deepest hunger is for justice (rightness) and the peace that comes from it.

First Reading: Exodus 16:2-4, 12-15

Slavery has its attractions, not the least of which is freedom from responsibility. When facing the hardships of responsible decision-making which is the price of liberation, symbolized by the desert experience of Israel, it is tempting to look back longingly at former comforts. Returning, however, has its price too: petrification — non-growth, settling for less than what we really are. This is what happened to Lot's wife (Gn 19:26; see also Wis 10:7; Lk 17:32). On the other hand, fidelity to the freedom that is God's gift to his faithful people, even if the struggle is arduous and uncertain, requires faith that God will sustain us to our need, but not necessarily according to our desires.

Responsorial Psalm: Psalm 78:3-4, 23-24, 25, 54

This psalm calls on a favorite teaching method of the ancient rabbis: to recall past events and draw from them lessons for the present. Response: "The Lord gave them bread from heaven."

Second Reading: Ephesians 4:17, 20-24

Following his plea for unity based on the reality of the Christian community's identity with the one Christ (vv 1-16), Paul here emphasizes that this new identity transforms our very selves into a new person. We often try to reduce Christianity into a mere possession of something or a code of behavior, rather than see our discipleship as a very basic change in what we are, accomplished through baptism and sustained in the eucharist.

Questions for thought, discussion, and prayer:
1. How does the eucharist signify (and accomplish) the unity of the Church?

2. Discuss the ways that we commonly use bread (or any other food) as a metaphor. How might this help us understand Jesus' use of bread here.

BREAD FROM HEAVEN

Gospel: John 6:41-51

Jesus, having presented himself as the bread of life (v 35), now begins to speak of the decisive choice that is before his hearers: discipleship or rejection. There is no in-between alternative.

True disciples come to Jesus because they recognize him for what he is: the true and full sign of the Father. They see God the Father in Jesus, and are drawn into that union (vv 36-40, 44-47).

By contrast, those who murmur recognize Jesus only in the human dimension (v 42), and fail to look beyond the surface. No matter what the reason, this failure is ultimately a rejection of the person of Jesus himself.

Jesus responds to their objections by repeating what he had already said (vv 44-50), but he abruptly advances to the next step in v 51: he adds a new dimension to his self-reference as bread of life, a dimension which unmistakably refers to what the Church has come to understand as the eucharist, the sacrament of the continuation of his personal presence throughout history.

First Reading: 1 Kings 19:4-8

The discouraged prophet Elijah, fleeing for his life, is strengthened by a miraculous gift of food and drink, and then walks for forty days to Mount Horeb (Sinai) to encounter the Lord. This journey echoes the exodus experience of the Israelites — it recalls the manna and the water from the rock, the forty years in the desert, and the meeting with God and establishment of the covenant on this same mountain. Looking forward from this event to Jesus' self-revelation as the bread of life, we can understand our own nourishment in the eucharist better as food for the pilgrimage. The meal is the sign that refreshes and gives hope, and so not yet possessing the fullness, we can still proceed with new vigor to the final goal of complete union with God.

Responsorial Psalm: Psalm 34:2-3, 4-5, 6-7, 8-9
    This psalm alludes to nourishment as a sign of God's care for the poor and oppressed. Response: "Taste and see the goodness of the Lord."

Second Reading: Ephesians 4:30-5:2
    The eucharist is brought about in the Church by the work of the Holy Spirit. Thus, as the eucharist is the nourishing foretaste and hope-filled pledge of eternal life, so the experience of the action of the Holy Spirit confirms (seals) us in hope. His action enables us to imitate God's compassion and love because we are God's children in reality, not just in name. God's love for us, revealed in Christ's self-giving, is the norm of our behavior as Christians. Nothing else is adequate.

Questions for thought, discussion, and prayer:
1.   Discuss the Sunday Mass obligation in the light of your understanding of the meaning of the eucharist. Is the Church right or wrong, wise or unwise, in keeping it as a hard and fast rule? Why or why not?

2.   How does food or mealtime company affect our spirits? What can this consideration contribute to our understanding and experience of the eucharist?

TWENTIETH SUNDAY OF THE YEAR — YEAR B

FLESH AND BLOOD

Gospel: John 6:51-58
    This passage is the climax of Jesus' teaching about the bread of life. Having shared bread with the crowd (6:1-13), he spoke of bread as sign of his relationship with the Father shared with us (6:27-50). Now he describes vividly the manner of our participation in this life. When these words were recalled among the Church, the actions of eating and drinking could only refer to the eucharistic sharing which the Christian communities were already experiencing regularly as the focus of their relationship with Christ.
    The use of the word "flesh" echoes the description of the incar-

nation itself in Jn 1:14 — "The Word became flesh and made his dwelling among us." Just as he originally "took flesh," so now through the eucharist he continues to take flesh in us. Through the sharing of the Lord's supper, the incarnation — "enfleshment" — of Jesus is continued through all times and all places. Through communion with his eucharistic flesh and blood we become one flesh and blood with him. It is important to see Christ not only in the eucharistic bread and wine, but as really present as well in the those who share them (v 56).

The eucharist is our link with the whole Trinity (v 57): as the Son lives by the Father, so the Christian lives by the Son through the medium of this bread; and this union is brought about in the power of the Holy Spirit. When parents offer bread to their children in their love and care for them, it can be described as a sharing of their flesh through the personal toil that went into it. What is given in love is always a sign and a bearer of the one who gives.

First Reading: Proverbs 9:1-6

In nearly every religion throughout history, the ritual meal has played an important role as a sign of communion with divinity. This is true of the Jewish tradition as well as the Christian eucharist. Eating in common creates bonds among the partakers, and insofar as the food is seen to belong to the divinity in some way — as either a gift of nature or a sacrificial offering — a favorable unity with the Beyond is established.

In this reading, the meal is seen as symbolizing the communication of God's wisdom to humankind. The banquet well expresses the richness of God's generosity (vv 1-2) and his eagerness to share by sending out servants to shout the invitation (v 3). Just as hunger is necessary to appreciate a meal, so poverty in spirit and awareness of our lack of wisdom are necessary to open us to God's wisdom (v 4).

Responsorial Psalm: Psalm 34:2-3, 10-11, 12-13, 14-15

These verse meditate on the openness of the poor, the hungry, and the ignorant to God's care. Response: "Taste and see the goodness of the Lord."

Second Reading: Ephesians 5:15-20

In chapters 5 and 6, Paul draws practical conclusions from the key verse: "Be imitators of God as his dear children" (5:1). Vv 8-14 are read on the Fourth Sunday of Lent, Year A. In these passages, he reminds us that we live in time, and the present moment is a precious, unrepeatable opportunity. In the life of the Spirit, the occasions of worship and praise (eucharist) are focal points, summing up the remainder of life and charging every moment with new and life-giving meaning. They are a challenge to live fully in time as the sacrament of God's presence, and not merely to pass time heedlessly or try to escape or evade the passage of time.

Questions for thought, discussion, and prayer:
1.   Does a Christian social conscience have anything to do with the eucharist? Can one satisfy one's own hunger and be heedless of the hungers of others, material or spiritual? Does sharing the eucharistic bread relate to the obligation to share bread with the poor?

2.   Reflect upon your own experience of time. How does it relate to the eucharist and the Church's liturgical year?

TWENTY-FIRST SUNDAY OF THE YEAR — YEAR B

WE HAVE COME TO BELIEVE . . .

Gospel: John 6:60-69
       The reaction of Jesus' hearers gives us a mirror in which to examine our own reaction to his presence and teaching. Faith is ultimately a choice to accept the full implications of Jesus' presence; a choice that is ours in complete freedom, and yet a choice made under the impulse of God's power.
       The hearers who murmur and turn away encounter Jesus' flesh as an obstacle — they see him only in human terms (v 42). They are very aware that their union in the flesh with Abraham, as his descendants, gives them the right to the same relationship with God that he had (see Jn 8:31-41). They cannot look beyond Jesus' human reality as sign of his relationship with God as Son, nor see the possibility of sharing that relationship themselves by union in the flesh, signified and brought about by eating and drinking.
       Throughout chapter 6, Jesus has emphasized the importance of a total union ("in the flesh") with himself as the only avenue to a full, life-giving relationship with God the Father. This union cannot be achieved by physical generation, but by a free choice of the will — full acceptance and adherence in faith (v 63).

The disciples who turn away see Jesus' flesh as a roadblock. The Twelve represent those open to faith, who have the power to look beyond the flesh and see the Spirit that gives life to the flesh.

The glorification of Jesus in his death and resurrection is pre-echoed here. His prediction of the completion in his return to the Father is accompanied by the scattering of his disciples in unbelief, and at the same time stronger adherence by the true disciples.

First Reading: Joshua 24:1-2, 15-18

Read all of chapter 24. It describes the covenant made between God and the people of Israel upon their settlement in the promised land. In contrast with the bloody covenant rites with Abraham (Gn 15) and at Sinai (Ex 24), which were based on the customs of nomads, this covenant at Shechem reflects the customs of a settled people beginning the process of civilization. Thus life's blood as a sign of the binding agreement gives way to the word carved in stone as a perpetual reminder of the terms. This liturgical reading, as part of the preamble to the event, emphasizes freedom of choice. The covenant between God and his people is not a contract that binds slavishly, but an agreement between free agents to establish a relationship of mutual commitment.

Responsorial Psalm: Psalm 34:2-3, 16-17, 18-19, 20-21, 22-23

This psalm praises God for his fidelity to the covenant. Response: "Taste and see the goodness of the Lord."

Second Reading: Ephesians 5:21-32

It wasn't easy for Christ to love us. Nor is it easy for us to follow his command to love one another as he loved us. Paul continues to challenge us to take Christ's love as the model for our own, and further to see in our own selfless love the actual love of Christ in operation. The self-gift-love of a Christian marriage is both the image of Christ's love for his Church as well as the place where this divine love is concretely shared.

It is unfortunate that many people fail to see beyond v 22! A careful reading can perceive the expression of a beautiful equality of husband and wife in the diversity of their roles. Genuine human love is a matter of mutual submission, and we can rejoice that this love is able to signify the depth and strength of Christ's relationship with us, his Church.

In reading the concluding chapters of Ephesians, it is important to understand that Paul was not out to change the social structures of his day, even if they were often at odds with the demands of human dignity. Rather, he was concerned to explore how Christians can make the kingdom of God present in their lives and their communities no matter what their situation. This does not, however, absolve us of the responsibility as Christians to work toward an ever more just society for all people in our day.

Questions for thought, discussion, and prayer:
1. How is faith in Jesus a necessary requirement for sharing the eucharist? What are some of the implications of this, for example, regarding the way we live our faith in union with the Church?

2. Love is fundamentally a choice. Reflect upon the cost of making Christ's love your own.

TWENTY-SECOND SUNDAY OF THE YEAR — YEAR B

WHERE IS YOUR HEART?

Gospel: Mark 7:1-8, 14-15, 21-23
    The lectionary now returns to Mark's Gospel, and presents the hardened attitude of the Pharisees as a continuation of the rejection by the disciples in last week's reading.
    Pharisees were by no means what we would call bad people. They were rightfully looked up to by all as being models of what it means to be good. Unfortunately they were so concerned with what was required to "be good" (that is, to keep the law in every detail) that they risked losing sight of God himself as the Giver of all goodness. Religious traditions are necessary to give concrete expression to religious spirit. But if these traditions assume greater importance than the spirit, they kill the spirit. This distortion of priorities in the name of religion is more dangerous than the more obvious forms of sin, which is why Jesus condemns the Pharisaic attitude harshly, and yet appears forgiving and lenient toward other sinners. Self-righteousness is a disease of self-centeredness that blinds one to deeper realities, and constitutes an insurmountable obstacle to repentance.
    Jesus gives examples of this attitude: a false dedication of goods

to the Lord's service (*korban*) and ritual purity. Tradition had developed numerous ways a person could become ritually impure, which had nothing to do with personal morality or sinfulness but was simply a temporary unfitness for performing a rite of worship. Elaborate rituals for cleansing were also created. Jesus' point is that these things do not touch the core of our being. But they are not mere harmless games either, for they can blind us to real moral impurity and the need for inner cleansing.

First Reading: Deuteronomy 4:1-2, 6-8

This passage is a preamble to the law as given in Deuteronomy. The law is seen here not primarily as a set of rules or commands, but as the peoples' way of fulfilling who they are by keeping the covenant. Because the continuance of the covenant depended upon observance of God's word as its necessary condition, the law itself could be viewed as giving life. The motive for obeying the law was not to bargain with a God who attached strings to his favors, but simply to respond to the God who had shown himself close to his people.

These words were recorded long after the time of the exodus, in an age when the nation was falling apart and exile in Babylon was approaching. They appear here with a sense of urgency and sad hindsight: "We have not been faithful to the covenant, we have not kept God's commands; and that is why we are experiencing dissolution, defeat, and death."

Responsorial Psalm: Psalm 15:2-3, 3-4, 4-5

This is a moralistic psalm describing the qualities of a person who treasures God's presence. Response: "He who does justice will live in the presence of the Lord."

Second Reading: James 1:17-18, 21-22, 27

In a sense, James takes up where Paul leaves off. Paul's foundational teaching is that all who profess faith in Christ are united in the Church as the one body of Christ. Faith therefore involves not only adherence to Christ and acceptance of his message personally, it also demands that we acknowledge, in word and act, our unity with one another in Christ. James insistently spells out the implications of this unity with each other as God's people, bound together by our relationship with God.

In the first chapter, James sets the tone for the entire letter. The one rule of life, which cuts through all traditions and practices, is to hear God's word and put it into action. This word is not a mere teaching of lessons, but the real presence of God in Jesus Christ among those who hear. Planting and keeping the word is not like burying a treasure for safekeeping, but like sowing a seed, which enables a new plant to come to life and bear fruit. The ground is made fertile by contemplative silence (v 26) because the chatter with which we fill our lives does not allow God to be heard. The word bears fruit in worship and in lives of loving generosity (v 27).

Questions for thought, discussion, and prayer:
1.   How is the Pharisee's attitude in the Gospel found in people you know? More importantly, in yourself?

2.   Is all tradition bad? Does tradition have any necessary function in our lives as Christians?

TWENTY-THIRD SUNDAY OF THE YEAR — YEAR B

HEAR AND PROCLAIM

Gospel: Mark 7:31-37
       Jesus' encounter with the Gentile woman (vv 24-30) is read in Year A, the Twentieth Sunday of the Year, from Mt 15:21-28. It is interesting to compare the two versions. Mark has more little details in telling the story, like "small daughter" and "crouched at his feet." Matthew builds to a dramatic climax in v 28 — Jesus' affirmation of the woman's faith.
       In the Bible, deafness and blindness are often taken to be the result of sin, and the healing of these senses a sign of salvation. The inability to speak, or confusion of speech, was often a prophetic sign in the Jewish Scriptures: the word of God could not be proclaimed because the people had closed their ears to hear it not (see Lam 2:9; Ez 3:22-27; Amos 8:11-12; Gn 11:1-9). Restoration of speech, hearing, and sight was understood to be a sign of the arrival of the messianic age. (See also the saga of Zechariah in Lk 1.)
       This cure of the deaf and mute man closely resembles the cure of the blind man in 8:22-26. In both instances (1) the afflicted man was brought to Jesus by friends; (2) Jesus took him away by himself; (3) he touched or laid hands on him; (4) he used saliva; (5) he restored the man to his family or friends, but ordered him to be

silent to others. Moreover, both cures are placed in a section of Mark that concentrates heavily on bread (6:30-8:26). It is likely that these cures were seen in the early Church as models for Christian initiation, and in turn, the rituals of initiation influenced by the way these miracle-stories were told. Ancient as well as modern rituals have a rite of purifying (opening) the senses. The baptismal sponsors are seen in the deaf mute/blind man's friends. Candidates were taken aside to be baptized in private, and then restored to the community, "enlightened." Saliva may have represented a materialized form of breath, and therefore symbolized the Holy Spirit. Finally, the newly baptized shared in the eucharist, represented here by the feeding of the multitude with the loaves. The parallels aren't perfect, but references and clues are clearly present. The meaning, then, of these cures is that the Christian, enlightened through baptism, becomes a prophet — a confidant of God, charged and empowered with speaking the word he or she hears in faith.

First Reading: Isaiah 35:4-7

The theme of this prophetic song (35:1-10) is the return from exile in Babylon and the restoration of the people in the land of promise. But the hope expressed here goes far beyond mere return to a former state of life. It is rather the consequences of Adam's sin that will be reversed. This prophecy could only be fulfilled in Christ. However, the prophecy is not merely something that we are on the receiving end of. As members of Christ's body, we are challenged to share in his mission — to continue rescuing the world from sin and restoring it to God's plan is our job in union with Christ.

Responsorial Psalm: Psalm 146:7, 8-9, 9-10

These words undoubtedly refer to the experience of the psalmist, either in person or as a member of the people as a whole. But in their simple trust and praise, they look forward to the messianic times as well. Response: "Praise the Lord, my soul."

Second Reading: James 2:1-5

It is easier to love humanity as an abstraction than it is to love the people we come into daily contact (and conflict) with. In James' day, as in our own, Christians were professing to worship God, but in reality proclaiming their worship to be a lie because of their refusal to treat other children of the one Father as their brothers and sisters. We must display Christian love every moment and in every place, but the place where we must be most Christian is in the celebration of the eucharist. How often our participation at worship is characterized by isolation and disregard for those around us. Is it any wonder that many young people see the lie in this are turned off? Words do not convince when actions say something else more forcefully.

Vv 10 and 11 should not be a cause for scrupulosity or despair at our imperfections. But these verses do warn us that we cannot pick and choose the elements of the Christian way that we find to our liking. We need to be open to the challenge to continue broadening our understanding of what it means to be members of God's people.

Questions for thought, discussion, and prayer:
1.   How can the practical advice of James be a sign to others that Christ has truly come?

2.   Think about and share any religious experiences you have had that are comparable to being cured of blindness, deafness, or muteness.

TWENTY-FOURTH SUNDAY OF THE YEAR — YEAR B

TAKE UP YOUR CROSS

Gospel: Mark 8:27-35
   Peter (vv 32-33) is us. A Messiah without the cross is a phony. This passage is the doorway leading from the beginning of Jesus' ministry, characterized by wonderful cures and firm commands to be silent about his power, into the inevitable progress toward the cross. The miracles might convince one that Jesus was the Messiah, but faith based on miracles alone would be incomplete and dangerous. People following a worker of wonders will wander elsewhere when the performance ceases to satisfy their curiosity. Don't many Christians do this? Their faith in Jesus is strong enough as long as they understand him or have him under their control. Jesus, however, demands a faith in him as a Messiah that is beyond our full understanding and above our control. That is the mystery of the cross, symbolizing not only his ultimate submission to God the Father, but ours as well. Thus the disciples — and ourselves — should be silent about a miraculous Messiah until our faith in the

crucified Lord is firm.

First reading: Isaiah 50:4-9
    Why suffering? Or more pointedly, what good can suffering be? This is a mystery that humankind has pondered since the beginning of time. All answers are inadequate, though not necessarily wrong, and so suffering remains a mystery. But a mystery can still be profitably explored, and small hints of understanding can come our way. Jewish scriptural reflections on this mystery range from Ecclesiastes ("all is vanity") to Job (God remains faithful even if we don't understand his designs), through the psalms (expressing many different attitudes, including perhaps the hope of a reward in after-life) to the servant songs of Isaiah (42:1-4; 49:1-7; 50:4-11; 51:13-53:12), of which this passage is the third in series.
    These songs give us a fore-glimpse of the role of the suffering Messiah, and put suffering in a new light as a means of redemption. Possibly echoing the scapegoat atonement ritual (compare 53:4-5 with Lv 16:21), as well as the sacrifice of the paschal lamb (53:7), the suffering of the Lord's servant comes from making the burdens of others his own, thereby relieving them. The servant's suffering becomes the model and the means for facing and conquering sin. (See also the first reading of Passion/Palm Sunday.)

Responsorial Psalm: Psalm 116:1-2, 3-4, 5-6, 8-9
    This is a heartfelt and picturesque prayer of a person who has recovered from a death's-door illness. Response: "I will walk in the presence of the Lord, in the land of the living."

Second Reading: James 2:14-18
    To anyone who might say that faith alone guarantees eternal life, or that God's favor can be bought or merited by performing certain works, James in this passage simply states the obvious: true faith unfolds itself in action, and good works are nothing more and nothing less than the outward sign of inner faith.

Questions for thought, discussion, and prayer:
1. What is the value and purpose of suffering in life? How do you see this in your own suffering?

2. Distinguish various types of suffering (or its causes) and their relationship to redemption; e.g., suffering caused by one's own sin or foolishness, or by the sin of another, sickness, natural calamities, etc.

SHARING HIS CROSS

Gospel: Mark 9:30-37

In the synoptic Gospels, the transfiguration (9:2-10) comes between the first and second prediction of the passion; in the liturgical year, these selections are read on the Second Sunday of Lent each year. For apparently no reason whatsoever, the dramatic account of the cure of the possessed boy, with its strong challenge to the faith of Jesus' followers, has been omitted altogether from the Sunday readings, even though it is found in parallel accounts in all three synoptic Gospels (vv 14-29; see also Mt 17:14-21 and Lk 9:37-43).

Each time Jesus speaks of his cross (see also Mk 8:31-9:1; 10:32-45), he also emphasizes the call of his disciples to share in his cross. Here he speaks of this sharing in terms of service and humility (vv 33-37). Most cultures in Jesus' time, including the Jews, had a rather ambivalent attitude toward children. They were seen less as individuals in their own right than as extensions of the family and, perhaps, potential adults. We may find this hard to understand, but their mentality was conditioned by an economic condition of family enterprise that required many helping hands, as well as a high infant mortality rate. It was simply expected that many children would die and therefore families had to be large in hopes that some would survive to be productive and carry on the family name. In some languages, including Aramaic, the word for child was the same as for slave!

Jesus here is saying not only that children — and therefore all despised and lowly people — must be valued as persons in their own right, but also that his followers must become like them, not merely look down upon them kindly from a superior position. This likeness includes both service and simplicity. A true and dedicated servant fulfills his or her life in serving. A child who is deprived and despised will be appreciative of everything in open simplicity. (At least ideally it seems like that should be true. Modern psychology would rightly dispute that assertion.) These are the models for entry into the kingdom.

Jesus' way of teaching about his passion is saturated with references to the prophetic servants of the Jewish Scriptures that must have struck a responsive chord in his hearers. "Son of Man," used so often in Mark, recalls the mysterious figure of Dn 7:13-14. "To be delivered" recalls the handing over of the lamb in Is 53:7, identifying Jesus with the suffering servant. "Into the hands of men" is from Jer 26:24, and associates Jesus with the persecuted prophet. Rejection echoes the stone rejected by the builders in Psalm 118:22, and alludes to Is 53:4 as well.

First Reading: Wisdom 2:12, 17-20

Since the book of Wisdom was written only about a hundred years before the time of Jesus by a Jewish writer in Alexandria, Egypt, it is unlikely that Jesus and his disciples were acquainted with it. Nevertheless, the reflections in this passage on the plight of the persecuted Alexandrian Jewish community correspond remarkably to the situation Jesus faced. We can see here an insight into the mentality of those who rejected Jesus. In their own arrogant self-righteousness, they misunderstood his claim to be the Son of God as a pretense of superiority rather than a pledge of love and service, and so they felt threatened and sought to remove this threat. As with Jesus, so with his followers.

Responsorial Psalm: Psalm 54:3-4, 5, 6-8

This psalm, attributed to David when being pursued by Saul, is a declaration of confidence in God's care and power. Response: "The Lord upholds my life."

Second Reading: James 3:16-4:3

James and Paul take different approaches to the same thing, and so provide a balanced view. Paul's writings concentrate on faith, and see behavior as the result of faith (or its lack). James concentrates on behavior as the sign and test of faith. The existence of conflict and jealousy within a community is a sure sign that natural desires and competition have the upper hand, even if the members claim to have faith. If true peace and gentleness characterize the life of a community, it is a sure sign that faith and God's wisdom must be there.

In the light of the common good, it becomes clear why James argues for restraint and order in the use of spiritual gifts, especially those involving speech, at the beginning of chapter 3. What possesses great power for good is all the more capable of being used for self-centered good, and therefore distorted into a force destructive of community.

Questions for thought, discussion, and prayer:
1. Who are the "little ones" (see also Mt 18:2-4, 10) in today's society that might correspond to Jesus' command in the Gospel?

2. What questions does the passage from James raise about your own life as a Christian, or your family's life, or your parish's?

TWENTY-SIXTH SUNDAY OF THE YEAR — YEAR B

WHOEVER IS NOT AGAINST US

Gospel: Mark 9:38-48
This passage contains various teachings of Jesus loosely connected by the theme of "little ones" and their relationship to the kingdom. First come commands about behavior (vv 38-42). Jesus' followers must show leniency toward good, and promote good wherever they find it. Just because we have the assurance that God does work in and through our own Church, both as community and as institution, we are not justified in restricting his activity to there alone. God is always bigger than whatever we make of him. Our attitude toward those who are weaker or who differ from us must be to build up faith, not to tear down (scandalize), to seek unity and solidarity, not to set up barriers.

V 40 and its parallel Lk 9:50 seems to contradict a stern warning of Jesus in Mt 12:30 and Lk 11:23: "He who is not with me is against me, and he who does not gather with me scatters." However, the context of both statements makes it clear that Jesus is speaking about two distinct attitudes. First, his disciples must accept true good wherever they find it — the work of the kingdom of God is always from God, even if it arrives through surprising quarters. Secondly, the disciples themselves have to decide to be firmly with Christ — they cannot be half-hearted or compromising in their commitment.

The following of Christ demands strict self-discipline in overcoming obstacles to the unity and harmony of the kingdom (vv 43-48). These words are not to be understood in a closed individualistic sense, as if one's own personal salvation were all that mattered. No one is ever part of God's kingdom alone. The hand that oppresses the other person, the foot that steps on or walks away from the other, the eye that sees the other only as an object of self-gratification — all are obstacles that must be rooted out. We can only enter the kingdom fully aware of our weaknesses and handicaps, in need of support as well as giving support. Refusal to admit dependence on others, and ultimately on the Other, is itself hell.

First Reading: Numbers 11:25-29

The book of Numbers presents both law and history with a definite emphasis on the legitimacy and authority of the religious and civil institutions of Israel. This incident is therefore curious and significant in that it presents a case in which Spirit-filled charisms outside the established structure are recognized as legitimate. It is very tempting to go from recognizing and affirming the Spirit's activity within the Church or one's own group or personal life, to restricting him to a particular institution or sphere — to try to make the Spirit the possession of a certain group and to exclude all others from his action.

Responsorial Psalm: Psalm 19:8, 10, 12-13, 14

The more we realize and accept God's dominion, and strive to keep his law, the more we know that we cannot grasp it or understand it fully. Response: "The precepts of the Lord give joy to the heart."

Second Reading: James 5:1-6

Then, as now, the wealthy of the world stood on the backs of poor, having acquired their surfeit of goods and power at the expense of those who must labor, whether in their own country or in "underdeveloped nations." Although the actual possession of wealth itself is not wrong, acquiring it by dubious means or using it solely for one's own further power or profit rather than the common good is a deadly obstacle to God's kingdom and deserves the strong language of James' condemnation.

The following verses, 7-10, which counsel patience as as one of the most important virtues for Christian community life, are read on the Third Sunday of Advent, Year A. Vv 14-16 are traditionally seen as alluding to the sacrament of anointing of the sick, but are more pertinent for us in affirming the healing power of solidarity in love, prayer, and mutual forgiveness.

Questions for thought, discussion, and prayer:
1. What is the purpose of self-denial and discipline?

2.   Discuss criteria by which the Spirit's activity and gifts may be discerned.

ONE FLESH

Gospel: Mark 10:2-16

Jesus' teaching on marriage confronts his followers with a bold challenge to reverse their thinking from what would seem reasonable and convenient to a realization of the cross in their lives. However, this teaching invites acceptance of the cross freely more than it allows outside authority to impose the cross. It must not be interpreted in a judgmental way that would add to the burdens of someone who may be already innocently suffering a traumatic breakup of marriage. It is all too easy to impose rigid answers to problems that we ourselves do not have to face!

First of all, Jesus affirms the basic oneness of the married couple, which no human agency, not even the law of Moses (see Dt 24:1), has the right to interfere with. This is of nature, inherent in the way things are, rather than anybody's rule or interpretation. Therefore it is absolute and unchangeable in principle. In practice, this ideal must primarily be seen as an obligation incumbent on both partners in a marriage — a call to both equally to live in fidelity even in the face of any difficulty. The infidelity of one partner does not automatically absolve the other of all responsibility for the marriage. Yet, maintaining this ideal in all its strength, Jesus gives no one any cause to judge or condemn another person in an unfortunate marital situation, nor any reason to hinder a Christian from seeking a stable and permanent marriage union after the breakup of a bad marriage, particularly if the first marriage never exhibited the qualities that must characterize genuine marital commitment. The ideal is absolute and cannot be set aside, compromised, or reinterpreted. Yet, in practice, the Church does seek a place for the discernment of individual needs and problems.

The deeper level on which Jesus is speaking adds further weight to the obligation of marital fidelity. He is teaching about God's kingdom here, and he emphasizes that the faithful married state is a strong and privileged manifestation of God's plan and a sign of the restoration of creation in Christ. In this light, divorce is not only an injustice to the abandoned partner, but to God himself. Just as childlike simplicity and acceptance is the prime requirement for entry into the kingdom (vv 13-16), so the same trusting mutual acceptance and fidelity are necessary for the successful marriage, which then becomes a sign of the kingdom's presence.

First Reading: Genesis 2:18-24

The account of the creation of woman in Gn 2 stems from a definite "man's world" view (in contrast to the equality of the simple statement of the creation of man and woman in Gn 1:27). Yet, in an age in which women were often seen as mere possessions to be used and disposed of at will, the degree of equality of man and woman here expressed was revolutionary. Although a certain dependence and subordination is envisioned here — and this is corrected to a certain extent in other scriptural teachings — woman is truly seen as man's "other self," not an inferior by any means.

Responsorial Psalm: Psalm 128:1-2, 3, 4-5, 6

This psalm extols fruitful and prosperous family life as the blessing of a life of fidelity to God. Response: "May the Lord bless us all the days of our lives."

Second Reading: Hebrews 2:9-11

The letter to the Hebrews is very different in style and approach from any of the writings of Paul, and appears to have been a lengthy sermon or instruction rather than a letter sent to a particular community or person. It is basically a commentary on the Jewish Scriptures in the light of the person and role of Jesus Christ in God's plan of salvation. The opening section, vv 1-6, reminiscent of the opening of John's Gospel in its exalted vision of Christ as the eternal Son of God, is read at the Mass of the Day on Christmas.

After affirming the divinity of Christ and his position as superior to all forms of creation, the author of this letter explores the significance of Jesus' solidarity with humanity — he calls us brothers and sisters, and became subject to the laws of nature with us, including death. In his becoming one with us, we truly become one with him in his overcoming the limitations of nature and his being made "perfect through suffering."

Questions for thought, discussion, and prayer:
1. How is Christian marriage a sign of God's kingdom?

2.   How is the creation of man and woman, as described in Genesis, brought to perfection in Christ, as described in Hebrews?

THE NEEDLE'S EYE

Gospel: Mark 10:17-30

This long and complicated passage poses many problems of interpretation, of which we can only touch the surface here for a small entry into understanding. Jesus is seen as surpassing the legalism of the current interpretation of the Jewish law, just as he did in the view of marriage presented in last week's reading (Mk 10:2-11), and at length in Mt 5:17-48. True life does not come from mere obedience to the law, but from abandonment of the heart to God. In fact, trying to earn points in God's eyes by legalistic scruples can be an excuse to cover up a lack of faith rather than a manifestation of genuine faith. Riches and possessions can erect a serious obstacle to this abandonment, but not an insurmountable one. The true willingness to place God first, and even to have that attitude tested by deprivation, is the first requirement for entry into the kingdom. Whatever the "eye of the needle" may be, it is small — and one cannot pass through carrying the baggage of egotism, pride, and worldly attachments. The question "what to do" to enter the kingdom has to be changed to "what to be": Jesus' disciple with no conflicting interests.

To say that those who have wealth must simply become materially poor risks falling into another sort of legalism. Wealth must be used responsibly, for the benefit of those truly in need, and this could not be done by mindless abandonment of the necessities of living, particularly if there are family responsibilities involved. Seeing wealth only in terms of profit and self-aggrandizement is anti-kingdom and damnable. But seeing wealth as an opportunity for advancing the common good in Christ advances the kingdom at the same time. (But, let's face it, the "more for me" temptation grows stronger even for the best of us as the dollars multiply!)

First Reading: Wisdom 7:7-11

Although written nearly a thousand years after the death of

Solomon, the book of Wisdom is put into his mouth to give it authority. Solomon's own request for wisdom centered more on the political savvy to keep his people in order than on the discernment of God's will for its own sake (see 1 Kgs 3:7-9), but the wisdom envisioned here is contentment with union with God's plan manifested in right judgment and correct moral action.

Responsorial Psalm: Psalm 90:12-13, 14-15, 16-17
This comparison between God's infinity and human limitations puts us properly in our place: our destiny is fulfilled only when we are united to God's will. Response: "Fill us with your love, O Lord, and we will sing for joy."

Second Reading: Hebrews 4:12-13
God's self-revealing word is one, manifesting the fullness of his presence. This word is a threat to those who are not open in faith, but at the same time is a promise of life to faithful hearers. This word is effective — it accomplishes what it says. Those who hate God flee from his word into self-destruction; those who love God come and are nourished. His word is a standard by which our own stature is measured.

Questions for thought, discussion, and prayer:
1. Discuss the responsible use of wealth today in accord with the Gospel.

2. What is wisdom, and how do you grow in it?

TWENTY-NINTH SUNDAY OF THE YEAR — YEAR B

TRUE GREATNESS: TO SERVE

Gospel: Mark 10:35-45
Jesus never speaks of his own suffering, death, and resurrection without connecting it in some way to the lives of his followers. We have seen this already is his first two statements (8:31-38; 9:30-37) in which he makes it clear that following him in the suffering of the cross and in service to all are essential requirements of participation in his kingdom. Here, following his third prediction of

the passion (vv 32-34), which takes place on the way to Jerusalem and very close to when the event will happen, the spirited dialogue with James and John not only reinforces his previous teaching, but also makes it clear to them the exact nature of his messiahship and kingdom.

The "cup" and the "bath" are both images of God's judgment in the Hebrew Scriptures. The cup of judgment is one which sinners will have to drink to the dregs (see Jer 25:15-29; Ez 23:31-35; Is 51:17-23). A bath of fire — sometimes seen as purifying, sometimes as merely destroying — awaits those who come under God's judgment (see Gn 19; Is 9:17-18; Jer 44:5-6; Zeph 3:8-9). Clearly Jesus is here identifying himself as the suffering servant of Is 53:4-11. He turns around the apostles' notion of judgment: they wanted to become judges with him, meting out punishments on their enemies. He tells them that he must stand as the accused, the judged, in place of the world in order to redeem the world. Rather than lust after the throne of power, his followers must identify with him precisely as rejected, judged, and put to death.

This understanding of judgment can shed some light on how to interpret a similar passage in Lk 13:49-53. Jesus takes upon himself the judgment and divisions of humanity in order to pardon and heal. Note also, in comparison with the parallel in Mt 20:20-28, that Mark omits the request of the mother, but is richer in preserving the images of judgment. In Matthew, the request seems to echo the promise of Jesus in Mt 19:28, which is omitted in Mark's account (see Mk 10:28-31).

First Reading: Isaiah 53:10-11
These verses about the suffering servant underscore the aspect of Jesus' messiahship as the substitute for the world in taking on himself the judgment and punishment for sin it deserves. We must, however, never allow this concept of redemption to be understood in an impersonal or mechanistic sense, as if Jesus did it all for us without us. What he accomplished in himself still needs to be fulfilled in us. As he identified with us by taking on our condemnation and misery, we must now identify with him by following him in his passage through redemptive death.

Responsorial Psalm: Psalm 33:4-5, 18-19, 20, 22
This psalm reaffirms God's goodness in creation as the reason to hope for merciful deliverance. Response: "Lord, let your mercy be on us, as we place our trust in you."

Second Reading: Hebrews 4:14-16

The letter to the Hebrews was written for Christians of Jewish background, and assures them that they have lost nothing of their original faith, but rather that it has been fulfilled in Christ. The function of a mediator is to represent two opposing parties to one another. In the relation of God and humanity, Jesus can do this perfectly because as fully a man he can represent humankind, and as truly Son of God, he is the face of God for us, even as glorified and seated at the Father's side.

This passage, plus vv 7-9, is read on Good Friday. Vv 7-9 alone appear on the Fifth Sunday of Lent, Year B.

Questions for thought, discussion, and prayer:
1.   How do the visual images of a cup being drained to its dregs and baptism of fire speak to you of God's judgment? or of Jesus' redemptive work? or of your own participation in it?

2.   What is a mediator? What does Jesus as mediator mean to you? Do you share in his function as mediator in any way?

THIRTIETH SUNDAY OF THE YEAR — YEAR B

I WANT TO SEE!

Gospel: Mark 10:46-52

This cure of the blind man occupies a central position in the plan of Mark's Gospel. It is the last of Jesus' healings reported by Mark, and its importance is emphasized by the fact that the man's name is given. This miracle climaxes the section in which Jesus reveals the nature of his messiahship as that of suffering servant (8:27-10:45), just as the healing of another blind man (8:22-26) marked the conclusion of Jesus' miracle-signs affirming that he was the Messiah foretold in Jewish prophecy.

A comparison of this healing with the cures of the former section (especially the deaf-mute of 7:31-37 and the blind man of 8:22-26) reveals a significant shift in both procedure and meaning. In the former, others brought the person to Jesus (7:32; 8:22); in this, the blind man already knows enough of Jesus to profess his own faith in him as the Messiah ("Son of David") and to seek the healing himself. Others try to hinder him — either because of their own lack of faith or, worse, their lack of concern for him. The former deeds were done through either a gesture or a process — Jesus used some medium for his work (7:33-34; 8:24-25); here Jesus works directly by his word (v 52). More significantly, Jesus took the others away from the crowds and outside the town (7:33; 8:23), and emphatically ordered them not to talk about it to the people (7:36; 8:26); this blind man, however, Jesus cures right in the midst of the crowd, and instead of being sent away, he is allowed to become a follower. In the early miracles, Jesus established the fact of his messiahship, especially for his close disciples to see. But he could not risk a huge following based solely on a misunderstanding of his mission. So he waited until the understanding of his messianic mission as suffering servant was clearly proclaimed and began to be understood. Then he invited recipients of his cures to become his followers, and opened himself for crowds to witness.

First Reading: Jeremiah 31:7-9
Jeremiah, for the most part a pessimistic prophet of destruction of captivity, turns his attention here to the restoration of God's people (chapters 30-31). Although his optimism regarding the reestablishment of the northern kingdom (Israel) was unwarranted (and unfulfilled), it nonetheless presents a valid and hopeful image of the messianic times. Noteworthy in this brief section is the initiative and call of God, which corresponds to Jesus' call of the blind man in the Gospel — not only to sight, but to discipleship.

Responsorial Psalm: Psalm 126:1-2, 2-3, 4-5, 6
This joyful hymn of returned exiles reflects our joy at the awareness of God's loving forgiveness. Response: "The Lord has done great things for us; we are filled with joy."

Second Reading: Hebrews 5:1-6
One of the concerns of the letter to the Hebrews is to show the superiority of the new covenant in Christ over the old covenant of the law of Moses. This section speaks of priesthood, demonstrating that the priesthood of Christ surpasses that of the Levites, the Jewish priestly tribe. Not only does he fulfill all the requirements — taken from among the people (see Num 8:6), delegated to offer sacrifices (Lv 4), and called by God (Ex 28) — but he is beyond them as the Son of God (v 5) and eternal in his priestly office (v 6).

Questions for thought, discussion, and prayer:
1.   What significance does clothing have as a sign of the person (see v 49 of the Gospel)? Discuss uniforms, liturgical vesture (including the baptismal garment), as well as choices of fashion in this light.

2.   In what ways do we share in the priesthood of Christ as described in Hebrews 5?

THIRTY-FIRST SUNDAY OF THE YEAR — YEAR B

HEAR, O ISRAEL!

Gospel: Mark 12:28-34

Mark, along with Matthew and Luke, compresses all the events of the Jerusalem ministry into one week (beginning with chapter 11), but there are indications that it was longer (see 14:49) including the witness of John's Gospel that there were multiple visits to Jerusalem (Jn 2:13; 5:1; 7:10; 10:23; 11:7). The import of his teaching during the final week in Mark's account is to present the "hard truths" about his kingdom that would arouse the opposition of the leaders of the Jewish establishment, and would lead to his death. Note that, although Jesus was openly critical of the Pharisees and disputed with them throughout his ministry (see 7:1-23; 8:11-21), Mark gives no indication of danger or open hostility until Jesus arrives in Jerusalem. Other Gospels, especially John, show an earlier build-up of antagonism, with plots against his life hatching early (see Lk 11:53-54; Jn 7:44-52; 8:59; 11:53).

The great commandment of love is often thought unique to Jesus' teaching, but he is only quoting the law of Moses, and showing that it is to be the foundation of love in the Christian life. These commandments are found in Dt 6:4-5 and Lv 19:18. In the parallel passage in Mt 22:34-40, Jesus explicitly teaches that the whole Hebrew Scriptures (law and prophets) may be summed up in this twofold commandment. Here in Mark, the perceptive and sincere scribe (contrast with Matthew's!) affirms that a life imbued with this sort of love is itself an act of worship (v 33) — an answer which Jesus heartily approved. However, this is not an insight proper only to followers of Christ — see also Amos 5:21-27; Is 29:13; Ps 50:23; 51:18-19.

First Reading: Deuteronomy 6:2-6

This passage is the beginning of the Jewish prayer, *Shema Is-rael* ("Hear, O Israel"), which pious believers recited three times a day. Vv 8-9 figuratively emphasized the wholehearted seriousness with which this commandment of love was to be received, but later these figures were literally followed in the phylacteries (boxes or bags containing a tiny scroll with these words worn on the forehead and wrist) and the mezuzah, which Jews today still put on their doorways. As a reminder to take these commandments to heart, these outward signs are good; but as empty substitutes for inner adherence, such signs are empty.

The commandment of love of God is primarily directed against idolatry, which throughout the Hebrew Scriptures is often described as adultery (see especially Hos 1-3).

Responsorial Psalm: Psalm 18:2-3, 3-4, 47, 51

This psalm sees the victory of King David over his enemies as the sign of God's fidelity, and conversely, the motive for him to be faithful to God. Response: "I love you, Lord, my strength."

Second Reading: Hebrews 7:23-28

This would be a good time to read carefully and reflectively the entire section of this letter about the priesthood of Jesus Christ (chapters 3-8). The concepts and images used are complicated and somewhat foreign to our mentality, but the basic idea is clear. No human religious activity can truly touch God as he is in himself. But Jesus Christ, the Son of God, because he is enthroned at the right hand of God in his full humanity as well as divinity, provides the unfailing point of contact with God, now and for all time.

Questions for thought, discussion, and prayer:
1.   What are the demands of the love of God in relation to the things that could be idols in your life, competing for allegiance of the heart?

2.   How do you conceive the perfection of Jesus Christ? What does this mean to you? Is your thought of Christ a source of hope or a discouraging unreachable ideal?

THIRTY-SECOND SUNDAY OF THE YEAR — YEAR B

THE GIVING THAT MATTERS

Gospel: Mark 12:38-48

In Mark's plan of the Gospel, when Jesus arrives in Jerusalem he is primarily concerned with speaking about the ultimate fulfillment of the kingdom, the re-establishment of God's order in creation. The principal theme of this is the reversal of earthly values and positions of power, which he sets in the parable of the tenants (12:1-11). The contrast between the scribes — highly respected officials who will find themselves outlaws in the kingdom — and the poor widow, a social outcast, who is in reality rich in the qualities that matter, continues and illustrates this theme. The meaning of this contrast for us is clear enough, as is our moral obligation of detachment from worldly values and genuine concern for the worth of those we usually consider worthless.

However, Jesus is speaking of more than moral obligation here. He is describing the nature of the kingdom. Those whose generosity extends only to giving away surplus cannot be a part of it. That may be a disturbing mirror for us, but it presents us with a hopeful and challenging image of God himself. His kingdom cannot be different than he is himself. If God gives only from superfluous abundance, then he would be no better than the wealthy donors Jesus condemns. But if his kingdom is based on his own self-emptying generosity, then God must himself be the model for those who would become part of it. We can begin to understand how God gives from his poverty if we accept Jesus-as-servant as the full manifestation of divinity. God emptied himself completely into humanity in Christ.

First Reading: 1 Kings 17:10-16

The two great prophets in the books of Kings, Elijah and Elisha, lived during a time of great apostasy, and their stories show them often finding greater faith among the inhabitants of foreign lands than among the Israelites. At the same time that Jezebel, the queen of Israel, was successfully introducing the worship of Baal into the kingdom of Israel, Elijah found this manifestation of faith in action in the generosity of a foreign widow. This story is an excellent Jewish prefiguring of the Gospel message because it too speaks of the reversal of human values and priorities by God's order.

Responsorial Psalm: Psalm 146:7, 8-9, 9-10
    This simple hymn of confidence meditates on the love of God shown in his care and sustenance of all creation. Response: "Praise the Lord, my soul."

Second Reading: Hebrews 9:24-28
    The long discourse on the priesthood of Jesus as fulfilling for all time the temporal priesthood of the Jewish order leads to an analysis of the sacrifice of Jesus. (Vv 11-15 are read on the Solemnity of Corpus Christi, Year B.) The Jewish sacrifices had their value as pre-images, but their limitation was evident from the insufficiency of matter — slaughtered animals could not redeem human sin — and from their being rooted in the recurring cycles of time. A sacrifice that needs to be repeated over and over cannot have any real value in establishing a lasting relationship between God and humankind. Jesus' sacrifice derives its value from the fact that he is fully both God and a man. Note that his sacrifice does not consist in his death on the cross, which was the outward expression of sacrifice, but in his perfect self-offering, which endures as one sacrifice for all time.

Questions for thought, discussion, and prayer:
1.   Do you picture God as being generous? How generous?

2.   Discuss how God's order — the establishment of his rule or kingdom — reverses human values and priorities.

THIRTY-THIRD SUNDAY OF THE YEAR — YEAR B

LORD JESUS, COME IN GLORY!

Gospel: Mark 13:24-32
    Read carefully the whole of chapter 13, remembering that in Mark's Gospel the events and teachings of Jesus in his last week in Jerusalem (chapters 11-13) are concerned with the fulfillment of the kingdom — the complete restoration of God's order in humankind. The conviction of the early Church, reflected in the Gospels, was that the "last days" had already arrived with the death and resurrection of Jesus, and that God's definitive judgment upon the old order

and his affirmation of the new and final age of humanity was demonstrated in the destruction of the Jerusalem temple in 70 C.E. This chapter needs to be understood with the memory of this event very much alive in the mind of the writer, as well as the first readers — this Gospel was compiled nearly at the same time.

The persecution faced by the early Church was seen as the means by which Christ's triumph would be manifested (vv 24-25). The coming on the clouds of the Son of Man in power (v 26) echoes Dn 7:13, and actually referred to the enthronement of Jesus as Lord of the world in the ascension to the Father. The angels (messengers) who assemble all the chosen (v 27) refer to the mission of the Church throughout the world. Mark's message, then, to his readers is not to look merely to some future cataclysmic event, but to see the triumphant Christ already operating within the Church as it presently exists, even as it is persecuted and in constant danger. Jesus' words about the nearness of the events of those "last days" (vv 28-30) pose no problem if we can raise our understanding above a narrow literal interpretation of vv 24-27, and refrain from seeing shooting stars, comets, or eclipses as omens. The signs mentioned are images of both ongoing persecution and the enduring power of the risen Christ among his people.

Finally, Jesus' words warn us not to interpret Biblical prophecy as predicting events of our own day (v 32). Fidelity to Christ demands that we not be concerned with the timetable of the end of the world, but make each day count fully as servants of the kingdom of God.

First Reading: Daniel 12:1-3
These verses are the conclusion of the description of the so-called Hellenistic wars between the Seleucid dynasty in Syria (king of the north) and the Ptolemaic dynasty in Egypt (king of the south) during the third and second centuries B.C.E., described in chapters 10 and 11. Of course, the Jews were in the middle of this — both geographically and politically. Some remained faithful to their heritage, often at the cost of persecution and death. Many others compromised for protection or profit. The fate of these unfaithful ones is the subject of this reading. Michael is seen as the particular protector of the Jewish people in later apocalyptic books like Daniel. This passage gives us the most definite reference to the resurrection of the dead to be found in the Jewish Scriptures.

Much of the book of Daniel is written in an apocalyptic style, similar to the Christian scriptural book of Revelation. This type of writing usually comes from an oppressed and persecuted people, and graphically depicts the horrors of destruction awaiting their enemies as well as the sweet triumphs and blissful rewards prepared for the faithful. In the light of the origin and nature of apocalyptic writing, we should be careful not to read into them a prediction of events to be fulfilled in a future age — or in our own day.

Responsorial Psalm: Psalm 16:5, 8, 9-10, 11

God's protection of those who are his own is the confident hope of this quiet and trusting psalm. Response: "Keep me safe, O God; you are my hope."

Second Reading: Hebrews 10:11-14, 18

These verses recall the points already made about the priesthood and sacrifice of Christ. Note that vv 5-10 are read on the Fourth Sunday of Advent, Year C. Of significance for us is the simple statement of v 18: forgiveness of sin is assured by Christ's sacrifice as an already present reality, not something to be hoped for or earned in the future. The concluding chapters appear in Year C, on the Nineteenth through Twenty-Second Sundays.

Questions for thought, discussion, and prayer:
1. What does Mark 13 say to us today?

2. What does "resurrection of the body" mean to you?

SOLEMNITY OF CHRIST THE KING — YEAR B
(THIRTY-FOURTH OR LAST SUNDAY OF THE YEAR)

HIS KINGSHIP SHALL NEVER END

Gospel: John 18:33-37

The Jewish leaders, anxious to find a charge against Jesus that might carry weight before a Roman official, accused Jesus of setting himself up as king in opposition to the Roman authority. When questioned by Pilate about this, Jesus curtly turned the question back on him, indicating that the question as Pilate put it was absurd — but hinting at a deeper meaning (see Mt 27:11; Mk 15:2; Lk 23:3). John's account turns into a dialog with the Roman procurator on the nature of the Messiah's kingship, which is distinct from all other forms of royalty. Pilate never took seriously that Jesus could be any earthly threat to imperial prerogatives, but he failed to distinguish and understand the worldly and non-worldly order of things.

The kingship of Christ comes from his sharing the divine life, and has its origin from eternity. His kingship has the power of truth, regardless of its interpretation or acceptance by the worldly. Truth, for John's Jesus, is the divine life itself, and the re-establishment of the order of all creation — beginning with human beings learning to love one another — according to God's will to fulfill the life he has given. Truth is what God alone can establish, but what the deepest human inner longing seeks as well. But pragmatism, a characteristic of the Roman mentality (and the American mentality as well!), blinded Pilate to the serious consideration of anything except the immediate response to the here and now according to what might prove profitable or convenient. For a Roman politician, truth in the abstract was something that philosophers liked to argue about, but was irrelevant in day-to-day life. Truth in the concrete was simply whatever was expedient. (Times and mentalities don't change much, do they?)

Vv 36-37 link Jesus' passion with his divine origin in Jn 1:1-18. Thus Jesus' kingship — his rule over all creation — stems from his divinity.

First Reading: Daniel 7:13-14

We do not know who this "son of man" was, for the author of Daniel was speaking in very figurative and poetic language of the approaching destruction of earthly kingdoms that held the chosen people in subjection. However, the fact that Jesus uses the expression to refer to himself enables us to employ these verses as an appropriate description of Jesus' proper dominion over all creation. This passage pre-echoes John's Gospel's affirmation of Jesus' kingship based on his divinity.

Responsorial Psalm: Psalm 93:1 1-2, 5

This is an enthronement psalm, celebrating God's lordship over all creation. Response: "The Lord is king; he is robed in majesty."

Second Reading: Revelation 1:5-8

This passage recalls what Jesus did in the past — he redeemed his people and made them priests like himself — and it looks forward to his future fulfillment in glory. "Seeing" (v 7) means two different things: for the Christian, it is the completion of faith and acceptance of Jesus; for the unbeliever, it is judgment and lament, the awareness of opportunity missed. V 8 refers to the eternity of God the

Father — without beginning or end. Reference to the Father as him "who is to come" stresses our unity with him for ever in Christ.

Questions for thought, discussion, and prayer:
1.   What does the image of "king" say to you? Reflect on and discuss how you picture Christ as King?

2.   What is truth? How would you answer Pilate's question?

YEAR C
ADVENT-CHRISTMAS SEASON
AND RELATED FEASTS

THE DAYS ARE COMING . . .

Gospel: Luke 21: 25-28, 34-36

The message of the First Sunday of Advent each year jolts us awake to be alert for Christ's coming. The frightening signs have been characteristic of all history, and should not be naively taken to refer only to our own day or any particular age. Originally, these events were seen as accomplished in the destruction of Jerusalem and the temple in 70 C.E., which signified for the early Christian communities the definitive end of the old order and the beginning of the new — thus vv 25-26 are simply the continuation of vv 20-24. The coming of the Son of Man on a cloud derives from the prophecy of Dn 7:13-14, and should be interpreted in the light of the entire prophecy. Jesus enthroned in glory now has fullness of dominion. It is up to us to clear away the obstacles to his lordship in our own hearts and in the world.

Thus, v 28 describes the posture that should characterize every Christian at all times — eager, joyful anticipation of the fulfillment of the new order that has already begun, even though we are now faced with the tragedy of suffering and persecution. Vv 34-36 offer concrete qualities of this life in the spirit — attentiveness, discipline, and prayer.

As Christians, we do not await the coming of the Messiah as did the Jewish people, and Advent is not for us a make-believe entry into pre-Christian times. However, we can still learn from how they expressed their anticipation and their spirit as recorded in the Scriptures can enrich our faith. We now wait as a people who have already tasted the reality of God's order, yet are seeking its fullness. The message of Advent is not merely that we must be watchful for something to happen, but that we are now filled with the presence of the glorified Christ, and must bring him into the world if his glory is to be fulfilled.

First Reading: Jeremiah 33:14-16

Vv 14-26 are a later addition by another author to this book, and are a commentary on the prophecy of Jeremiah in 23:5-6. The royal dynasty of David ended with the Babylonian exile in the time of Jeremiah. After the return and restoration, it was no longer possible to have a king who was a direct descendant of David, and so the prophecy of Nathan (v 17, see Sam 7:8-16) came to be reinterpreted — the Lord himself would raise up a true descendant of David, in spirit rather than merely physical, whose kingdom would endure. Note vv 25-26 as a beautiful image of God's faithful care.

Responsorial Psalm: Psalm 25:4-5, 8-9, 10, 14
God's goodness and constancy are seen in this psalm as motives for trust in his guidance. Response: "To you, O Lord, I lift up my soul."

Second Reading: 1 Thessalonians 3:12-4:2
In writing to the young Christian community of Thessalonica which he had himself instructed, Paul was fearful that they were not fully grounded in faith and were being led astray by false preachers as well as the danger of persecution. He prays that their faith and love may be strengthened so that they may stand firm until Christ's coming and the new life begun in them may achieve its completeness.

Questions for thought, discussion, and prayer:
1. How should watching and waiting be balanced with activity in a Christian's life?

2. How does Christian love hasten the coming of Jesus?

SECOND SUNDAY OF ADVENT — YEAR C

MAKE READY THE WAY

Gospel: Luke 3:1-6
The Second Sunday of Advent follows last week's alarm to wake up with John the Baptist's call to repentance. Luke, as a careful historian, situates the beginning of John's proclamation of God's word at a precise moment in time (vv 1-2). All four Gospels quote the passage from Isaiah (40:3-4; see Mt 3:3; Mk 1:2-3; Jn 1:23) to refer to the mission of the Baptist, but each one abbreviates it or modifies it. Luke is the only one who includes Is 40:5 (v 6), which

emphasizes that John's mission is for the benefit of all peoples.

Repentance, which opens one to receive God's forgiveness, is precisely the act which clears a straight path for the Lord, into the heart of the individual and into the life of the community. Repentance is not just a "God and me" peace treaty, but a genuine turning away from sin in all its aspects, especially those which erect barriers within God's people. Thus, repentance is a turning from self-centeredness to others as well as to the Other. John the Baptist makes the implications of this sort of repentance clear in the following verses (vv 7-14).

First Reading: Baruch 5:1-9

The book of Baruch (attributed to the secretary of Jeremiah, see Jer 32:12-16; 36:4; 45:1-5) appears to be a late (second century B.C.E.) compendium of earlier prophetic teaching for Jews living in Greek speaking areas outside Palestine (i.e., Jews of the Diaspora). This chapter expresses well their attitude of longing for Jerusalem as the mother who will gather her children from all lands of exile. This sentiment strikes a responsive chord in the hearts of Christians who await the fulfillment of Christ's coming.

Responsorial Psalm: Psalm 126:1-2, 2-3, 4-5, 6

This processional song, intended to accompany the march of freed exiles as they approach Jerusalem, expresses confidence that the Lord who brought them back will restore prosperity. Response: "The Lord has done great things for us; we are filled with joy."

Second Reading: Philippians 1:4-6, 8-11

Paul established a Christian community at Philippi, a wealthy center of commerce, on his second missionary journey, about 50 C.E. (see Acts 16:10-40). Although he suffered a brief imprisonment there, his apostolic efforts met with success, and when he wrote this letter (either 53 or 62 C.E., also from prison), he was pleased with their adherence to the way of Christ. In this greeting to them, he could happily point to their experience of God's gifts — the good work he had begun (v 6) — as the sure sign that God would be faithful to his promises and bring them to the rich harvest of justice (v 11).

Questions for thought, discussion, and prayer:
1. How can you clear the way for the Lord in your life?

2. How can Paul be so happy in prison? What works of God in

your life, even in the midst of adversity and disappointment, can you see as sign of growth in Christ?

REJOICE IN THE LORD!

Gospel: Luke 3:10-18

The message of the Third Sunday of Advent turns from the call to watchfulness and repentance to a consideration of Jesus as the Messiah proclaimed by John the Baptist. The call to repentance is not a generic "turn away from sin" but a specific set of demands on each person in every walk of life (vv 10-14), and John's picture of the Messiah reflects this. His image is primarily one of judgment. Remember that to baptize means to plunge oneself into something. John's baptism is an immersion into water as a sign of plunging deeply into oneself in personal change of heart and way of life. Isaiah often presents God's judgment as a thresher or a fire (Is 29:5-6; 30:27-28; 33:11-14; 41:15-16; 66:15). John conceives the coming Messiah as a similar manifestation of God's judgment. His baptism will immerse one into the Spirit (v 16) just as the thresher "immerses" grain into the wind to separate the wheat from the chaff, and into the fire of judgment just as the metal worker plunges silver into fire to burn away impurities. This judgment is not for destruction but for purification — that which is sinful in the individual life as well as in the life of society are to be destroyed. The baptism of the Messiah, however, will have the power to accomplish what John's plunging into water merely signifies. Luke sees this baptism continued in the work of the Church, which is to immerse humanity into the full reality of God (see Acts 1:5; 11:16).

First Reading: Zephaniah 3:14-18

This brief prophetic book, consisting of three distinct but closely related oracles, was composed just prior to the time of Jeremiah (about 630 B.C.E.), at a time of internal corruption that had sapped the moral strength of the Jewish nation and exposed them as weak before the powerful Assyrians. The language of destruction is remarkably strong and complete in this whole book, and is directed both to the nation itself (chapter 1) and their enemies (chapter 2).

However, God's threats do not seek revenge but conversion (3:7), and the book concludes with a renewed promise of God's favor, again in strikingly vivid language (3:9-20).

Today's reading, a promise of the saving presence of the Lord with his people, contains expressions that are quite similar to the words of greeting which Luke attributes to the angel appearing to Mary announcing the birth of the Messiah through her (see Lk 1:28-30). Note especially "rejoice," "fear not," "the Lord is with you" as echoes of vv 14, 16, 17.

Responsorial Psalm: Isaiah 12:2-3, 4, 5-6

This short and exuberant song of thanksgiving is a fitting conclusion to the prophecy of messianic restoration in Is 11. Response: "Cry out with joy and gladness: for among you is the great and holy one of Israel."

Second Reading: Philippians 4:4-7

As we saw in last week's reading, Paul had reason to rejoice in the strong faith of the Philippian community. This joy in the Lord is no mere superficial emotion at the mercy of winds that change, but a deeply rooted posture of life resulting from an overwhelming awareness of God's nearness. We have to reflect on the qualities of this rejoicing. First and most basic is unselfishness. Anxiety and placing our own needs above all else are manifestations of selfishness that restricts our vision and narrows our horizons. We find little reason to rejoice if our vision cannot rise above the satisfaction of our own needs. Peace is the other side of prayer, the sort of prayer that stems from a profound and all-embracing perception of God's goodness in our world and in our lives.

Questions for thought, discussion, and prayer:
1. Discuss the meaning of your own baptism in the light of this Gospel reading.

2. Think about and discuss "joy" and "rejoicing" as reflected in the lives of people you know. And in your own life.

BLESSED ARE YOU

Gospel: Luke 1:39-45

Mary's journey of about sixty miles (on foot!) from Nazareth to the vicinity of Jerusalem to visit and care for Elizabeth may be seen as an outstanding act of charity, as well as a very human indication that she could not keep good news to herself. But Luke, of course, probes this event more deeply and finds also the fulfillment of scriptural symbolism. Mary, in carrying Jesus, is the new ark of the covenant, the sign of God's presence among his people. This journey resembles in broad outline the transfer of the ark to Jerusalem in 2 Sam 6. Note especially the cry of David in 2 Sam 6:9 and his dance in vv 14-16 as corresponding to Elizabeth's greeting and the activity of her unborn baby. Mary is a source of blessing for the house of Zachariah and Elizabeth, just as the Lord blessed the house of Obededom — and the duration of the stay is the same, three months (2 Sam 6:11).

Another echo from the past is the image of Mary as the victorious woman. Elizabeth's blessing-greeting (v 42) recalls the blessing of Deborah upon Jael after she had killed Sisera (Jdgs 5:24) and, more remotely, that of Judith after she had beheaded Holofernes (Jdt 13:17-18; 15:9-10), Thus Mary is seen from the very beginning as the woman who assures final victory of the enemies — sin and oppression.

First Reading: Micah 5:1-4

Micah succeeded Isaiah in prophetic spirit, and the content of his message was basically the same: the sinful and corrupt Jewish nation would be destroyed in a violent judgment, but a select remnant would emerge, and the messianic promises would be fulfilled in them. This prophecy looks back to the origins of king David — a young shepherd boy from a tiny town (see 1 Sam 16) — in contrast to the empty vainglory of the present king in Jerusalem (Zion, chapters 1-3). David's simple origins are to be the model for the future king who would restore Jerusalem to her true strength and glory in the Lord.

Responsorial Psalm: Psalm 80:2-3, 15-16, 18-19

This psalm sets side by side two different metaphors for the Lord's rule and care — that of shepherd (vv 2-7) and vine-grower (vv 9-20). Each is developed beautifully in its own right, but they do not mix well (as this selection of verses attempts to do) because they represent two completely distinct and often antagonistic types of people: shepherds, who were nomads having little regard for property boundaries; and farmers, who were settled folk whose existence depended on the integrity of their fixed parcels of land. Nevertheless, a sense of confidence in God's care for his own comes through. Response: "Lord, make us turn to you, let us see your face and we shall be saved."

Second Reading: Hebrews 10:5-10

A genuine religious spirit sees sacrifice as an outward sign of an inner recognition of God's lordship over all creation, an act of submission to him. This often degenerates into a manipulative view of sacrifice as having value to "buy" God's favor. This is at the heart of the distinction made in the letter to the Hebrews between Christ's sacrifice and and the Jewish sacrifices. His is perfect because it does not depend on the offering of some external thing but consists in the total acceptance of the divine nature into humanity by the human will of Jesus Christ. His fidelity and love is the one effective model for all time of our acceptance of God into our lives, and so a repetition of limited sacrifices is no longer needed nor even possible.

Questions for thought, discussion, and prayer:
1. How do the qualities and actions of Mary, as the bearer of Christ, speak to your life as a Christian?

2. How can Jesus' accomplishment of the Father's will be the model for your own following of God's will?

SOLEMNITY OF CHRISTMAS — DECEMBER 25

VIGIL MASS
MIDNIGHT MASS
MASS AT DAWN
MASS DURING THE DAY

See YEAR A for all the readings, pages 29-34

* * * * * * *

FEAST OF THE HOLY FAMILY, SUNDAY AFTER CHRISTMAS — YEAR C

LET THE WORD DWELL IN YOU

Gospel: Luke 2:41-52

The emotions surrounding the thought of a lost child should not overwhelm the deeper significance of this event: this first journey of Jesus to Jerusalem as a legal adult (twelve years old) foreshadows the final journey there for his passion and death. The time of the passover is the time for the fulfillment of the Father's will; the three days of being lost pre-image the time in the tomb. Jesus is shown here at the beginning of his adult life placing the accomplishment of God's plan above all else.

See YEAR A for the first and second readings, pages 34-35.

SOLEMNITY OF MARY, MOTHER OF GOD — JANUARY 1, YEAR C

See YEAR A for all the readings, pages 35-36.

SOLEMNITY OF THE EPIPHANY — YEAR C

See YEAR A for all the readings, pages 36-38.

See YEAR A for all the readings, pages 38-39.

SPIRIT AND FIRE

Gospel: Luke 3:15-16, 21-22

Luke's Gospel account of the baptism of Jesus de-emphasizes the role of John, the meaning of whose baptism was clearly described earlier (v 3). In contrast to John's baptism signifying personal repentance leading to, but not accomplishing, forgiveness of sins, Jesus baptism would have the power of God acting within it. Luke here is actually describing in a nutshell the whole messianic ministry of Jesus, not just a baptismal rite alone. Spirit and fire (v 16) allude to God's judgment, separating the good from the evil and purifying — just as the harvester uses the wind to separate the grains of wheat from the chaff, and fire to get rid of the waste (v 17). There are many roots of this image in Jewish Scriptures (see Is 41:15-16; 29:5-6; 30:33; 33:11-16; 66:15-16; Dn 7:10; Amos 1:14) which would already be familiar to John's hearers, and would make it clear to them that he was proclaiming the arrival of the messianic times — the final days of God's judgment and purifying powers were at hand.

Luke's story also gives an important place to the prayer of Jesus (v 21). Jesus' prayer at significant moments of transition is a theme dear to Luke (see 5:16; 6:12; 9:18, 28-29; 11:1; 22:41-45) and is a model for the Church's prayer (see Acts 1:14; 2:1; 3:42; 4:31).

See YEAR A for the first and second readings, pages 39-40.

YEAR C
LENT-EASTER SEASON

See readings for YEAR A, pages 42-43.

FIRST SUNDAY OF LENT — YEAR C

PUT TO THE TEST

Gospel: Luke 4:1-13

As we embark on Lent's forty-day journey in the desert of self-denial, this Gospel reminds us that we are to look face-to-face at our sinful self. This is the same road traveled by the people of Israel during their forty years of wandering in the desert before entering the land of promise. And we are assured that Jesus walked this way as well. He, like us a descendant of Adam, faced the same temptations that Adam and the wandering Israelites did — and that we do. But he faced them "full of the Spirit" (4:1) — just as we do as his disciples.

We can best understand these temptations not as a grand dramatic scene but as the ongoing inner struggle that Jesus engaged in to remain faithful to his messianic mission (v 13). He could have misused God's power for selfish ends — for possessions, for power, or for fame. Each of these would have brought an illusion of God's kingdom, but would actually have been a distortion of it.

It is important to notice that none of these temptations is to moral evil as we usually understand it, like theft, murder, or adultery. These are temptations to wealth, power, and fame — and we do not consider the wealthy, the powerful, or the famous to be automatically immoral. The temptations that Jesus faced — and that give us the most danger — are more subtle than overt immorality. And more deadly. These are the temptations to rest in the goods and goals of this world rather than to seek the reality of God behind them. Our basic temptation is to go for something second best, and ignore the designs of God the Creator and Giver of all good.

The way that Jesus deals with these temptations has to be our model: each time the devil wants Jesus to put his needs and desires first, Jesus puts God first.

First Reading: Deuteronomy 26:4-10
   The book of Deuteronomy presents a view of law as servant of the covenant. The central fact of Israel's existence as a people was the call by God to enter into a binding relationship with him. This covenant imposed a choice upon people, between the way of good which leads to life and the way of evil which leads to death — a choice repeated many times, especially in Dt 4-11. The specific laws which follow this central section may then be seen as norms of behavior in keeping with the new life of a people bound to God by covenant.

   This liturgical selection, which closes the section of laws, is an ancient profession of faith which clearly distinguishes the Israelite religion from pagan religions. The pagan religious spirit saw God or gods only in terms of control of natural forces. They worshiped god(s) as responsible for seasonal changes, fertility, good weather, abundant crops, victory in war, etc. The Israelite religious spirit saw the one God as the God of history, who showed himself in definite events that radically altered the destiny of his people. He called the people to be his own, and it was their place to submit to him unconditionally, not to try to manipulate him or gain his favor. Compare a similar but more developed profession of faith in the God of history in Joshua 24, which also serves as a prelude to the ritual renewal of the covenant.

Responsorial Psalm: Psalm 91:1-2, 10-11, 12-13, 14-15
   This prayer of confidence in God's protection is based on a mutual relationship of fidelity between God and his servant, and cannot be distorted into an excuse for presuming that God will make up for one's own folly, as Satan tempted Jesus. Response: "Be with me, Lord, when I am in trouble."

Second Reading: Romans 10:8-13
   This reading contrasts well with the passage from Deuteronomy. Israel's confession of faith was an acknowledgment of God's saving activity in history. The Christian confession of faith extends to an acknowledgment of God's activity in one's own personal life through Christ, as well as one's relation to the Christian community and to the world. "Jesus is Lord" (v 9) sums up this confession of faith. Note that "heart" here (vv 9-10) does not mean

mere feelings, but that center of our being from which all activity flows. Thus, Christian faith accepts Jesus as the driving and guiding force of one's life.

Questions for thought, discussion, and prayer:
1.   Note v 13 of the Gospel reading. Can you point to any other events of Jesus' life that might be called temptations? What were their significance in his life, and do they relate to your life in any way?

2.   We often talk in general terms about faith and hide from the fact that we often don't really know what we believe. Discuss: What do you really believe, and how does it affect your life? What difference does your personal belief make to the community of the Church? to the world around you?

SECOND SUNDAY OF LENT — YEAR C

PASSAGE TO GLORY

Gospel: Luke 9:28-36
    This surprising and striking vision is best approached as myth in the true meaning of the word — not a story that is necessarily untrue, but a story that leads to a deeper insight into realities beyond the power of mere words to express. It would be hard to dismiss this story as a fanciful invention of the Gospel writers. In fact, 2 Pet 1:16-18 gives strong witness in addition to the Gospels that this event was known and accepted as literal fact in the earliest days of the Church. But it is the meaning beyond the details that is important.
    Read this passage within its context: Peter had just professed faith in Jesus as Messiah (vv 18-20); Jesus then began to reveal that messiahship centers on the cross (vv 22 and 44) and true discipleship means following him in the cross (vv 23-27). In the midst of the message of the cross, this vision was intended to confirm the faith of the disciples, but the following incidents (see especially vv 41-42 and 45) show their continued weakness in faith.
    How could the transfiguration of Jesus confirm their faith? It was more than just an impressive display of divine power. Anyone familiar with Israelite history knows that, for a Jew, the central

event of all history was the exodus from Egypt and the establishment of the covenant on Mount Sinai. So many of the Jewish scriptural images were brought to a focus here — the mountain, radiance, the law (in the person of Moses), the prophets (in Elijah), the overshadowing cloud — that it became an unmistakable sign that the fulfillment of God's deliverance (note that the Greek word for passage in v 31 is "exodos") was to take place through the cross of Christ. (Read Ex 19; 24; 34:27-35.)

Peter's first reaction was to build a "dwelling" there (see Ex 40) to prolong the experience. This temptation, which reflects on our own attitude as well, sought to capture and take possession of the divine presence, and was countered by the testimony and affirmation of God in v 35. Peter, like ourselves, was in danger of drowning out Christ's voice with his own.

First Reading: Genesis 15:5-12, 17-18
God's call of Abraham and his covenant with him is regarded as the foundation of the people of Israel — his descendants — just as the Sinai covenant would be the confirmation of their identity as God's people. This covenant, whose terms focus mainly on land and progeny, may be more clearly understood if the sections relating to it are read consecutively, leaving aside other Abraham stories that are not directly connected. Thus, read together as one unit: Abraham's call (Gn 12:1-8), the sealing of the covenant (chapter 15), circumcision as the permanent sign of the covenant (chapter 17), and the beginnings of the fulfillment of the covenant in the birth of Isaac (18:1-5; chapter 21).

The bloody and mysterious ritual described here is based on the ancient covenant rite of the people of that time and place. The leader of each tribe making the covenant agreement (usually concerning division of land or pledging mutual support against common enemies) would walk among the slaughtered carcasses and declare: "May this happen to me if I break this covenant." Note that in this reading God alone passes between the remains of the animals, signifying his fidelity even if Abraham's descendants should prove unfaithful.

Responsorial Psalm: Psalm 27:1, 7-8, 8-9, 13-14
This is actually two distinct psalms. The second half (vv 7-14) is a patient and confident prayer of an oppressed person (or the whole people), calling upon God to be faithful to his covenant. Response: "Be with me, Lord, when I am in trouble."

Second Reading: Philippians 3:17-4:1

The Christian life is truly an imitation of Christ — not in a superficial way, as we usually understand the word "imitation" (something not real), but in a way that recognizes that we fully share in Christ's life. Read all of chapters 2 and 3 as a mediation on the implications of this challenge of imitation.

Questions for thought, discussion, and prayer:
1.   What does Jesus Christ as crucified Savior mean to you? What signs in your life strengthen your own faith in the meaning of the cross?

2.   Discuss what it means to imitate Christ by carrying his cross.

THIRD SUNDAY OF LENT — YEAR C

URGENCY AND PATIENCE

Gospel: Luke 13:1-9

A sense of urgency pervades the message of Lk 12-13. It is not so much that final judgment is imminent, but rather the urgency that comes from the realization that the opportunity for repentance and conversion presented today will be forever gone tomorrow, and that ultimate judgment depends on what we are and what we do in the present moment.

The two examples in vv 1-4 are not found in any non-Biblical historical source, but they certainly fit the times. Pontius Pilate was a tyrant whose excess cruelty got him in trouble with higher Roman authorities — and they were not noted for their gentleness either! The tower was likely a part of the water project for Jerusalem which was being built with funds confiscated from the temple treasury. The Jews who worked on it may have been considered traitors, and therefore any work-related casualties would have been seen as God's punishment on them.

Jesus' message here is twofold. First, we should not look for signs of God's wrath in every such event. Secondly, we are all guilty, we are all in need of conversion. We cannot withhold compassion from victims of disaster (or discrimination or poverty) in an attitude of self-righteous moral superiority ("they had it coming"), nor can we fail to realize that, in view of the demands of God's kingdom, we must look to our own change of heart rather than concern ourselves about what sort of punishment others may deserve.

Although the call to conversion demands immediate and earnest response, the second part of this reading affirms that the actual accomplishment of reform is a slow, growth-oriented, painstaking process. Although God will not tolerate delay in taking the decisive first steps, once those steps become clear, he shows infinite patience in bringing them to completion.

First Reading: Exodus 3:1-8, 13-15

This religious experience of Moses at the foot of Mount Horeb (Sinai) marked the beginning of the decisive event of liberation which established the people of Israel as a nation. It is best not to be too concerned about incidental outward features of the narrative, such as the bush, the fire, or the angel, for the important thing is the inner change (conversion) that took place within Moses himself. Inner realities are often expressed in metaphorical language in the Bible. The essence of this event is that Moses came to the realization that the ancestral God of his people, whom they had forgotten during the long years of slavery, still cared for them and wished to set them free. Moses recognized his responsibility as leader and liberator, but also feared the difficulty of the task, and was strengthened by his vision of God's presence and power.

The divine name revealed here "I Am Who Am," in Hebrew YAHWEH, is obscure in its exact meaning. As it stands, it says nothing except to affirm the existence of God as Supreme Being — it is not really a name. Yet, if this means that the name itself is in fact a refusal to give a name, it has even deeper meaning. Knowing the name of someone or something gives a certain control over them (see Gn 2:19-20; 32:27-31). Pagans invoked their deities by name, expecting favors in return. God, on the other hand, in declaring that he is Lord over his people, emphasized that they could not dominate or manipulate him. Some see an active significance in the name, meaning not just "I Am," but "I Am with You (to deliver you)."

Responsorial Psalm: Psalm 103:1-2, 3-4, 6-7, 8, 11

This psalm continues the theme of God's faithful, active, loving presence. Response: "The Lord is kind and merciful."

Second Reading: 1 Corinthians 10:1-6, 10-12

Paul, writing to a Christian community torn by factions and not living united in Christ, appeals to the experience of the Jews in the desert to show that salvation is not merely the automatic consequence of baptism or the receiving of the eucharist, but demands living in accord with what is received.

Questions for thought, discussion, and prayer:
1.   Discuss what may be meant by "the grace of the present moment." What does the urgency of Christ's call mean to us two thousand years later?

2.   By what names or titles do you invoke God? What do these have to say about how you understand your relationship to him?

FOURTH SUNDAY OF LENT — YEAR C

THE LOVING FATHER

Gospel: Luke 15:1-3, 11-32
Jesus' critics could identify with a common but wrong-headed proverb: "There is joy before God when those who provoke him perish from the world." The point of the three parables in Lk 15 is that God's true joy is found in forgiving. Many "religious" people, in their self-righteousness, tend to dole out forgiveness sparingly, and then only if paid for in the blood of humiliation. Jesus affirmed that this is not the way with God — he loves sinners and searches them out and rejoices at their return — nor may it be with us.

The traditional title of this parable, "the prodigal son," distorts its meaning. Considering the attitude of the hearers (vv 1-3), it more pointedly portrays the older son as their mirror image in contrast to the love shown by the father. The joyful and lavish banquet is an image of the eternal, and the response of the elder son should give us pause. Even though he felt he had earned the banquet as a faithful family member, in the moment of truth he cut himself off by his own resentment of the treatment given the younger son. Even though the father went out to plead with him, the elder son created his own bitter hell by his refusal to take part in the joy of forgiveness. Note that the father did not take sides, and he affirmed his love for both sons equally. But by his refusal of the father's love, the elder brother showed himself more lost than the younger ever was.

First Reading: Joshua 5:9, 10-12

The events surrounding the entry of the people of Israel into the land of promise, recounted in Jos 3-5, may not be as famous or as striking as the passage through the Red Sea and the covenant as told in the book of Exodus, but in many ways they are of equal significance. The passage through the water of the Jordan marks a decisive transition, the covenant is renewed in the circumcision rite, and the passover banquet is celebrated as the sign of new independence in their own land.

Forty years in the desert was a period of cleansing and strengthening under the Lord's direct nourishment — manna. Now they had achieved maturity, able to settle on their own land (even if much of it remained to be conquered!) and produce their own sustenance. Henceforth, the sign of the Lord's providence would not be direct gifts but the fruitfulness of the work of their hands. This passover meal was the sign of the dawn of a new age.

Responsorial Psalm: Psalm 34:2-3, 4-5, 6-7

The experience of God's goodness, especially his protection of those faithful to him, inspired this song of confidence. Response: "Taste and see the goodness of the Lord."

Second Reading: 2 Corinthians 5:17-21

The dilemma of those who realize their sinfulness and sincerely want to repent is similar to that of the young son reduced to eating pig's fodder, and desiring to return home. Can one be sure of acceptance? Ultimately, repentance demands an act of trust — a trust founded on Christ. We do not have to hope that God will change his mind about us. Our minds are in need of change to accept the God who has already extended his arms to embrace us.

Questions for thought, discussion, and prayer:
1. Reflect on the effect of forgiveness — or lack of forgiveness — in your own life.

2. How does your concept of God's justice square with the picture of God's mercy presented in these readings?

GO, AND SIN NO MORE

Gospel: John 8:1-11

Scholars agree that this incident is a later addition to the original Gospel, but nevertheless it is certainly an authentic part of earliest tradition. It does not indicate that Jesus was soft on matters of sexual morality nor that he passed over guilt lightly. Forgiveness requires a genuine facing up to guilt with an honest conversion and intention of amendment: "Go and sin no more."

The question here is not whether the law is valid, but the dishonest use of the law by the scribes and Pharisees. Their intention was not to seek justice but to trap Jesus. (It is quite possible that the woman herself was lured into a trap by a jealous husband — such an accusation required two eyewitnesses to the act itself — see Dt 19:15; and the closely related story of Susanna in Dn 13). References to the death penalty for adultery are in Lv 20:10; Dt 22:21-22; Ez 16:36-41. However, there are indications that capital punishment was not always invoked, and that reconciliation was possible on the initiative of the husband (see Hos 1-3).

The writing in the dirt remains an enigma — we simply have no way of knowing what Jesus wrote. It could not have been considered important to the story, but it does stimulate our idle curiosity. Conjectures range from a list of accusers' sins, through some pertinent Hebrew proverbs, to simply doodling to show that he was not perturbed by the trial — whether the trial was of him or of her.

First Reading: Isaiah 43:16-21

The only way it is possible to foretell the future is by reference to the past. One does not live in the past, but one should see in it the pattern of the future. Israel was in exile when this part of Isaiah was written, and would naturally look nostalgically at past glories. The prophet here announces to the people that future restoration will be even greater. This in turn gives us an image of repentance and forgiveness that echoes the Gospel reading. The sinner (or sinful nation) who repents recovers true dignity. The past is not whitewashed, but is truly dead, and life is regained (v 19), which makes possible the activity proper to the redeemed: to praise God (v 21).

Responsorial Psalm: Psalm 126:1-2, 2-3, 4-5, 6

This is a song of the restoration: praise springs not merely from a recollection of the past but from the experience of God's saving power in the present. Response: "The Lord has done great things for us; we are filled with joy."

Second Reading: Philippians 3:8-14

This letter is somewhat rambling, which leads some scholars to believe that it may be a composite of several messages written at different times. Nonetheless, one thread of meaning that runs through the whole letter is that the suffering of Christ is the source of our life. In this reading, "knowledge" of Christ is the hope and goal of Paul and of all Christians. This knowledge is no mere abstract intellectual matter, but an active participation in his sufferings. One cannot really know another at a distance. Knowledge is communion — sharing what that person is and does.

Questions for thought, discussion, and prayer:
1.   What does forgiveness teach us about the human worth and dignity of even the worst sinner? Can you concentrate on the dignity of person of those who have hurt you?

2.   How does "knowledge of Christ," as St. Paul describes it, influence your understanding of your relationship with him?

PASSION/PALM SUNDAY — YEAR C

PEACE AND GLORY

Gospel for Procession: Luke 19:28-40

The emphasis of this day is on the passion of Jesus, with the triumphal entry into Jerusalem seen as its prelude. Putting the two together in such close connection creates an intentionally jarring effect: the shouts of acclaim give way immediately to the clamor for crucifixion. This should give us pause — our own high-spirited devotion of one moment does not in itself guarantee fidelity. Pilgrim Jews spoke of coming to Jerusalem for the feast as an "ascent." This entry was, for Jesus, his ascent to the sacrifice. For us, the procession with palms is our ascent as a pilgrim people with Christ to the summit of the cross.

Gospel of the Mass: Luke 22:14-23:56

Thea Passion according to Luke. Luke's account of the passion and death of Jesus brings to a climax the major themes of his Gospel. In particular he emphasizes love and forgiveness in the details peculiar to Luke. He is the only evangelist who notes the healing of the high priest's servants ear (22:51); he alone records Jesus' words of forgiveness on the cross (23:34) and the promise of paradise to the repentant thief (23:39-43). The source of this love and pardon is the union of Jesus with the Father, which Luke always portrays in a most intimate way. He alone records the Father's sign of comfort in the presence of an angel at the agony in the garden (22:43) as well as Jesus' final word of self-commendation in 23:46.

The cross is seen as the link between Jesus and his followers with Christians down through the ages. The various persons who figure in the story are presented as models of our own relationship with Christ. Peter is an example of repentance in response to the healing glance of Christ (note especially 22:61). Luke is the only one who records this encounter. Simon of Cyrene (23:26) and the women along the way (23:27-31) are people whose lives are changed by their meeting with Christ. Even the Roman soldier does not merely exclaim that Jesus was the Son of God, as in Mt 27:54 and Mk 15:39, but shows his change of heart by praising God as well (23:47). Even the crowd experiences a change (23:48). Through these persons, Luke personally invites us also to become one with the Event taking place.

As with the other Gospels' passion accounts, the story line maybe divided into four basic sections:

(1)   the Lord's supper and prayer in the garden (22:14-46);
(2)   the arrest, the religious trial, and Peter's denial (22:47-71);
(3)   the civil trial and sentencing (23:1-25);
(4)   the cross and death (23:26-56).

See YEAR A for the first and second readings, pages 53-54.

THE SACRED TRIDUUM

HOLY THURSDAY, MASS OF THE LORD'S SUPPER

See YEAR A for all the readings, pages 54-55.

GOOD FRIDAY, CELEBRATION OF THE LORD'S PASSION

See YEAR A for all the readings, pages 55-56.

EASTER VIGIL

See YEAR A for all the readings, pages 56-58, except:

Gospel: Luke 24:1-12
　　The early Church was faced with a need to give clear witness to the event of the resurrection in expressing its faith in Jesus. Luke agrees with the other Gospel accounts that the discovery of the empty tomb was made by the women who went there with the intention of completing the preparations for burial, therefore the resurrection was not simply a story made up by the apostles. In fact, they were at first incredulous (v 11). In addition, Luke's account has the formula of faith, "he has been raised up," spoken by two heavenly men (v 6) because legally the agreement of two witnesses was necessary to establish the truth. Finally, the inclusion of Peter as eyewitness underscores his position as foundation "rock" of the Church, and assures that the resurrection is at the heart of the faith of the whole Church.

See YEAR A for all the readings, pages 58-60.

SHALOM!

Gospel: See YEAR A, pages 58-60.
First Reading: Acts of the Apostles 5:12-16

This reading gives us another insight into the spirit of the early Christian community in Jerusalem under the leadership of the apostles. (See also the Second Sunday of Easter, Year B.) They were seen as having the power to continue the messianic ministry of Jesus by performing the same signs he did. These miracles were also an indication of the victory over evil and the restoration of order in creation that had been accomplished in Christ.

Responsorial Psalm: Psalm 118:2-4, 13-15, 22-24

This hymn of praise recounts God's deliverance of his faithful servant from death, and glorifies God for it. Vv 22-24, while referring to the oppressed nation of Israel directly, is also a beautiful summary of God's power in raising Jesus to life, and establishing him as Lord of all creation. Response: "Give thanks to the Lord for he is good, his love is everlasting."

Second Reading: Revelation 1:9-11, 12-13, 17-19

The book of Revelation, which is read throughout Easter season this year, opens with John's vision that is connected with the eucharist, celebrated on the Lord's day (v 10). The Son of Man, recalling the visions of Dn 7 and 10, and Ez 1:24-26, is the Lord of all history, and therefore he will be the judge on the last day. At this time, however, he is unfolding his view of the world. The book begins with an inspection and evaluation of seven churches (chapters 2-3), and continues with the assurance of victory of God's power over the forces of evil that was then being experienced — and continues to be experienced to this day.

Questions for thought, discussion, and prayer:
1. How have you seen Christ in the Christian lives of others?

2. Can we recapture in our day something of the spirit that characterized the early Church as told in the Acts of the Apostles?

PETER, WITNESS AND SHEPHERD

Gospel: John 21:1-19
This chapter aims at defining the role of Peter in the early Church as both chief witness to the resurrection and shepherd of Christ's sheep. The story as told here shows a definite relationship to the call of the disciples in Lk 5:1-11, but is placed after the resurrection in John so the details become symbolic of the ongoing role of Peter and the other disciples in the Church. Although Peter is clearly given authority, it is equally obvious that he does not fulfill this work alone. "The disciple Jesus loved" (presumably John) is the one who identifies Jesus in v 7, and the other disciples actually haul in the load of fish in vv 8-9. The catch of fish represents the saving work of the Church, which by human effort alone accomplishes nothing (v 3), but at the word and power of Jesus brings overwhelming results (v 6). The nourishment that Jesus gives for their task (vv 9-13) is his own gift rather than the fruit of their labors. And in this meal, which recalls the eucharist in a way similar to the Emmaus meal (see Lk 24:30-31), they grow in their recognition of him (v 12).
The triple question, response, and commission could perhaps be seen as a counterbalance to Peter's triple denial (18:15-18, 25-27), but more probably is a ritual indication of the solemnity of this investiture to the office of shepherd. Repetition emphasizes the importance of the moment. Peter's shepherding and witness would be to the point of suffering the violent death of a martyr, the ultimate act of following Jesus in his cross.

First Reading: Acts of the Apostles 5:27-32, 40-41
Read this passage in conjunction with the first trial (4:5-22) and the whole second trial (5:17-42). The emphasis here is upon wit-

ness, and it focuses on Peter. He is fulfilling the commission given to him the Gospel reading. While he affirms that they must obey God rather than the human authority that contradicts God's sovereignty, he is careful to give legal basis to his witness, calling upon two sources of testimony, his own and the Holy Spirit's (v 32, see Dt 19:15). This appeal to the Holy Spirit undoubtedly refers to the evidence of the works they performed (vv 12-16). The advice of Gamaliel (vv 34-39) is good advice for the present as well, when we must live with many apparently contradictory trends in the Church and in the world. Finally, the irrational punishment of the apostles indicates the strength and effectiveness of their witness, and was therefore cause for rejoicing (vv 40-41). What is weak and ineffective does not provoke violent antagonism.

Responsorial Psalm: Psalm 30:2, 4, 5-6, 11-12, 13
     This prayer of thanksgiving for recovery from a serious illness echoes the confident thanks of the disciples after experiencing God's power in their witness. Response: "I will praise you, Lord, for you have rescued me."

Second Reading: Revelation 5:11-14
     Chapters 4 and 5 depict a majestic heavenly liturgy, patterned after early forms of Jewish and Christian ritual, but elevated to the splendor of the heavenly court. As the eucharist culminates in the communion with Christ in his sacrificial death and resurrection, so this apocalyptic liturgy comes to a climax in Christ as the Lamb slain but triumphant.

Questions for thought, discussion, and prayer:
1.   How does, or should, the Pope today as successor of Peter, exercise the power given him by Christ? What does reflection on the Gospel reading tell you about his responsibility?

2.   How can pain, opposition, rejection, or apparent disregard be a sign of the effectiveness of God's power in witnessing to the death and resurrection of Christ, and therefore be a cause for rejoicing?

FOURTH SUNDAY OF EASTER — YEAR C

HEAR MY VOICE

Gospel: John 10:27-30

Some Christians would like to see faith as an intellectual exercise, going no further than acceptance of certain truths as divinely revealed. Others want to use faith as a tool to manipulate the Divine Mind around to their own way of thinking and the mold the Divine Will to conform to their own desires. The image of a shepherd and his sheep, as given by Jesus in Jn 10, draws us above these mechanical and self-serving conceptions of faith. Faith is a matter of belonging. The decisive question of faith is: "To whom do you belong?" Thus the words of Jesus cannot be accepted on the basis of human argumentation and reasoning. We can accept his word only because we accept him: "My sheep hear my voice" (v 27). Those who demand conclusive proof (v 24) will never be convinced because they want only knowledge without commitment. Knowledge of a person demands the price of commitment; otherwise this knowledge cannot go beyond surface impressions. Our experience of human friendship tells us this. Only if we take the trouble to accept the other person into the fabric of our lives — in a sense to belong to him or her — can we say that we are beginning to know him or her. Without such a commitment, knowledge cannot reach the inner person of the other because we would not really care about the inner person of the other.

In today's Gospel reading, Jesus opens up the other side of that relationship as well. Not only do his sheep know him and hear his voice, but he knows them and he gives them eternal life. The intimate knowledge of Jesus that comes as a result of belonging to him is itself eternal life because "the Father and I are one" (v 30).

First Reading: Acts of the Apostles 13:14, 43-52

The apostles continue to witness to the Shepherd who gives his life for the sheep and enables them to have eternal life. The long sermon of Paul to the Jews in the synagogue at Antioch in Pisidia (in the heart of present-day Turkey) (vv 16-41) announcing the good news is favorably received (vv 42-43) — until they began to realize its full implications. Once it becomes clear to them that salvation is not an exclusive possession of any one people (that is, themselves!)

but a gift to be shared with all, even the Gentiles, they will hear no more of this. The opposition from the Jewish leaders begins to mount. But, as many Jews say no to the word, many Gentiles begin to welcome it and respond to it. The Good Shepherd wants to draw all into his fold. We cannot try to make his flock into our own private club by harboring our own opinions as to who should included and who should be excluded.

Responsorial Psalm: Psalm 100:1-2, 3, 5
This is a song of praise to the Lord who faithfully shepherds his people. Response: "We are his people: the sheep of his flock."

Second Reading: Revelation 7:9, 14-17
This apocalyptic vision of John depicts the fulfillment of the Gospel promise, and pointedly indicates that all peoples are called to share in this eternal life. The white garments represent the cleansing of baptism in the death of Christ and the Christian life of faith. Martyrdom — witness to Christ in the midst of trial and suffering — is the call given to each of us, not just a special few. Roots of this passage in the Hebrew Scriptures are Ps 23 and Is 49:10.

Questions for thought, discussion, and prayer:
1. Why should faithful witness to Christ necessarily involve trials and suffering?

2. What are the various things "belonging to someone" can mean? How does this help us understand our relationship to Christ?

FIFTH SUNDAY OF EASTER — YEAR C

GLORY AND LOVE

Gospel: John 13:31-33a, 34-35
John 13 is the prelude to the majestic yet intimate farewell of Jesus to his disciples. This final discourse, comprising Jn 14-17, spells out the terms of both Jesus' union with the Father and the disciples' union with him. If we want to know the meaning of the death and resurrection of Jesus and of the Christian life, it is necessary to be familiar with the whole picture presented in these chapters.

In today's passage, the two key words — glory and love — are difficult to understand properly. Both words are commonly used for something other than what they really are, and so the meaning of Jesus' words can be easily distorted.

Glory is a recognition of true worth — the clarity in which all reality is seen as it really is. Therefore, God's true glory is the acknowledgment of his lordship over all. This acknowledgment is not merely intellectual assent or lip service, but wholehearted submission involving every aspect of one's being. Jesus, as a man, perfectly fulfilled this submission in his life, even though this cost him rejection and the cross. Here we encounter the heart of the paradox of the cross: the sufferings of Jesus were not something merely to be endured on the road to glory, but precisely in the sufferings was the glory of God revealed.

Christ's followers have recognized this pattern in themselves as well. When Christians suffer persecution or martyrdom, the glory of God is revealed in full strength. This glory reveals perfect love at its heart. A love willing to give up all — even the satisfaction of possessing the beloved, even life itself, even all personal hopes and dreams — on behalf of the beloved cannot fail to have the power of God behind it. This is the love Jesus had (and has), and he commands (not merely suggests) that this same love be ours.

If God's glory is obscured in the world today, it is because Christians do not in fact love in this way.

First Reading: Acts of the Apostles 14:21-27

The Acts of the Apostles tells of the spread of the Christian faith from its tiny beginnings with the band of disciples in Jerusalem to its planting in Rome, then the capital of the world. On the one hand, the power behind this rapid growth is seen to be the Holy Spirit. But the paradox of the cross is never absent — persecution and rejection cause the Church to grow in two ways. First, the witness of the courage and steadfastness of the missionaries demonstrates the power of their conviction; and secondly, they are always being driven forceably from place to place, and cannot settle comfortably into an easy "established" Christianity. The key statement in this reading, echoing the Gospel, is v 22.

Responsorial Psalm: Psalm 145:8-9, 10-11, 12-13

This psalm is a good example of glorification in the sense of the Gospel. God's position in relation to ourselves and all creation is explicitly acknowledged. Response: "I will praise your name for ever, my king and my God."

Second Reading: Revelation 21:1-5
 The final two chapters of Revelation depict the fulfillment of God's glory in the eternal new creation. This glory is not merely outward splendor, but the rightness of the new order — this is the way things ought to be, the way God intended them, and the way things will be when sin and death are fully overcome.

Questions for thought, discussion, and prayer:
1. How does the Christian — as an individual and as community (Church) — show forth God's glory today? What are the obstacles to this glory?

2. How is loving as Jesus commanded a cross in the lives of those you know? In your own life?

SIXTH SUNDAY OF EASTER — YEAR C

FAREWELL PEACE

Gospel: John 14:23-29
 The key to this passage, as well as to the whole farewell message of Jn 13-17, is found in v 24. The word that Jesus shares is not his own (that is, according to human reckoning), but God the Father's. The peace that Jesus is concerned to share with his followers is based on a right ordering of one's life before God — the result of keeping Christ's fundamental command to love one another as he did. The Holy Spirit shows how this can be done and therefore reveals the power to love.
 The farewell which signals the end of one sort of presence of Jesus on earth also spells the beginning of a new presence — he is in his Church formed by the Spirit. The risen body of Jesus is not just his previous physical body brought back to life as before, but is a totally new, spiritually charged body. Whatever the physical elements of the body the disciples saw after the resurrection, this much is clear: the early Christians saw themselves as one with this very body. The risen Jesus continued to work on earth through their bodies united in the one body, the Church.

First Reading: Acts of the Apostles 15:1-2, 22-29

The account of the council of Jerusalem in Acts 15 brings us down to earth about the way the Church actually strives to love in the presence of Christ. The power of the Spirit does not take away the need for human organization or human powers of deliberation, decision, and action. The human situation becomes the field within which the Spirit worked, and thus human responsibility is raised to a new level, that of cooperation with the divine will.

Responsorial Psalm: Psalm 67:2-3, 5, 6, 8

This psalm looks to the reign of God throughout the world through the presence of Christ in his Church. Response: "O God, let all the nations praise you."

Second Reading: Revelation 21:10-14, 22-23

City of God versus city of man is an age-old theme in religious writings. Human civilization, as we experience it, is founded upon pride and greed, and cannot be considered an environment worthy of human dignity, nor is it able to survive the limitations of time. The final realization of the city of God is recognition of God's sufficiency (v 23) over and above all the strivings of human wisdom and effort.

Questions for thought, discussion, and prayer:
1. Reflect on the meaning and value of Christ's peace in the world today.

2. "The glory of God is man and woman fully alive." Comment.

SOLEMNITY OF THE ASCENSION — YEAR C

FULFILLING HIS PROMISE

Gospel: Luke 24:46-53

In Year C both the Gospel and the first reading contain Luke's account of the Ascension of Jesus, but they are very different. For a description of the differences, see the commentary on the first reading for Year A.

The end echoes the beginning. In his telling the story of Jesus' origins in chapters 1-3, Luke is careful to point out the ways that he fulfills the Jewish Scriptures, he ends his Gospel with the Scriptures not only being fulfilled but, equally important, opened up to the disciples and understood by them (vv 44-46). As the preaching of John the Baptist called the nation of Israel to repentance in preparation for the kingdom of God (3:2), and as Jesus announced the kingdom's presence in his person (4:16-21), so now the disciples are commissioned to make the same proclamation throughout the world (v 47) as they themselves have experienced it (v 48), and are promised the power to accomplish this work (v 49). The farewell itself is touching and simple, and there is no hint of sadness or fear (vv 50-52); the disciples are confident that the Lord will fulfill his promise.

See YEAR A for the first and second readings, pages 69-70.

SEVENTH SUNDAY OF EASTER — YEAR C

THAT ALL MAY BE ONE

Gospel: John 17:20-26

The last supper farewell of Jesus (Jn 13-17) concludes with prayer — for the consecration of his disciples (17:9-19) and for unity and love among all believers (17:20-26). The unity of all believers is accomplished by the death of Christ (11:50-52; 12:32) because the reconciliation of humankind with God enables all people to be reconciled to one another (see Eph 2). This unity brought about by the sacrificial death of Christ becomes real and effective among Christians in the sharing of the eucharistic bread and cup (1 Cor 10:16-17; 11:26-29). Love, which means full openness of one person to another, is the result of this eucharistic sharing in the one body and blood of Christ. Note that Paul's great teaching on the unity and love of Christians (1 Cor 12-14) stems directly from his teaching on the Lord's supper (1 Cor 11:17-34). Unity and love in celebration is both the expression and the source of unity and love in the Christian life. Through this unity and love, the "name" (i.e. the full reality) of God continues to be revealed to the world. On the other hand, to the extent that Christians fail to become one with what they celebrate in the eucharist, the revelation of God is obscured in the world today.

First Reading: Acts of the Apostles 7:55-60

The account of Stephen's martyrdom bears many similarities to the trial and death of Jesus as told in the Gospels. In the trial, false witnesses accuse him of profaning the temple (6:13-14; see Mk 14:53-59), his hearers violently take him outside the city, and during the stoning, Stephen's words echo those of Jesus: giving up his spirit (see Jn 19:30), forgiveness (see Lk 23:34), and a loud cry (see Lk 23:46). Stephen not only dies for Christ, he dies with him and in him. The power of martyrdom is not merely one of example but of participation in the same reality of Christ's sacrifice. The conversion and missionary work of Saul-Paul (v 58, see 8:1-3; 9:1-29) is clearly seen as the fruit of Stephen's blood shed.

Responsorial Psalm: Psalm 97:1-2, 6-7, 9

The courageous witness of the good who suffer at the hand of evil is itself a sign of the judgment of God and a cause for rejoicing. Response: "The Lord is king, the most high over all the earth."

Second Reading: Revelation 22:12-14, 16-17, 20

These final verses sum up the message of the whole book of Revelation — Christ is the center of all human history, and he personally is the reward and goal of all who persevere in holiness and faith in him. The Church, living in the power of the Spirit, is the Bride of Christ, longing for union with him and crying out, "Come!" The eucharist is the pledge of his coming. Those who hear his word and taste his banquet of sacrifice live in a posture of anticipation. "Come, Lord Jesus!"

Questions for thought, discussion, and prayer:

1. What obstacles are there to Christian love and unity in the Church today? In your own life?

2. What signs should the Christian life give of longing for Christ's coming in fullness?

THE SOLEMNITY OF PENTECOST — YEAR C

VIGIL and MASS OF THE DAY

See YEAR A for all the readings, pages 72-75.

SOLEMNITY OF THE HOLY TRINITY — YEAR C
(SUNDAY AFTER PENTECOST)

THE SPIRIT OF TRUTH

Gospel: John 16:12-15

The Gospel of John expresses the relationship of the Persons of the Trinity to each other most clearly of all the Gospels. Catholics who have been brought up learning little more about the Trinity than "Three Persons in One God" would do well to study the way John speaks of this mystery, and listen carefully to the way we pray in the Mass. The three Divine Persons are equal as one God, but it is important to know in what ways they are portrayed as distinct in Scripture and to understand each one's proper activity in relation to each other and to our own lives. The last supper farewell of Jesus (Jn 13-17) is exceptionally rich in teaching about who and what the Father, Son, and Holy Spirit are, and what they do. Read the whole of this discourse again (you should already be familiar with it from the past few weeks). This time, ask yourself what exactly is Jesus saying about himself as the Son of God, and his relationship to the Father and the Holy Spirit, and what this means for his followers.

This passage focuses on the activity of the Spirit to continue what Christ has begun. In Christ, God the Son become a man, the fullness of God-ness is shared with us. However, we will always receive only in part because our capacity is limited, and we must continually grow. A once-and-for-all full revelation on God's part must necessarily be received by us as an ongoing and never-ending process because of our human limitations. Although Christ has the fullness of the Father, the revelation of this fullness needs to be carried on through the Spirit in the Church. The Spirit's work is not a new work, distinct from Christ's, but the very same revelation made present ever-new in all ages and places.

The truth which Jesus and the Spirit speak is more than a teaching or doctrine to be understood and/or believed; it is the full acceptance of the person of Jesus as revealing God the Father and his love.

First Reading: Proverbs 8:22-31

This beautiful hymn personifying God's wisdom in creation is echoed in Jn 1; Col 1:15-20; and Rev 3:14. It is not a literal portrayal of God's wisdom as a distinct person, as though it were a Judaic prefiguring of Christ as God's wisdom. However, as an allegory, it invites us to contemplate the great work of God in creation and reveals a stage in the preparation for the full revelation of God's love in the Son and through the Spirit. In a sense, this passage expands the repeated phrase in Gn 1: "And God saw that it was good."

Responsorial Psalm: Psalm 8:4-5, 6-7, 8-9
     This "hymn of the universe" presents a somewhat more down to earth, but no less beautiful, reflection on the creative wisdom of God. Response: "O Lord, our Lord, how wonderful your name in all the earth."

Second Reading: Romans 5:1-5
     Paul, as well as John, speaks often of the distinct roles of the three Divine Persons in the Christian life. In fact, Paul's teaching is in a much more practical vein, describing how the Father, Son, and Holy Spirit relate actively to us here and now, and how we respond concretely. It is very important for us to have a sense of living within the sphere of the Trinity's life, rather than to be content with worshiping from afar.

Questions for thought, discussion, and prayer:
1.   Compare the prayer, "Glory be ..." with the "Through him, with him, in him ..." of the Mass. How do they differ in the way they speak to or of the persons of the Trinity, and what might account for that difference?

2.   Is prayer to the Father different from prayer to the Son or to the Holy Spirit? How?

SOLEMNITY OF CORPUS CHRISTI — YEAR C
(IN U.S.A., SUNDAY AFTER TRUTH)

BREAD OF LIFE

Gospel: Luke 9:11b-17
     The first generation of Christians understood this event of the multiplication of loaves and fishes as speaking of the eucharist. This is most obvious in v 16, in which the actions of Jesus are depicted precisely as the actions of eucharistic consecration. But the details of

this miraculous banquet point also to the implications the eucharist has for the Church that celebrates it.

The first condition for us to share the eucharist is a sense of our own inability to provide for ourselves. The eucharist is the bread of the poor, of those who realize the insufficiency of their own resources. Only those who have followed Jesus into "an out-of-the-way place" (v 12) can partake. The hungry can be filled at the Lord's table. The rich, secure in their own self-sufficiency, cannot receive from the Lord what they neither want nor seek. Jesus in the Gospel entrusts the sharing of his food to others — and now to us. He is the source, but he depends on our cooperation for equal and just distribution. If his gifts are not properly shared, if some still go hungry, it is our fault, not his. When he gives, he gives in over-abundance (v 17), which clearly indicates that his gifts are to be shared, not hoarded. People go hungry when those who have more goods than they need are more concerned about their own profit and security than the needs of their neighbors.

The food of the eucharist is primarily spiritual: the nourishment of God's word, bestowed lavishly upon us in the person of Christ himself. But spiritual nourishment cannot be divorced from the physical. Conditions of deprivation and unjust oppression cannot be tolerated if the Gospel is truly received and lived. A healthy spirit cannot flourish in a hungry body, or in an undernourished society. To partake freely of God's gifts oneself, and then to refuse to share them with those in need, is supreme dishonesty and ingratitude.

First Reading: Genesis 14:18-20

Melchizedek (the name means king of righteousness) appears almost from nowhere — no ancestry and only an uncertain and probably symbolic location (Salem means peace). Along with a gift of food, he pronounces this blessing over Abraham, who gives him a tithe in return for priestly service. Then he disappears without a further trace in Scriptures. The mysteriousness and ambiguity of this figure give rise to the equally mysterious phrase in Ps 110:4, which probably referred originally to the establishment of king David in Jerusalem (see 2 Sm 5) and his appointment of priests (2 Sm 8:17), especially Zadok (righteous). Later tradition has seen Melchizedek as an image of Christ. Heb 7 capitalizes on the mysterious origins to explain Christ's priesthood as as being of divine origin. Only in post-biblical times, around 200-300 C.E., did the bread and wine of Melchizedek begin to be seen as forerunner to the eucharistic sacrifice.

Responsorial Psalm: Psalm 110:1, 2, 3, 4

This psalm is likely a ceremonial dialogue in which Zadok the priest confirms David's kingship (vv 1-3, 5-7), and king David in turn confirms Zadok's priesthood (v 4).

Second Reading: 1 Corinthians 11:23-26

This familiar passage, echoing the institution of the eucharist at the last supper, should be read in its entirety to provide proper context: vv 17-34, and chapter 12. In giving the body and blood of his sacrifice, Jesus provides nourishment for the health and vitality of his body, the Church. If we who partake of the eucharist do not seek to live as one in mind, heart, and action, we are being unfaithful to the body of Christ itself (vv 27-29), and are destroying the health of this body.

Questions for thought, discussion, and prayer:
1. The Lord's prayer, sign of peace, and breaking of the bread are all elements of preparation for communion at Mass. What is the significance of each in your own participation in the Mass?

2. How can the presence of Christ in the eucharist be echoed and reinforced in your own family meals?

SOLEMNITY OF THE SACRED HEART — YEAR C
(FRIDAY AFTER THE SECOND SUNDAY AFTER PENTECOST)

GOD FIRST LOVED US

Gospel: Luke 15:3-7

In the three parables of divine mercy in Lk 15, of which this is the first, Jesus addresses a mentality that restricts salvation to a legalistic observance of certain norms, and which thereby excludes those who do not (or cannot) fulfill those norms precisely. Jesus shows the outcast as a result of this attitude to be the special object of God's concern. It is not true that the sinner is loved more than the faithful. Instead, Jesus affirms that sinful straying or out-group status does not sever the bonds that unite one to the Christian family, and that those very bonds give rise to the obligation of seeking the lost, not disowning them. The faithful have an obligation to maintain a lively sense of acceptance and concern for the unfaithful, even to the extent of going out of their way to seek them, in imitation of God the Father and Jesus. And their return is the cause for rejoicing because family unity has been restored.

First Reading: Ezekiel 34:11-16
God was often described as a shepherd in the Jewish Scriptures, as also were the leaders of the people. In this case, Ezekiel, having witnessed the scattering of the people into exile and into diverse regions as refugees because of the incompetence and infidelity of their leaders, now looks forward to the time when God himself will draw the people back together. Reliance on God as the leader is occasioned by the experience of the crumbling dynasty of the earthly kings as much as by an awareness of God's concern shown in the past. Often when things go well according to our plans, we feel we don't need God. God's time of calling us back to reliance on him is when things fall apart around us.

Responsorial Psalm: Psalm 23:1-3, 3-4, 5, 6
This most famous shepherd psalm carries the marks of the psalmist's experience of "walking in the dark valley" and struggling to keep his faith in God. Response: "The Lord is my shepherd; there is nothing I shall want."

Second Reading: Romans 5:5-11
Today's feast is a celebration of God's love manifested concretely in the human nature of Jesus Christ. In Year C, the image of the shepherd faithfully tending, unifying, and protecting all his sheep (first reading) and actively seeking our even the lost sheep (Gospel) embodies this love. Paul here meditates on how God's love embraced us even when we were unmindful and straying. The assurance that God continues to care for us is the experience that he has cared for us even when we didn't care.

Questions for thought, discussion, and prayer:
1.   Does devotion to the Sacred Heart of Jesus appeal to you personally? Why or why not?

2.   Discuss the meaning of "heart" and the many ways we use this word.

YEAR C
SEASON OF THE YEAR

278

SECOND SUNDAY OF THE YEAR— YEAR C

THE LAMB AND HIS BRIDE

Gospel: John 2:1-12

As with all of John's Gospel, this story will provide the patient, careful, and prayerful reader with rich rewards of understanding. This "first of Jesus' signs" (v 11), in which he graces the wedding celebration at Cana, reaches across all history to touch the eternal marriage of the Lamb and his Bride (the Church) in Rev 21. The "third day" clearly connects this sign to the life-giving paschal sacrifice of the Messiah (see Hosea 6:2; Jn 11:6-7; Lk 24:7). Similarly, although the final "hour" of Jesus has not yet come (v 4), it is time for the preparation in sign, telling of and leading to that hour. The condition for proper preparation is simply "do whatever he tells you" (v 5). It is significant that Mary, who is in the background throughout, is nevertheless the one who both impels Jesus toward his "hour" and sets the stage for it — a pattern of her continued role in the Church.

What is this sign? In this transformation of water into wine on the particular occasion may be seen the "good wine" of messianic fullness — the wisdom and happiness of renewed creation — now present in abundance to those who are aware of emptiness and need (see Is 55:1-3; Joel 2:21-27).

Our approach to Jesus' signs — in John's Gospel and in our own lives — must be with a proper sense of mystery. It's wrong to think that a mystery is merely something that we cannot understand. Rather, it is the beginnings of an understanding of something that we cannot get enough of! Mystery is an invitation to explore and experience the never-ending riches of God's self-revealing presence and action. Mystery always escapes being defined or explained. The only tool for probing mystery is symbol — a deeper reality contained within and expressed by an outward sign, which may be a person, an action, or an event. And while this tool is usually experienced in community with others, it becomes our own and effective through quiet reflection and prayer.

The wonder of the marriage feast at Cana is not merely that water became wine, but that this sign still speaks to us of God's saving love in Christ.

First Reading: Isaiah 62:1-5

The return of the small remnant of Jews from exile is described here as the espousal of God with his formerly abandoned people. The marriage relationship is a fitting sign of the relationship of God to his people because the committed-in-love partners are fulfilled in one another's presence, and yet never cease to seek fulfillment.

Responsorial Psalm: Psalm 96:1-2, 2-3, 7-8, 9-10

This is an eloquent hymn of praise to God, Creator and Lord of all. Response: "Proclaim his marvelous deeds to all the nations."

Second Reading: 1 Corinthians 12:4-11

Many problems plagued the church at Corinth. In addition to factions and immorality, there was also a temptation to adopt a pagan attitude towards spiritual gifts. Pagan cults could also claim to know God through various trances and ecstasies, resembling the gifts of the Spirit. Paul gives criteria for discernment: signs must be accompanied by (1) true faith in Jesus Christ (vv 1-3), (2) a spirit of unity (vv 4-31), and (3) unfailing love (chapter 13). Gifts claiming to be "of the Spirit," even if they are very impressive, that sow scandal or discord are by that very fact proven false.

Questions for thought, discussion, and prayer:

1. Reflect on the role of Mary in the life of a Christian in the light of the Gospel passage.

2. What does it mean to discern and understand signs in your relationship as a Christian to God and to others?

THIRD SUNDAY OF THE YEAR — YEAR C

TODAY IT IS ACCOMPLISHED

Gospel: Luke 1:1-4; 4:14-21

By using the first four verses of chapter 1 as a prologue, the Mass reading emphasizes that this event constitutes the real beginning of the Gospel (the proclamation of the good news of God's saving love) of Jesus Christ. The intervening chapters may be considered "pre-history" — background and foundation for the actual mission of Jesus. Chapters 1-3 are read for the most part during Advent and Christmas seasons; 4:1-13, the dramatic account of the temptation in the desert, appears on the First Sunday of Lent.

As recorded in today's reading, Jesus gave what must be the shortest yet most intensely meaningful homily in history. It conveys the essence of the good news: "Today it is accomplished." This is a good example of what a homily should be (in more ways than brevity), as well as a model to every Christian for proclaiming the Gospel in his or her own life. The homily (and the day by day proclamation of God's word in life) is not a doctrinal lesson, nor a moralistic exhortation, not a mere commentary on the Scripture, nor even a repetition of God's promises. It is rather the firm and true declaration of God's saving action here and now. It involves a glance at the past, but does not dwell on it. It is full of hope in the future, but requires more than just patient waiting for "pie in the sky by-and-by." The Sunday homily — as well as the witness of the Christian life — must aim at being nothing other than an eloquent testimony that God is at work here and now.

The synagogue liturgy was based on two readings. The first was from the law (from the torah or pentateuch, the first five books of the Hebrew Scriptures) and would be commented upon by a rabbi or teacher of the law. This commentary often was the sort of meticulous interpretation that Jesus frequently criticized (see Mk 7; Lk 11:45-52; Mt 7:28-29) or a dispute about fine points of the law. The second reading, taken from the prophets, could be read and interpreted by anyone over thirty years of age. We don't often think of Jesus as an ordinary Jewish layman, but it was in this capacity that he read and preached on this reading from Isaiah.

First Reading: Nehemiah 8:2-4a, 5-6, 8-10

This promulgation of the law after the restoration of Israel is cast in the form of a well-planned celebration in which the proclamation prompts the people to assimilate the law and respond to it. Read this section in its proper context by following this sequence: Ezra 7-8; Neh 8; Ezra 9-10; Neh 9-13 (portions of the books of Ezra and Nehemiah got dislocated and mixed together in history). This feast of the renewal of the covenant (feast of tabernacles or booths) became the most popular feast of Jewish religious life down to the time of Jesus.

The law was proclaimed not merely for the people to hear and follow, but to be inscribed on their hearts (see Dt 5-6; 6:6 — note that Deuteronomy was written not more than two centuries before this event, and was probably the basic text proclaimed at this time).

The word of the law was seen as constitutive of the people — having the power to give them their identity, to make them what they are. God's word proclaimed today in the Mass has the same function. We do not merely listen to it for instruction. In hearing it and taking it to heart, God's word forms us as his own people, as well as informs us with his truth.

Responsorial Psalm: Psalm 19:8, 9, 10, 15

This psalm makes explicit the relationship between God as Creator and God as Lord and Lawgiver. His redeeming law is seen as the fulfillment of what he began in creation. Response: "Your words, Lord, are spirit and life."

Second Reading: 1 Corinthians 12:12-30

If the Church is to be alive with Christ's life, it is necessary that we not be isolated individuals, each doing our own thing — even if that's a "holy" thing. On the other hand, to consider the Church as a massive homogeneous conglomeration of indistinguishable individuals who should think, act, and feel exactly the same is equally erroneous. The essence of the Church, rather, is a community life striving for harmony in one Spirit among those — individuals as well as groups — who possess differing gifts and capabilities, each supporting and being enriched by one another. A healthy body needs a unifying spirit as well as many diverse members working together.

Questions for thought, discussion, and prayer:

1.   How can you in your own life be a proclamation of the Gospel, the good news? What is this "good news" to be proclaimed? What does it mean to proclaim?

2.   Are you comfortable with those who are different from you? Think of examples; discuss why or why not.

FOURTH SUNDAY OF THE YEAR — YEAR C

REJECTED BY HIS OWN

Gospel: Luke 4:21-30

In this passage, Jesus breaks with the environment of his own upbringing, and definitively expands the horizon of his ministry. While acknowledging and accepting his heritage — he does not turn his back on his own — he also refuses to be bound by the limitations they want to impose on him (to be merely Joseph's son, the carpenter; or at best, the town wonder-worker, vv 22-23 — think of the tourist business he'd attract!). And so his own reject him. This rejection, in turn, becomes the open door for his ministry to reach out beyond.

Luke sees this event as establishing the pattern for the full meaning of Jesus' entire ministry. Nazareth, a tiny provincial town, symbolizes the "lost sheep of the house of Israel" (see Mt 15:24). Their rejection foreshadows the rejection of the Jewish leaders in handing Jesus over to the Roman authority to be put to death. His transfer of his "home base" to Capernaum, a prosperous commercial center of mixed population, embodies the same direction that the apostles took in expanding their preaching of the Gospel to the Gentiles because of persecution in Jerusalem (see Acts 8:1-4).

Jesus presents a difficult model for his followers here. The true Christian cannot flee from the world. We must accept the world as our own and must care for it with the love of Christ. But, by the same token, the world will reject us because our standards and ideals transcend those of the world, and point to what is beyond. To be in the world (to love and care for the well-being of all creation) and yet not be of the world (to be limited by the world's self-centered, shortsighted standards) is the genuine test of love for a Christian, a love that endures in the face of trials, rejection, and suffering.

First Reading: Jeremiah 1:4-5, 17-19
The prophetic call of Jeremiah, echoed in the heart of every Christian, is a fearsome challenge. Yet, God gives the assurance of strength to the prophet to fulfill his calling.

Responsorial Psalm: Psalm 71:1-2, 3-4, 5-6, 15-17
The praise of this psalm derives from the realization that God has been with his faithful servant through trials. Response: "I will sing of your salvation."

Second Reading: 1 Corinthians 12:31-13:13
This eloquent hymn on Christian love is deservedly one of the best known passages in all Scripture. It ties together all that Paul has said or will say about Church order and spiritual gifts. Vv 12:31-13:3 show that all other gifts depend on love if they are to have any value whatsoever. Vv 4-7 show the personal obligation of

this love, and vv 8-13 show the limited nature of other virtues and gifts in distinction to love which is enduring.

Chapter 14 can be understood only in the light of chapter 13. All spiritual gifts, no matter how striking or seemingly important, have value only when subordinated in a spirit of love to the order and building up of the Christian community as the body of Christ.

Questions for thought, discussion, and prayer:
1. Discuss your own relationship, as a Christian, with the values of the world.

2. Discover and evaluate as many synonyms as you can for the concept of love as described by St. Paul.

FIFTH SUNDAY OF THE YEAR — YEAR C

THE FISH OF GOD'S KINGDOM

Gospel: Luke 5:1-11

The cure of the man possessed by a demon and the healing of Simon Peter's mother-in-law (4:31-44) are read during Year B from Mk 1:23-39, on the Fourth and Fifth Sundays of the Year.

The simple and direct story of the calling of Simon Peter and the other disciples by the shore of the lake as told in Mk 1:16-20 (see the Third Sunday of Year B) and Mt 4:18-22 (see the Fourth Sunday of Year A) is expanded by Luke here to include the highly symbolic miraculous catch of fish (which may be a different telling of the same incident as the post-resurrection story in Jn 21:1-8). This catch is clearly seen to result from the command and power of Jesus, and it foretells the eventual mission of Peter and the apostles to draw all peoples out of the water of sin into the boat of salvation.

In the Jewish tradition, water was a powerful symbol of evil. The sea was the dwelling place of Satan and all the forces opposed to God. Water represented the primal chaos before creation, and was the afterlife abode of the dead (see Gn 1:2; Job 26:12-13; 38:16-17; Ps 69:2-3; 74:13-14; 89:10-11; Is 51:9-10; Jonah 2:2-10). Water, therefore, became the place where God's salvation was most needed, and most manifest. In water, the power of God confronted the forces of evil (see above references, also the great flood of Gn 6-8; the liberation from Egypt through the Red Sea, Ex 14-15; and Ps 107:23-32). The work of the apostles — and the missionary Church following them — to fish for men and women would be to rescue by the saving power of God all humanity engulfed by evil. The expression "fishers of men" has further roots in Jer 16:16.

This Gospel story emphasizes the ineffectiveness of human effort alone in accomplishing God's mission (v 5), contrasted with the surprising and overwhelming effect of reliance on God's power (v 6). Note the stages of Simon Peter's conversion: "Master" (v 5) recognizes Jesus' human authority, but "Lord" (v 8) has a definite religious meaning — Peter accepts Jesus as the Lord of his own life.

First Reading: Isaiah 6:1-8

Isaiah lived in the eighth century B.C.E., and prophesied at a time when the northern kingdom of Israel was about to fall and the southern kingdom of Judah — the focus of his prophecy — was failing to live up to its calling as God's people. The main thrust of Isaiah's prophetic oracles was to keep alive the hope that God would show his own fidelity through a remnant of faithful Jews even though the majority appear headed for well-deserved destruction.

This account of the call of Isaiah appears to take place at a temple ceremony during which the prophet goes into an ecstatic trance. The vision centers on the holiness of God — he is the Totally Other — making his prophet share in his holiness (separation from the limitations and evil of the world) to form a people that is holy (set apart), even if these will be just a tiny remnant. The six-winged creatures (v 2) may relate to figures in the ancient near eastern religions who were considered bearers of God's fire to consume sacrifices (seraphim means burning ones). Their "triple holy" hymn (v 3) cannot be stretched by us to contain an ancient pre-Christian inkling of the Trinity, but simply emphasizes the complete and above-all holiness of God. This verse, along with Ps 118:25-26, is the source of the "Holy, holy, holy . . ." acclamation in the eucharistic prayer of the Mass.

Responsorial Psalm: Psalm 138:1-2, 2-3, 4-5, 7-8

This psalm thanks God for his fidelity: the God who calls us to proclaim his name will respond to his faithful ones who call upon him in their need. Response: "In the sight of the angels I will sing your praises, Lord."

Second Reading: 1 Corinthians 15:1-11

Apparently one of the factions in the community at Corinth

had difficulty accepting the final resurrection of the body for Christians at the last day (v 12). The reason for this was probably a common Greek philosophical idea that the body was a hindrance to the soul's perfection, and therefore would have no place in the final state of perfect life. Paul does not attempt to counter this with logical reasoning — he might have appealed to the Jewish idea of wholeness of the human person requiring both body and soul to reach perfection. However, just before coming to Corinth in the first place, he had a bad experience in Athens trying to present Christian faith in a "reasonable" way (see Acts 17:16-34). Now he simply points to Christ as the model. If one accepts in faith the Christ preached by the apostles and in their witness of the resurrection, as the Corinthians professed to believe, then the Christian's own sharing in the full event of Christ, including both death to sin and rising to a fully new life, cannot be denied. Vv 3b-4 give us one of the earliest formulas of a creed, from which later expressions of faith were built.

Questions for thought, discussion, and prayer:
1.   Think carefully about v 11 of the Gospel. Discuss how Simon might explain this event to his wife, or James and John to their father. What objections might wife and father raise, and how would you answer them?

2.   Write a letter to someone — fictitious or real — who does not believe in the resurrection of the body, and explain what you believe and why.

SIXTH SUNDAY OF THE YEAR — YEAR C

BLESSINGS AND CURSES

Gospel: Luke 6:17, 20-26
Everything between last week's reading and today's reading (Lk 5:12-6:16) is found in Matthew and Mark as well, and is read in other years (see Year B, Sixth through Ninth Sundays; Year A, Tenth and Eleventh Sundays).
The sermon on the plain of Luke's Gospel (6:17-49) is roughly comparable to Matthew's sermon on the mount (Mt 5-7). Each author arranges Jesus' teachings in a way that reflects the basic re-

quirements of the kingdom of God according to his view. Although both insist on a radically new way of thinking and living, Luke is unique in his emphasis on absolute poverty. Note that the blessings focus on various aspects of poverty, while the curses concern the fate of the rich (vv 24-26) who are equated with false prophets, blind to realities beyond this world's goods.

First Reading: Jeremiah 17:5-8
This passage repeats a favorite theme of the Hebrew Scriptures: the human person (or the nation) stands at a fork in the road and chooses which way to take, the way of good or the way of evil. The way of good, difficult as it may be, leads to life. The way of evil, attractive as it may be, leads only to death. The root of this distinction of the two ways goes back to the very origin of the Israelites as a nation in the covenant, expressed in Dt 30:15-20; see also Dt 11:26-32 and chapter 28.

Responsorial Psalm: Psalm 1:1-2, 3, 4, 6
This psalm, based in large portion on the above passage from Jeremiah, forms the introduction to the entire collection of psalms, setting the theme of the two ways that will be developed by the rest of the book. Response: "Happy are they who hope in the Lord" (Ps 40:5).

Second Reading: 1 Corinthians 15:12, 16-20
The Corinthian Christians did not doubt that Jesus had been raised from the dead. As we have seen, their difficulty lay in connecting his risen life with their own destiny. They were blinded by their own preconceived ideas of a "perfect" afterlife being totally spiritual, and saw no necessity for the body — to them a hindrance and imperfection — to take part in eternal happiness. Paul's way of answering this problem was to emphasize that salvation itself is victory over bodily death, and if our bodies do not rise to life again, we are not saved. Insofar as Jesus has shared our human nature, his resurrection is the pattern and the cause of our own. Be sure to read carefully all of chapter 15. (See also the second reading for the Solemnity of Christ the King, Year A; and the Solemnity of the Assumption.)

Questions for thought, discussion, and prayer:
1.   What connection does the way of Christian living proposed in Luke's Gospel have with eternal life and our final resurrection?

2.　In the light of what Paul says about the resurrection, do you think the expression "to save one's soul" is adequate or appropriate to describe the goal of the Christian life?

LOVE YOUR ENEMY

Gospel: Luke 6:27-38

The son or daughter bears the image of the parent. If we are truly children of God the Father, Jesus warns us, we must adopt God's outlook as our own. The motivation behind our love for one another transcends personal attraction and sociological considerations. We learn love from the way God loves us. The first sign of his universal love that goes beyond human barriers is in creation (see Mt 5:45), and we are called to open our eyes to see God's way so that we can make it our way.

Family love or love based on attraction always draws lines which include some and exclude others. Society always requires some group or race to be "the enemy," a scapegoat on which the ills of the majority can be blamed. Jesus' challenge of love for our enemies cuts directly to the heart of our sinful way of loving that we consider both normal and necessary.

Love of enemies is the criterion of true, all-embracing love. To do good to those who do not reciprocate or who respond with injury tests the extent of our love. But this love should not be confused with a weak, naive attitude that condones evil or tolerates injustice. Love means seeking the other person's true good, not just their comfort or appeasement. Love of enemies does not come automatically — it has to be learned; we need to discover the ways it can be done. This is the task ever before us.

First Reading: 1 Samuel 26:2, 7-9, 12-13, 22-23

David, convinced that he had been chosen by the Lord to unify the nation of Israel (1 Sm 16), led a guerilla band to overthrow the rule of Saul, who had failed to lead the people properly (1 Sm 15). Two occasions are recorded in which David had the opportunity to kill Saul, but did not take advantage of it (1 Sm 24 and 26). David's compassion was not a sign of weakness, but of strength — only his assurance of the Lord's power behind him could give him the confidence to love his sworn enemy in this way.

Responsorial Psalm: Psalm 103:1-2, 3-4, 8, 10, 12-13
   This psalm of praise extols the Lord's mercy toward us as the motive for our imitating his kindness. Response: "The Lord is kind and merciful."

Second Reading: 1 Corinthians 15:45-49
   Paul, in teaching the resurrection of the body to people who were influenced by Greek philosophy to see death as freeing the soul from its bodily prison, speaks of Christ's Spirit as giving new life to the body. The Spirit of divine life does not reject our bodiliness, but transforms it in the image of Christ to be perfected and incorruptible.

Questions for thought, discussion, and prayer:
1.   How would following Christ's command to love enemies transform the society in which we live?

2.   What are the signs of God's way of love in your own life?

EIGHTH SUNDAY OF THE YEAR — YEAR C

WOOD AND WORD

Gospel: Luke 6:39-45
   In Luke's Gospel, the Christian ethic may be summed up as a love that admits no boundaries or exclusions. This passage presents us several sayings of Jesus that are loosely bound together around this theme.
   The relationship of Jesus to his disciples is not like that found among the Pharisees, whom he calls "blind guides" (Mt 15:14). A teacher can communicate only what he or she has been taught — and all that Jesus has received is from the Father (see Jn 17:8). In sharing everything, he forms his disciples into images of himself (vv 39-40).
   He frequently criticized the Pharisees' hypocrisy, and here counters it with a somewhat humorous image of how a teacher can be blind to his own glaring faults and still try to reform someone

else. In this image, we catch something of Jesus' early training as a carpenter (vv 41-42).

The ultimate test of discipleship, and therefore of one's love, is in what is accomplished. The type of fruit reveals the type of tree; the outward result reveals the inner attitude. Actions, not mere words, tell where the heart is (vv 43-45).

The concluding verses of the sermon, vv 46-49, are parallel to Mt 7:21-27, and are read on the Ninth Sunday of Year A.

First Reading: Sirach 27:4-7

The power of the word for good and for evil is a basic concern of Sirach, as it is in the letter of James (James 3). Quarreling (8:1-19; 28:8-12), taking false or hasty oaths (23:7-15), gossiping and lying (19:5-12; 20:22-26), and insincerity (5:14-6:1; 28:13-16) are all sins revealed through the tongue. Speech is a gift that must be in harmony with an inner sense of truth; inner decay is revealed when what we say is superficial and detached from what we are.

Responsorial Psalm: Psalm 92:2-3, 13-14, 15-16

This psalm of praise concentrates on how the good and the evil, and the wise and the foolish, respond to God's works. Response: "Lord, it is good to give thanks to you."

Second Reading: 1 Corinthians 15:54-58

Paul concludes his discourse on the resurrection of the body with this hymn of praise to God for having overcome death in the victory of Jesus Christ (vv 54-57) and a final word of encouragement to his hearers (v 58). The trumpet (v 52) is a call to assembly, and assures us that the Church of which we are now a part will be fulfilled in the final union of all who will have been raised to new life. Being with Jesus is not a matter only of individual salvation or resurrection, but of togetherness with all his faithful in him.

Questions for thought, discussion, and prayer:
1. How well or poorly do you feel that your own tongue reflects you?

2. Do you feel confident or uneasy in thinking about Jesus' victory over your own death? Why?

COMMAND TO BE HEALED

Gospel: Luke 7:1-10

Three Gospel writers record this healing — Mt 28:5-13 and Jn 4:46-54, in addition to Luke. All three place great emphasis on the cure being brought about at a distance by Jesus' power to command obedience (from sickness-causing demons? from healing spirits?), and all three indicate that Jesus' concern extends beyond the confines of Jewish religious nationalism.

There are only two healings from a distance recorded in the Gospels, and both are for foreigners. The other is the Canaanite woman's daughter in Mt 15:21-28. Although Jesus seems to be restricting his mission now only to Israel, he makes it clear that he is paving the way for his followers' mission to all peoples.

The centurion was obviously sympathetic towards the Jews (v 5) and respected the law forbidding a Jew to enter a Gentile's house (v 6). This sort of respect is behind the adoption of his words as part of the invitation to communion in the Mass. But we have to be careful not to take Jesus' display of power from afar as the norm. He usually accomplished healings by personal presence and contact, and is careful to exclude any hint of magic or mere mechanical action in his acts. For the centurion as well as for us, the "Lord, I am not worthy . . ." is an acceptance in faith of Jesus as he is present, not a desire to keep him at a distance.

First Reading: 1 Kings 8:41-43

After Solomon had built the temple and the Lord had manifested his presence in it (vv 10-13), Solomon uttered a solemn prayer of dedication. Only a small portion of the prayer as recorded here (vv 23-53) is actually his. Most of it can best be dated from the time of exile, after the destruction of the temple in 587 B.C.E. Today's brief passage reflects the thinking of the Jews after the exile about the universalist dimensions of their religion. They began to realize that God chose them not just for their own benefit, but to be a source of salvation for all people. The temple (to be restored) was to signify God's sanctifying presence for the whole world.

Responsorial Psalm: Psalm 117:1-2

This shortest of all psalms calls on all humanity to praise God for his faithfulness. Response: "Go out to all the world, and tell the Good News."

Second Reading: Galatians 1:1-2, 6-10

The "other gospel" (v 6) was the message of the Judaizers — those Jewish Christians who felt that it was necessary to maintain the full Jewish law, including circumcision, in order to follow Christ and be saved. For them, it would seem, the way of Jesus was frosting on the cake, simply another way of being Jewish. And therefore, everybody, including Gentiles, who wanted to be Christian had to be Jewish first. Paul, however, was struggling to keep Jesus at the center of the Gospel. Jesus, not the law, is the full revelation of God's love, and therefore the source of salvation. If Jesus is at the heart, Paul maintains, whether of not one personally chooses to follow the law of Moses makes little difference. Paul himself personally chose to keep the law; he never repudiated his Jewish identity. But he insiste that the law not be imposed on non-Jews as essential for salvation because that would impose unnecessary conditions on them, put the emphasis in the wrong place, and hinder their growth in faith in Christ Jesus.

Questions for thought, discussion, and prayer:

1. Do we sometimes look to Jesus as a "super-genie" who can fulfill our wishes rather than as Messiah and Lord to whom we are faithful without conditions? How can the way you pray reveal your real attitude toward Jesus?

2. What sorts of people are some present-day equivalents of Judaizers in the Church?

TENTH SUNDAY OF THE YEAR— YEAR C

GOD HAS VISITED HIS PEOPLE

Gospel: Luke 7:11-17

The anticipation of the Messiah in late (third-second century B.C.E.) Judaism included the belief that pious Jews who had died

would rise from the dead to be part of the Messiah's reign (see Dn
12:2-3; 2 Mac 7:9-36). Jesus alludes to this expectation in his
answer to John the Baptist's disciples in v 22. It is precisely to verify
this statement that Luke includes this raising of the widow's son to
life at this point in his Gospel.

Her status as a widow losing her only son is significant to Luke
— she had just lost her sole means of support, and as a woman alone
would be a virtual outcast from society, having no more claim as a
productive member and dependent on others' charity for her support. Jesus' intention to remove barriers of division and gather all
people as one is evident here, as it is in passages detailing his involvement with foreigners, lepers, and sinners.

This passage consciously alludes to Elijah's miracle in the first
reading, and Elisha's in 2 Kgs 4:18-37. But there are differences. The
prophets were sought out, and the widows each had a claim on their
concern; Jesus approaches the funeral procession and raises the
young man of his own accord without being asked. The prophets
worked in private, and performed an action that carried traces of
magic; Jesus works in full view of the crowd and simply touched the
bier and spoke. Jesus both echoes and surpasses the work of the
prophets.

Nevertheless, this is not yet a true resurrection, but a resuscita-
tion or recovery of of the same life as before. The resurrection of
Jesus, promised to his followers, is a passage to a completely new order of life.

The following section concerning John the Baptist (vv 18-35) is
paralleled in Matthew (11:2-19), and the major portion of it is read
on the Third Sunday of Advent, Year A.

First Reading: 1 Kings 17:17-24

The miracle stories of the prophets Elijah (1 Kgs 17-18) and
Elisha (2 Kgs 2, 4-6) vindicate the prophets as speaking and acting
with the Lord's power in face of the wickedness and duplicity of the
kings. They are signs that God's reign is present in spite of the infidelity of Israel's leaders. The raising of the widow's son from the
dead, in particular, proclaims God's will to life, not death.

Responsorial Psalm: Psalm 30:2, 4, 5-6, 11, 12, 13

This psalm speaks praise from one who has just returned from
death's door because of a serious illness. The psalmist is filled with
gratitude for the Lord's response to prayers and gift of healing. Response: "I will praise you, Lord, for you have rescued me."

Second Reading: Galatians 1:11-19

In order to counter the teaching of the Judaizers, Paul here establishes his authority as a preacher of the true Gospel of Jesus Christ. He emphasizes that he was faithful as a Jew, but that his conversion came directly by means of a revelation from Christ (v 16). His call to go to the Gentiles came directly from Christ, not through the other apostles or the Jerusalem community, but it was confirmed by them (vv 18-19). Therefore, he maintains that he does not depend on them for the correctness of his Gospel, although he is careful to maintain union with them.

Chapter 2 begins with an account of the council of Jerusalem, described in Acts 15, at which the leaders of the Jerusalem church, including Peter, gave full approval to Paul's mission to the Gentiles, and confirmed his conviction that it was not necessary to observe the Jewish law in order to become a Christian. (See the first reading of the Sixth Sunday of Easter, Year C.)

Questions for thought, discussion, and prayer:

1. A sign is something that is meant to point beyond itself. Can we misunderstand Jesus' miracles in a way that limits him rather than opens us up to greater things? What does this question have to do about signs?

2. Discuss unity in diversity as a principle that Paul seems to affirm.

ELEVENTH SUNDAY OF THE YEAR — YEAR C

FORGIVENESS AND LOVE

Gospel: Luke 7:36-8:3

In Luke's Gospel, meals are significant moments of teaching and revealing (see also 5:27-39; 6:1-5; 7:31-35; 9:10-17; 10:38-42; 14:1-15:32; 19:1-27; 22:14-38; 24:13-35, 41-49). All these references carry some eucharistic connotation — what Jesus did at mealtime during his earthly ministry, he continues to do when the Church gathers for the meal of the eucharist.

The point of the comparison Jesus made between Simon the Pharisee and the unnamed sinful woman is not who has the greater sinfulness. It is rather, who has fulfilled the conditions for forgiveness. To be forgiven requires first the realization of one's sinfulness, and one's overwhelming need for God's loving pardon. Selfrighteousness, although it breaks no law, is in many ways the greatest sin because it is the final door by which persons lock God out of their lives. Those who are perfectly satisfied with their own goodness do not need God. But climbing to heaven on one's own ladder is an illusion, and is really what hell is all about. Only faith — unconditioned acceptance of God into one's life — has the power to raise one out of self-centeredness, and that is the heart of forgiveness (vv 48-50).

The Pharisee's indignation at Jesus' acceptance of the woman's act of service came from an interpretation of Dt 23:19, prohibiting the acceptance of votive offerings from prostitutes. Laws such as this are needed in a society, and the law itself was not criticized by Jesus. But, he emphasized that laws are not the ultimate standard of right and wrong — they must reflect what is right, they cannot create what is right. Laws must serve reconciliation between God and people, not substitute for it.

The final few verses (8:1-3) offer a delightful and challenging view of the place of women in the life and ministry of Jesus — a subject especially dear to Luke. It is certain that the Twelve (apostles) were men — they are all named in the Gospels; but it is also obvious, even though we don't often think about it, that whenever the word "disciples" is used in the Gospel, it refers to both women and men. Contrary to the Jewish traditions of his day, Jesus fully accepted the participation of women in his ministry. By the way, there is no indication whatever that Mary Magdalen is the woman who anointed Jesus' feet, nor is she Mary of Bethany (see Lk 10:38-42; Jn 11), although John gives a similar anointing story about her (Jn 12:1-8).

The rest of chapter 8 and first part of chapter 9 are omitted from the liturgical readings this year, but parallels are found in Year A, Fifteenth Sunday; and Year B, Tenth, Twelfth, Thirteenth and Fifteenth Sundays. The important event of casting out the "Legion" of demons from the Gerasene man (vv 26-39; see also Mt 8:28-34 and Mk 5:1-20) is omitted altogether from the Sunday lectionary. The event arouses antagonism in the neighbors, but inspires discipleship in the man who has been healed, who seeks to follow Jesus like the woman of 8:12. However, Jesus has other plans for him — to proclaim the work of God among his own people.

First Reading: 2 Sm 12:7-10, 13
Read all of 2 Sm 11-12 which tells of David's sin and repen-

tance. The few verses chosen for this reading do not do justice to the event, but do reflect both themes of anointing (pouring oil on a person) and wholehearted repentance found in the Gospel. Among the Israelites, kings (see 1 Sm 10:1; 16:12-13) and priests (see Ex 29:7; 30:30; Lv 8; Ps 133:2) were anointed as the initiation into their ministry. Prophets were said to be anointed by the Spirit (see Is 61:1). In fulfillment of these three roles, Jesus is called the Christ (the Messiah, the Anointed One). A good antidote to our self-righteousness would be to reflect that the only actual, physical anointing that Jesus received was from an admittedly sinful woman.

Through the prophet Nathan in this reading, the Lord assures David — and us — that he does not seek revenge or retribution for sin, but he does challenge us to acknowledge our sinfulness and turn to him in repentance to be healed.

Responsorial Psalm: Psalm 32:1-2, 5, 7, 11

This penitential psalm emphasizes the importance of admitting one's sinfulness as the condition of forgiveness. Response: "Lord, forgive the wrong I have done."

First Reading: Galatians 2:16, 19-21

The New American Bible titles this section "Paul's Basic Teaching." Paul concentrates on the death of Christ as the pattern for the whole Christian life. As the pattern from which the Christian life takes its shape, the death of Christ is the source of justification, which means being made in right order before God. Life in union with Christ's death leads to resurrection, and challenges every Christian to rise above human limitations embodied in law.

Questions for thought, discussion, and prayer:
1.   How is true repentance like "dying a little"? Could it be, then, that the refusal of salvation (as the Pharisees did) is refusing to die?

2.   According to Paul, why did Jesus die?

JESUS, THE MESSIAH OF GOD

Gospel: Luke 9:18-24

The multiplication of loaves, vv 11-17, is found on the Solemnity of Corpus Christi, Year C; and the Seventeenth Sunday of Year B.

The profession of faith and Jesus' prediction of his rejection and death in today's reading are put in contrast to Herod's reaction to news of Jesus in vv 7-9. We have here in a nutshell the implications of faith in Jesus as Lord. He is not just the Lord in general — he must be my Lord in particular. If we profess him to be the Messiah — our Savior (v 20) — we must accept him as the crucified Savior (v 22), not as some nice, self-serving creation of our own fancy. The crucifixion is a disgraceful, painful, bloody mess of a way to die — and Jesus commands us to face the implications of that squarely, just as he did. If we accept him as crucified Savior, we cannot escape union with him precisely as the Crucified One (vv 23-24). Union in sacrifice of life, not mere admiration, is the only key to salvation. Grace that has any eternal value is not cheap!

The account of the transfiguration, vv 28-36, is always read on the Second Sunday of Lent each year from the Gospel of the current cycle. For a commentary on the events that conclude this section, vv 37-50, see Year B, Twenty-Fifth Sunday.

First Reading: Zechariah 12:10-11

John's Gospel applies this passage to Jesus (Jn 19:37). The identity of the man who was "thrust through" in the prophet's mind is uncertain. He may have been referring to the prophetic office in general: prophets were usually persecuted because they spoke the truth (an act seldom appreciated by those who cling to positions of authority), and yet their words and works have power precisely because they were willing to place themselves on the line and accept the consequences of them — disbelief, ridicule, rejection, persecution, and death. This passage obviously alludes to the suffering servant of Isaiah 53, and the effect of the people's realization of the wrong they have done becomes a saving grace leading to conversion. Jer 6:26; 31:15-20; and Ez 36:16-38 appear to be related passages.

Responsorial Psalm: Psalm 63:2, 3-4, 5-6, 8-9

This is the psalm of one who is carrying a cross of suffering in the desert — without consolation, yet struggling to maintain confidence. Response: "My soul is thirsting for you, O Lord, my God."

Second Reading: Galatians 3:26-29

Read the whole of chapter 3, of which these are the final few verses. Keep in mind that Paul is not speaking against law in general, but responding to a particular Jewish mentality that held observance of the law of Moses to be in itself the source of salvation.

In defending his teaching that Christ alone is the source of salvation, Paul appeals to several images in this reading. As clothing both envelops the whole body and expresses our identity to others, so Christ embraces our total reality, and renders differences among us insignificant. Note that differences are not removed — male and female remain male and female — but they can no longer be a barrier to unity in the body of Christ. Nor can they be considered a criterion for judging superiority or inferiority. Finally, identity with Christ allows all people to share in the essence of Jewishness — in Christ the whole world is now the recipient of the promises God originally made to the Jewish people, beginning with Abraham.

Chapter 4 unfolds the terms of the promise as fulfilled in Christ. Paul maintains that the Jewish law locked the people into slavery by its powerlessness to release humankind from sin, even though it made us aware of sinfulness. Christ as Son of God broke the bonds of this slavery by making us free sons and daughters of God. (See the second reading for the Octave of Christmas.)

Questions for thought, discussion, and prayer:

1. How is baptism related to the cross?

2. How is baptism related to faith?

THIRTEENTH SUNDAY OF THE YEAR — YEAR C

THE TURNING POINT

Gospel: Luke 9:51-62

In the first verse, Luke depicts a solemn moment: the point of turning from the announcing of the kingdom of God by Jesus' ministry of preaching and healing in Galilee to the work of bringing about the kingdom by his death and resurrection in Jerusalem. There is a sense of urgency in the "approaching time," and also a sense of total control in his "firm resolve." Jesus is clearly not a victim of circumstances but is truly master of his fate, and as Master will ultimately hand himself over to the Enemy, yielding in order to overcome.

Look at the map of the Holy Land in your Bible to get a clear idea where Galilee, Samaria, and Judea are. Jews and Samaritans shared a common origin in the twelve tribes of Israel, but their "family feud" went back at least six hundred years, perhaps with roots hundreds of years ealier. We all know that hatred within a family is often far more bitter than hatred among strangers. The Jews looked on the Samaritans as heretical and false worshipers of the God of Israel, and detested them far more than the pagans. The feelings were mutual. (This is what gives great significance to the story of the good Samaritan in Lk 10:25-37, and the encounter with the woman at the well in Jn 4:4-42.) Note that at the beginning of his journey to Jerusalem, Jesus faced hatred and rejection — a foretaste of his passion — which he met with love and tolerance. And, as if disciplining unruly children, he instructed his followers to do the same (vv 53-55).

The answers of Jesus to the three would-be followers in vv 57-62 exemplify the wholehearted constancy that the Christian mission requires. Look also at Lk 9:23-26 and 14:25-35. The point is that lesser loves must be seen in the light of God's love, and true followers cannot be half-hearted or flighty in their commitment.

First Reading: 1 Kings 19:16, 19-21

Elijah could confidently preach to kings and overcome the prophets of false gods, but when Jezebel got mad at him — watch out! (Read 1 Kgs 18-19.) In Elijah's discouragement, God told him he needed a co-worker and successor, Elisha. In vv 19-20, notice how few spoken words are exchanged, yet how full of meaning are the actions. Imagine the old prophet approaching the younger man in the field, taking off his cloak which was the sign of his prophetic office, and putting it on the other's shoulders — all in complete silence. Yet both are well aware of exactly what was happening. Elisha's parting gesture — truly a turning point — signifies stripping himself of all signs of his old life and sacrificing them to symbolize the finality of his turning.

Responsorial Psalm: Psalm 16:1-2, 5, 7-8, 9-10, 11
This psalm has traditionally been used to exemplify the commitment to ordained ministry or religious profession, but it more accurately reflects the commitment of baptism of all Christians. Read it slowly and prayerfully. Response: "You are my inheritance, O Lord."

Second Reading: Galatians 5:1, 13-18
This passage reinforces the message of the other two readings. Paul seems rather exasperated at having to remind his hearers of the obvious: living the new life of freedom in the Spirit means abandoning the old ways of sin. The "lust of the flesh" should not be understood only in a sexual sense, but refers to all worldly impulses that are opposed to true love of neighbor (and self) — that is, all that leads to destruction.

Questions for thought, discussion, and prayer:
1. What does this Gospel tell you about the cost of being Jesus' disciple?

2. Why is true freedom incompatible with sin?

FOURTEENTH SUNDAY OF THE YEAR— YEAR C

THE HARVEST IS RICH

Gospel: Luke 10:1-12, 17-20
For the sake of brevity, the lectionary does an unfortunate job of editing the text in this passage. Vv 13-15 merely elaborate on v 12 and are not too important, but v 16 is at the heart of the mission of the disciples.
Jesus, having already called and instructed the disciples, now sends them on a "practice mission." The specific directives of vv 4-8 reinforce the demands already made in 9:57-62 — useless baggage is literally a drag! V 9 tells what they are to do: proclaim the kingdom in word and action just as Jesus has done. Vv 10-12 are a way of saying in action: "he who hears you hears me." Vv 17-20 may be understood: "Congratulations, you were successful. But don't get big heads! It was my power that did it, not yours. Remember, the Giver

is more important than his gifts." That last point is developed by Paul in 1 Cor 12-14.

Notice that Jesus' prayer is one of response to the manifestation of God's power. Vv 16 and 21-22 reflect very strongly the farewell discourse of Jesus that is proclaimed during Easter season (Jn 13-17). Vv 23-24 state that the kingdom of God established by Jesus fulfills the entirety of God's work in forming the people of Israel.

First Reading: Isaiah 66:10-14a

Read all of Isaiah 66. The prophet's image of the old Jerusalem (Zion) giving birth to the new in vv 7-9 is essential as a basis for the maternal images of vv 10-13. The beauty of the picture speaks for itself, and is a fitting conclusion to the greatest book of Hebrew prophecy. This passage is related to the Gospel reading because it exemplifies God's power bringing forth new life. The conclusion of the chapter gives both sides of the picture: those who seek to be part of this new life, will; those who don't, won't.

Responsorial Psalm: Psalm 66:1-3, 4-5, 6-7, 16, 20

Praise and worship are based on a realization of God's past works and a confidence that God is still at work. Response: "Let all the earth cry out to God with joy."

Second Reading: Galatians 6:14-18

Paul again reflects the theme of the Gospel: all that really matters is being renewed by the power of God — and to live in accord with this new creation as the rule of life.

Paul's "boasting" in v 14 is to counter the Judaizers who boast of their circumcision. Similarly, the "brand marks of Jesus" do not refer to what we call "stigmata" — the miraculous appearance of the wounds of Jesus in a person's hands, feet, and side. They can be more simply and realistically explained as the scars of what Paul had suffered for the name of Jesus (see 2 Cor 11:23-33). These are his "badge of honor" with which he opposes those who glory in the mark of their circumcision. A brand was used to mark slaves.

Note that the word "apostle" is from a Greek word meaning "one who is sent forth", while "disciple" comes from Latin, "one who learns from another."

Questions for thought, discussion, and prayer:
1. How can a Christian in the modern world fulfill the requirements Jesus imposed on his disciples?

2.   What might be some present-day trends among Christians that are similar to the Judaizers in Paul's day, replacing the essentials with secondary concerns?

WHO IS MY NEIGHBOR?

Gospel: Luke 10:25-37

The story of the "good Samaritan" is so familiar that it is easy to miss its point. The Samaritan's charity has deep meaning, especially in contrast to the contempt and negligence of "proper Jews" (vv 31-32), because of the intense and long-lasting hatred Jews and Samaritans had for each other. This act of charity was like being kind — at considerable personal risk — to the very person one considers most obnoxious, contemptible, and unworthy of consideration.

It is precisely in this expansion of the concept of neighbor to include not only one's townsfolk and follow citizens, but one's enemies and outcasts as well, that the uniqueness of Jesus' law is to be found. Although the relative importance of the many and various laws of the Jewish Scriptures was a frequent subject of discussion, the way of summarizing them into love of God and love of neighbor was common.

For us, it is noteworthy that Jesus here does not give a law or a counsel when asked what one must do "to inherit everlasting life." He gives an example; an unexpected and discomforting example; an example that continues to challenge us also to take a second look at the question, "who is my neighbor?"

First Reading: Deuteronomy 30:10-14

The best of the Jewish tradition was not hemmed in by the sort of narrow legalism that characterized the scribes and lawyers of Jesus' time. Law, for the most part, was not seen as an end in itself, but an attempt to reorder things according to God's will. Thus a person who is sensitive to the way things are and sees the way things ought to be can discover God's law already in his heart. The problem is that sinful self-centeredness blinds us to reality and hardens our hearts, requiring the constraint of external laws and rules to curb

our pride and greed, and enforce at least the minimals of construc-
tive social behavior. But true law is a matter of vision rather than
force — we love those we can look on as worthy of love, and therefore we will treat them properly. Jesus says that God sees everyone
as worthy of love, and he challenges us to adopt God's vision of
things. In the ever-deepening rifts among peoples, and the
wholesale shirking of mutual responsibility and commitments that
we find around us, it is more important than ever that Christians
nurture this vision and give true example of it.

Responsorial Psalm: Psalm 69:14, 17, 30-31, 33-34, 36, 37

The source of most of our problems is our failure to love properly; the solution is found in turning to the Lord, not in self-seeking
petition but in true change of heart and openness to him and one
another. Response: "Turn to the Lord in your need, and you will
live."

Second Reading: Colossians 1:15-20

Many scholars doubt that Colossians was actually written by
Paul because neither the style of writing nor the situation seems to
fit what we know of his character and ministry. If this is the case,
this letter joins a rather sizable body of ancient literature, both scriptural and non-scriptural, actually written by unknown authors "in
the name of" or "in the tradition of" a recognized authority to give
their own work greater weight. (Other examples include the letter to
the Hebrews, often attributed to Paul, the book of Wisdom, attributed to Solomon but written many centuries after him, and
chapters 40-66 of Isaiah.)

As Galatians addressed the problem of Judaizing Christians
leading an immature community into a sort of slavery to the Jewish
law, Colossians appears addressed to a more mature community
beginning to dabble in a form of Gnosticism. This "secret wisdom"
type of religion blended elements of Judaism, Christianity, and
paganism in an effort to unlock the "mysteries" of cosmic, elemen-
tal powers in order to gain control over them.

The hymn in today's reading, extolling Christ as the center of
all creation, directly opposes any worship of or allegiance to lesser
powers, whether they be angels or forces governing the cycles of nature. In addition, it is a call for everyone to participate in Christ's
saving mission: that of reconciling all things in himself. Reading on
(vv 21-22), we find that he overcomes the alienation that is sin. One
cannot claim to be reconciled to God (that is, saved, or seeking salva-

tion) and remain alienated from others. (See also the Solemnity of Christ the King, Year C.)

Questions for thought, discussion, and prayer:
1. Try to figure of a cast of characters to make the "good Samaritan" parable relevant for today.

2. Discuss what is reconciliation as the word is used by Paul and exemplified in the Gospel.

SIXTEENTH SUNDAY OF THE YEAR — YEAR C

THE BETTER PORTION

Gospel: Luke 10:38-42
This charming scene stands in contrast to the circumstances of the Samaritan parable. In the first instance, a professor of the law failed to listen to Jesus; in this case a woman — who was commonly held to be incapable of understanding higher religious values — sits at the feet of Jesus in attentive discipleship.

There is no real opposition between the contemplation of Mary and the activity of Martha. However, this incident serves as a warning to the Church (that is, to us!) that Christian mission cannot "be anxious and upset about many things." All activity must begin with and be nourished by attentive listening to the Lord in prayer, or it will be a futile exercise in self-deception. Substituting activity for prayer, instead of basing activity on prayer, is a real temptation against which the Christian must always guard. The "one thing required" (v 41) is a call to the right ordering of priorities and to simplicity.

First Reading: Genesis 18:1-10
This story bears some resemblance to the Gospel, not in detail but in the overall message that hospitality is basically attentiveness to the guest (that is, to the Lord) and that this spirit of genuine listening is fruitful. To receive a guest properly, one must be prepared to share everything. This type of hospitality is the image of the incarnation — in Christ, divinity and humanity welcome each other fully, and give their all. It is also the image of the continuation of the

incarnation in us, the Church. If we truly welcome God into our lives, this hospitality will bear fruit.

Responsorial Psalm: Psalm 15:2-3, 3-4, 5

The beginnings of religious sentiment would see the temple sanctuary as God's house, and consequently upright and moral behavior would be an element of etiquette to enter this house. A deeper understanding of revelation sees the human heart as God's chosen dwelling, and a just and upright life flows from the realization of God's power and presence. Response: "He who does justice will live in the presence of the Lord."

Second Reading: Colossians 1:24-28

If we apply our common understanding of the word "mystery" to the way it is used here, we will miss its meaning. We use the word in a very loose sense as a problem whose solution is hidden (as in a murder mystery) or something that is so completely beyond us as to be completely unknowable (as "it's a mystery to me!"). The author of Colossians, however, uses the word to describe the fullness of God's revelation which is now made available to us in Christ. God can never be fully grasped because he is infinite; but that doesn't mean that we cannot begin to know him, and continue to grow in that knowledge forever. Mystery does not indicate a locked door with a hidden secret behind it. Rather, it is an open door which invites us to explore unending riches within.

V 24 is often a problem. There is nothing lacking in the sacrifice of Christ in his own person. However, his Church, as his body, is as yet incomplete. It is this body which is built up through ministry — and this ministry always involves suffering in union with Christ. As Christ was transparent to God shining through him, so all those called to serve within the Church must be transparent to Christ, allowing him to be fully perceived in word and action. And the Church itself must present the living face of Christ to be seen by all the world.

Questions for thought, discussion, and prayer:

1.   How can or should contemplation enter into your own active life?

2.   How can you make the Church more hospitable? your place of work? your home? What does this hospitality have to do with Christianity?

SEVENTEENTH SUNDAY OF THE YEAR — YEAR C

WHEN YOU PRAY . . .

Gospel: Luke 11:1-13

Followers of any great teacher or prophet or leader want to model themselves after their master. Jesus' disciples naturally would ask for a glimpse into his own prayer in order to learn how to pray. It is important for us to understand that Jesus was not so concerned here to give instructions on how one ought to pray as he was to invite the disciples to share his own spirit of prayer, and to show them what sort of God it is who hears and answers our prayer.

Both versions of the Lord's Prayer, given in Mt 6:9-13 and here in Luke, are brief outlines of what the content of our own prayer should be. Matthew's text, which is more familiar to us, is expanded somewhat, but adds nothing important that is not found in Luke's briefer form. The simpler version in Luke, which is probably closer to the original words of Jesus, seems to be more personal and direct — an individual child in communion with his or her Father. Matthew's is a bit more formal and communal — it is more appropriate to be recited aloud by a liturgical assembly.

The parable in which the persistence of the neighbor wins out over the unwillingness of the bedded-down householder happens in a type of one-room dwelling in which all family members — parents, children, and animals — sleep on mats on the floor. To unbolt the door and raid the pantry would necessitate disturbing everyone, and would create an extremely unpleasant commotion in the middle of the night. The humor of the situation is the whole point of the parable. God is the exact opposite of the sleepy father. He is willing to give what his people need and does not need to be persistently or violently besieged in order to get him to act.

Why, then, must prayer be persistent? It is because of our poor perception of what we need — we often don't see our own most basic needs because our vision and understanding is clouded by our wants and desires. God wants to nourish us with his Spirit, and we so often prefer the stones and scorpions of material possessions and pleasures to the bread and fish of love and understanding. Persistent prayer opens us to get to know our needs as God sees them so he can fulfill them. True prayer as Jesus taught leads our wills to conform to God's will rather than try to bend God's will to our own wants.

First Reading: Genesis 18:20-32

This dialogue between God and Abraham gives us another picture of the way we should pray with persistence and confidence. The prayer that is answered is the one which displays a passion for the fulfillment of God's will, which is to save the just and to bring sinners to conversion. Although Abraham may seem to be trying to change God's mind here, what he really does is to remind God of his own intention to show mercy and reward justice. In praying for the salvation of others, Abraham shows his concern for them and concretely fulfills the prophecy just made that the would be a source of blessing for all nations (v 18, see 17:16).

Responsorial Psalm: Psalm 138:1-2, 2-3, 6-7, 7-8

This psalm praises God for showing his faithfulness by being attentive to our prayer. Response: "Lord, on the day I called for help, you answered me."

Second Reading: Colossians 2:12-14

The author of Colossians continues to assert the centrality of Jesus Christ in salvation. Rather than try to manipulate cosmic forces through a variety of superstitious practices, we need to realize that Christ has once and for all broken the hold that any sort of mysterious forces may have on us. This is still relevant today because so much of what passes for religion is no more than a thinly veiled superstitious attempt to serve our own interests rather than seek salvation in becoming one with God's vision.

For the Jew, circumcision was the physical sign and assurance of God's favor. As the identifying mark of the covenant, it reminded its bearer that God was faithful, and it expressed as well his own fidelity to God. But Paul maintained that Christ himself — God in the flesh — is now the full and true sign of the covenant, and the Christian's "mark" of incorporation into him is baptism.

Questions for thought, discussion, and prayer:
1. How do you pray? In the light of the Gospel message, how should you pray?

2. What does God's faithfulness mean to you? to what is he faithful? how does he show faithfulness?

EIGHTEENTH SUNDAY OF THE YEAR — YEAR C

WHERE IS YOUR TREASURE?

Gospel: Luke 12:13-21

Read the rest of chapter 11, from where we left off last week, and the beginning of chapter 12 up to the present reading. Jesus followed his teaching on confident and persistent prayer with counsel on the attitude and behavior of one who prays as a member of God's kingdom. Note that he very frequently formulates his teaching in response to questions or statements from others (11:1, 15, 27, 45; 12:13). In every case, his answer goes far beyond the expectations of the questioner.

One of the key statements in this section is in 11:31-32. Jesus was wiser than Solomon and a more effective proclaimer of the prophetic word than Jonah. Jonah's unwilling preaching brought a great and sinful pagan city to repentance. Jesus holds up a mirror to the self-satisfied leaders of his day (11:37-54) and proclaims the true response to God's love to the world (represented by the crowds — 12:1-12). He was then asked to give a Solomon-like judgment (12:13 — see 1 Kgs 3:16-28; for Jesus' use of a similar situation involving inheritance, see the famous parable of the loving father, Lk 15:11-32). Jesus here shows the nature of true wisdom by simply putting aside the importance of the division of wealth and concentrating on the spirit of greed as the root of the problem.

This story of the landowner who fancies himself secure because of his wealth helps us understand the difficult incident and teaching of Lk 18:18-30. One who grasps material possessions has his heart set on the here and now, and is unable to grasp eternal life with God simply because it is beyond his area of interest. Such a misplacing of attachments is the height of foolishness (v 20). Note the grossly egocentric way that the man constantly refers to himself. He sees nothing beyond what could benefit himself.

First Reading: Ecclesiastes 1:2; 2:21-23

The book of Ecclesiastes (or Qoheleth, which means presider or preacher to an assembly) is the darkest and most pessimistic book in the whole Bible. Its theme is well summed up in 1:2. The writer, an astute critic of the human condition, observed 2300 years ago what has become more obvious with the passing of time — to those who do not blind themselves — that humanity cannot be satisfied with itself as its own ultimate goal.

Responsorial Psalm: Psalm 95:1-2, 6-7, 8-9
   The spirit of this psalm is the direct opposite to that of Ecclesiastes. Optimism comes from confidence in the Power beyond us — God. But to understand and receive this, our hearts must be open. Response: "If today you hear his voice, harden not your hearts."

Second Reading: Colossians 3:1-5, 9-11
   Although different in many stylistic respects from the letters known to be written by Paul, this letter adopts an overall format typical of his letters. The first part is concerned with the meaning of the mystery of Christ in the life of the Christian, and the second part draws practical advice from that meaning. This reading is the beginning of the second, practical part of this letter. If our hearts are truly with Christ, we will live accordingly, and avoid those mentalities and actions that introduce divisions and alienation into the Christian community. (The following section, vv 12-21, is read on the Feast of the Holy Family each year.)

Questions for thought, discussion, and prayer:
1.   Discuss the lives of some famous people who appear to have yielded to the temptation described in the Gospel, as well as those who seem to have resisted it successfully. Do not be judgmental, but try to see in their lives a lesson for yourself.

2.   Would you like to invite Mr. Ecclesiastes to a dinner party? Why or why not?

NINETEENTH SUNDAY OF THE YEAR — YEAR C

DO NOT FEAR

Gospel: Luke 12:32-48
   Peace — freedom from fear — is of the very nature of God's kingdom. It means the reordering of all creation as God intended it to be. Only by accepting his rule as the guiding force of all life, rather than our own interests and desires, can true peace be found.

Jesus shows the way to this peace — the way to take the kingdom to heart — as a form of "spiritual dieting": giving up worldly goodies in order to lose the ugly fat of materialism for the sake of a trim and healthy life in the kingdom.

True charitable giving is more beneficial to the giver than to the receiver because it frees one from the burden of care for passing things, and allows one to pay greater attention to what is really important.

The type of waiting that Jesus recommends cannot be merely an idle passing of time, expecting something better to come along by-and-by. Rather, Christian waiting is an active life of service to prepare for and bring about the kingdom. The fullness of the kingdom ought to come as a surprise. But we should live so that it will be a pleasant and welcome surprise, like a promotion from a job well done to something better. If our total treasure is in the here and now, we will find the coming of God's kingdom unwelcome and threatening because we will have neglected to set our hearts on it and prepare for it.

Trustworthiness is an element of membership in the kingdom (v 44). God trusts us now with the preparation for the fullness of his kingdom. For eternity he will trust us if we prove trustworthy now.

Jesus does not answer Peter's question (v 41) directly, but implies that his words are for everyone in accord with each one's proper role. Some have a particular role of service within the Christian community, but all Christians have a ministry to the rest of the world to be a continuing sign of Christ to them.

First Reading: Wisdom 18:6-9

This brief selection is part of a longer section of the book of Wisdom (ch 11-19) in which the author recalls God's providence for his people during the exodus as reason for hope in present difficulties. The theme of night — the night which meant death for the Egyptian first-born and salvation for the Israelites (see Ex 11:4-12:36) — is the point of connection with the Gospel.

Responsorial Psalm: Psalm 33:1, 12, 18-19, 20-22

This praise-filled hymn of confidence in the Lord is based on a recollection of his past works of creation and of salvation for his people. Response: "Happy the people the Lord has chosen to be his own."

Second Reading: Hebrews 11:1-2, 8-19

Today we begin a series of readings from the last part of the letter to the Hebrews (the first part is read in Year B). The theme of the entire letter is that the whole revelation of God in Jewish history and Scriptures is summed up and fulfilled in Jesus. In this reading, v 1 gives a succinct and well-known definition of faith. Following that, we see examples of this faith in the great figures of ancient Israel. For them, faith was a constant search for the Lord; for us, it is the possession in Christ of what they sought.

Questions for thought, discussion, and prayer:
1.   What does the image of night convey about the condition of the Church in pilgrimage to the fullness of God's kingdom? the condition of your own heart on this pilgrimage?

2.   In what ways can Abraham's faith be a model for yours?

TWENTIETH SUNDAY OF THE YEAR — YEAR C

FIRE AND SWORD

Gospel: Luke 12:49-53
Many people are puzzled by these words. Yet their meaning is quite clear if we grasp the true nature of Jesus' mission as Messiah. Jesus' call to be one with the kingdom of God demands an all-or-nothing response, so it cannot fail to bring about dissension and division. Jesus is not happy about this — you can detect a deep sigh in his voice — but he foresees it as a necessary part of the struggle for perfection.

V 49 alludes to the fire imagery of Pentecost (see Acts 2:3-4). The "baptism" of v 50 reflects Mk 10:38-39. Both fire and water, powerful in their life-giving as well as their destroying capabilities, symbolize purification and passage from one state to another.

The dissension caused by his message was foretold in the prophecy of Simeon (Lk 2:34-35) and may be compared to a sword cut (see Mt 10:34-36). Further references to God's word as a cutting edge are in Heb 4:12; Eph 6:17; Rev 1:16 and 19:15. The divisions within a household may shed some light on the interpretation of the harsh words in Lk 14:26 (see also Mt 10:37 where both sayings are placed together).

First Reading: Jeremiah 38:4-6, 8-10

Poor Jeremiah! He was called to proclaim God's word to a people unwilling to hear it, and who were headed toward destruction in their obstinacy. He didn't want the job (read chapter 1). The Lord imposed on him a celibate and detached life-style as a sign of his displeasure with the conduct of the royal house of Judah (see chapter 16). Jeremiah was sad and often discouraged because of the message he conveyed and his lack of success (see 20:7-18), yet he was consistently faithful. Although seeing destruction and exile as unavoidable, his message is never hopeless, and often filled with great promise (especially chapter 31).

This reading concerns an attempt to murder him, perpetrated by influential citizens of Jerusalem (the "princes") shortly before the invasion of Jerusalem by the Babylonians (Chaldeans). The king, Zedekiah, was favorably impressed by Jeremiah and his message, but was weak in the face of opposition from these wealthy and comfortable people of power who saw Jeremiah's warnings as a threat to their own position of and power. The warning in 38:2-3 is what infuriated them. Read the whole story, chapters 37-38. At the beginning of chapter 39, the Babylonians invade, destroy Jerusalem, and lead all but the very poor into captivity.

The enmity between the king and the leaders provoked by Jeremiah's preaching pre-echoes the division that Jesus spoke about in the gospel.

Responsorial Psalm: Psalm 40:2, 3, 4, 18

This psalm is a cry of faith and confidence in the midst of affliction. Response: "Lord, come to my aid."

Second Reading: Hebrews 12:1-4

Christians have the example of Christ and their ancestors in faith to follow. This book — like most of the Christian Scriptures — was addressed to a church feeling the threat of persecution for its faith and way of life. The motive of encouragement is very strong: "Keep up the struggle as Jesus did."

Questions for thought, discussion, and prayer:

1. How would you encourage and console someone who is facing family divisions because of Christian faith or practices?

2. What would Jeremiah be like today?

THE NARROW DOOR

Gospel: Luke 13:22-30

Luke continues to make it clear that Jesus is on his way to Jerusalem — and to his sacrificial death. His words have the special significance of the final teaching of the Master who is about to fulfill in deed the kingdom of God that has been the subject of his words. (13:1-9 are read on the Third Sunday of Lent, Year C.)

Somebody asks Jesus the same question that we often like to ask: "How many are going to get to heaven? Do you think God's going to let everybody in, or will it be reserved for just a chosen few, and everybody else will be damned?" Jesus' answer is something of a put-down: "That's a wrong and dumb question! Don't bother with idle speculation about such things. What is really important is what place you allow the kingdom of God to have in your life."

In speaking of entry into the kingdom, Jesus gives two figures of speech: a narrow doorway and recognition of someone as one's own.

It is impossible to get through a narrow door carrying a heavy load of baggage. Salvation will depend on what a person is rather than on anything he or she has acquired.

The basis for recognition as a member of the kingdom is one's real association with Christ. All are invited and welcome, but membership is not automatic. The mere fact of being a Christian does not assure salvation any more than being physically a descendant of Abraham assured God's favor to the Jews of Jesus' time. Finding the way to the kingdom depends upon sincerely seeking it.

Compare the accounts of these same teachings in Matthew's Gospel. The emphasis is a bit different, but the meaning is largely the same. See Mt 7:13-14, 21-23. The idea of the narrow door echoes Jesus' teaching about riches and the kingdom found in all three synoptic Gospels: Mt 19:23-26; Mk 10:25-27; Lk 18:24-27.

First Reading: Isaiah 66:18-21

This prophecy is the final vision of the book of Isaiah — actually written long after the time of Isaiah, but "in his spirit." It holds out a promise of future glory to the impoverished remnant of the Jewish people returning from exile. This hope looks beyond the limitations of self-centered nationalism and sees the Jewish nation as an instrument of salvation for the entire world.

Responsorial Psalm: Psalm 117:1, 2

This is the shortest of all the psalms, consisting of only these two verses. It is an invitation for all humankind to praise God because of the works of his mercy. The response reflects the mission of God's chosen people to be an instrument of salvation to the whole world. Response: "Go out to all the world and tell the Good News."

Second Reading: Hebrews 12:5-7, 11-13

Faith is easy when everything is going well. Under persecution — or even under the crises that hit every life — a strength born of training and discipline is needed to insure its survival. We have the example and wisdom of our ancestors in faith as a precious heritage to encourage us.

Questions for thought, discussion, and prayer:
1.   What does the image of the narrow door, or the door locked because it is too late, say to you?

2.   How are you a part of God's invitation to all people to enter his kingdom?

TWENTY-SECOND SUNDAY OF THE YEAR — YEAR C

HUMILITY AND HONOR

Gospel: Luke 14:1, 7-14

The warning about Herod (13:31-33) is found only in Luke's Gospel. Not all the Pharisees were opposed to Jesus, but most of them seemed at least to find him discomforting and preferred not to have him around. More importantly, this little incident emphasizes that Jesus is fully in control of his own destiny, and is not in any way subject to worldly political or military power.

The lament over Jerusalem (13:34-35) foreshadows what Jesus would say again as he entered Jerusalem (Lk 19:41-44; see also Mt 23:37). At this point in the narrative, it seems to underscore Jesus' resolve to go to Jerusalem to die. V 34 gives a stiking image of maternal concern, which helps balance an overly masculine imagery of God in the Scriptures.

The Sabbath cure repeated a recurring theme in Jesus' teaching about the priority of life over law. See also Mk 3:1-6; Mt 12:1-15; Lk 6:1-11; 13:1-17.

Chapter 14 of Luke gives a "table talk" of Jesus. Frequently in ancient times as now, a formal dinner was the occasion for making speeches or engaging in significant conversation. When Luke put this speech of Jesus in gospel, he was very likely addressing a problem in the church of his day: the relationship of the rich to the poor in the gathering to celebrate the eucharist. Only if all members feel at home with one another can it truly be called the Lord's supper.

The advice to sit in the lower place in hopes of being invited up higher is simply a bit of "sage" wisdom, and in itself no new teaching (see Prov 25:6-7). It takes on Christian meaning only when seen not as a lesson in humility but as a plea for equality. All who share the Lord's table are equal in his sight, and we should treat all as brothers and sisters equally, regardless of their wealth or position.

First Reading: Sirach 3:17-18, 20, 28-29

The first part of the book of Sirach is a collection of popular proverbs, little pearls of wisdom attributed to Jewish sages, but many of them common to the best wisdom of all cultures. These sayings on humility center on the relative insignificance of everyone, even the wise and the powerful, before the awesome wisdom and power of God.

Responsorial Psalm: Psalm 68;4-5, 6-7, 10-11

This is a processional song celebrating God's leading his people to victory over their enemies. However, the verses chosen here reflect God's care shown through the gifts of nature. It echoes the theme of hospitality towards all found in the Gospel reading. Response: "God, in your goodness, you have made a home for the poor."

Second Reading: Hebrews 12:18-19, 22-24

Read Hebrews 12:14-29 for a better picture of what is being said. The person who lives by faith need not fear the wrath of God. The new city of God is a sign of hope for those living under fear, whether of persecution and oppression, or of the inner forces and demons that torment us.

The fulfillment of faith is, of course, love. The letter concludes with a counsel to love — in practice not just in word — as the foundation of the Christian life.

Questions for thought, discussion, and prayer:
1. Discuss the meaning and implications of "the Lord's Supper" in the light of the Gospel passage.

2. Do you find the image of God as judge to be comforting or threatening. Why?

TWENTY-THIRD SUNDAY OF THE YEAR — YEAR C

THE COST OF DISCIPLESHIP

Gospel: Luke 14:25-33

Must we really turn our backs on all those we love in order to follow Christ? Throughout the centuries, many Christians have taken this command quite literally, completely separating themselves from the ways of the world and even from their family relationships, and finding a seemingly assured way to eternal life. But must everyone do this? If every Christian followed the command literally, they would be denying the sacredness of marriage and family life which the bulk of Scripture strongly underscores. Is there a way to another valid interpretation?

The parallel passage in Mt 10:37-39 (see Thirteenth Sunday, Year A) indicates that the basic understanding of this command of Jesus is to keep all earthly matters, including the deepest family relationships, subordinated to the following of Christ. Often we can harmonize human realities with the divine — in fact, human relationships can become signs of God's love, and can serve to deepen our relationship with him. But if any earthly attachments stand in the way of God's kingdom, we cannot avoid the choice: turn our backs on these attachments . . . or turn our backs on the kingdom.

Jesus has just spoken about the equality of all members of his kingdom (vv 7-14), and declared that all humankind without exception is invited, although not all will accept the invitation (vv 15-24 — see Twenty-Eighth Sunday, Year A). Now he tells about what is required to accept. Notice that the occasion has changed from a relatively intimate dinner table conversation to an address to a large crowd. Crowds are usually motivated by superficial attractions. A good show will bring a starry-eyed following today, but tomorrow those raving fans will find something new to get wild about.

Jesus says that this sort of flighty following is not enough. The kingdom requires selfless dedication and constancy. The way of Christ must be placed before all else, even life itself. (Recall that when the Gospels were being written, the persecution of the Church had already begun. Christians were being called to follow Christ quite literally in carrying the cross to death.)

Discipleship demands a price, and those who seek to be disciples must be ready to pay the price, or they shouldn't bother (vv 28-33). Christians are called to be in the world and to change it, as salt becomes part of the food and yet transforms it (v 34). Salt is both a seasoning and a preservative. But if Christians fail — either by separating themselves from the world, like salt that remains in the shaker, or by merging indistinguishably into the world, like a stale or phony seasoning that lacks the power to improve the character of the food — then it would have been better had they never undertaken discipleship.

First Reading: Wisdom 9:13-18

Chapter 9 gives us a prayer for wisdom attributed to king Solomon, who lived eight hundred years before the book was written and was famous for his wisdom. The roots of this prayer are in 1 Kgs 3:9 and 1 Chron 1:10. V 11 begins a long hymn in praise of wisdom, leading to a summary of God's care for his people in history (chapters 11-19).

God's ways are above and beyond human wisdom. This reading relates to the Gospel insofar as the call of Christ is to step out of the limitations of human nature and to share in the reality of God.

Responsorial Psalm: Psalm 90:3-4, 5-6, 12-13, 14-17

This psalm recognizes God's dominion over all creation and seeks his powerful protection and help. Response: "In every age, O Lord, you have been our refuge."

Second Reading: Philemon 9-10, 12-17

Read the whole letter, it is very brief. Attempting to mediate between a wealthy Christian and his runaway slave presented a dilemma to Paul which put his preaching to a severe practical test. His response is a reflection on the Christian's role as a transforming presence in the world.

Questions for thought, discussion, and prayer:
1. Discuss the cost of being a disciple of Christ in your life; in the livess of people you know and admire.

2. How can Paul's advice to Philemon apply to the situations we face today?

TWENTY-FOURTH SUNDAY OF THE YEAR — YEAR C

PARABLES OF GOD'S MERCY

Gospel: Luke 15:1-32
The parable of the prodigal son is so well known that many of us are unaware that is is the climax of a trilogy of parables about God's mercy — the other two being brief stories about the lost sheep and the lost coin. These parables unfold further what Jesus had already said in 14:21-24, that even sinners and other "undesirables" are invited into God's kingdom.

Because these parables follow immediately after Jesus' teaching about the demands of discipleship, and were spoken in answer to the murmuring of the self-righteous, we may conclude that Jesus is not only speaking about God's mercy and forgiveness, but is insisting that his followers imitate God's attitude.

The heart of these parables is that being a disciple of Jesus requires more than merely counting oneself a member of the "saved." Rather, true discipleship means participating actively in the *saving community*. It is consoling for us as sinful humans to be able to identify also with the shepherd, the housewife, and the father in these parables — we must seek the lost as they sought, rejoice in the restoration of wholeness as they rejoiced, and accept the rejected as one family with us.

See also the commentary for the Fourth Sunday of Lent and the Solemnity of the Sacred Heart, Year C. For foreshadowings of this spirit of forgiveness in the Jewish Scriptures, check the books of Jonah and Hosea.

First Reading: Exodus 32:7-11, 13-14
Wandering around in the desert for forty years, with Moses spending a lot of time on mountaintops, the Israelites were frequently inclined to say: "If *this* is what it means to be God's free people,

we'd rather be slaves in Egypt!" When the demands of the Christian life weigh heavily on us and God seems distant, and the attractions of becoming mindless slaves to our feelings and inclinations is strongly felt, aren't we ofter tempted to say the very same thing?

Moses is shown here as an effective mediator between the wayward people and a God who seems to be giving up on them. "Look, Lord," he is saying, "you have already invested your power and love. If you give up now, what will it do to your credibility?"

If God seems to capricious here, remember that this is a dramatization of the conflict between human feelings and the divine reality.

Responsorial Psalm: Psalm 51:3-4, 12-13, 17, 19
This is the great prayer of David's repentance after his adultery with Bathsheba and murder of her husband Uriah (see 2 Sam 11-12). Both Jews and Christians have always found this psalm a perfect embodiment of their own spirit of repentance. Response: "I will rise and go to my father."

Second Reading: 1 Timothy 1:12-17
Timothy, a disciple of Paul, became the bishop of the Christian community at Ephesus. This letter is an instruction on how to carry out that office properly. In this introductory section, Paul (or more likely an author writing later in the tradition of Paul) recalls the great mercy and love that God showed him in his own conversion from unbelief and pride to a life of faith and service.

Questions for thought, discussion, and prayer:
1.   Which character of the Gospel do you most identify with? Why?

2.   Have you experienced God's mercy in a way that makes you more merciful to others? How?

DEDICATION TO THE KINGDOM

Gospel: Luke 16:1-13

In attentively reading the Gospels, we find Jesus often saying or doing something totally unexpected by his hearers and frequently foreign to our own expectations as well. Familiarity has softened the impact of much of Jesus' message and has enabled us to concentrate on the comforting words while conveniently ignoring the challenging or disturbing. Yet, it is almost impossible not to be disturbed by Jesus' apparent praise of this dishonest man. (Note that the "owner" of v 8 is not the owner of the estate, but is better translated "master," referring to Jesus.)

First, we might ask how dishonest was the manager? Certainly he must have misused his position of responsibility (v 1), but his reducing of the debtors' bills was very likely only an elimination of his own profit from those deals. Thus he would have been foregoing his own money in return for the good will of people who may previously have hated him for his hard business practices. In a sense he was using the profit they owed him to buy his way into their hearts.

The point, however, is not to justify the manager. The whole parable leads up to Jesus' lament that worldly people devote more energy and intelligence to their pursuits, which will end in dust, than we who have committed ourselves to God's eternal kingdom.

All the gifts of creation are good when ordered according to God's design, but become death-dealing when exploited for a profit that stops at one's own personal gain. To serve money is in essence to serve only oneself — and self-centeredness is incompatible with God-centeredness.

First Reading: Amos 8:4-7

In today's world, we can appreciate the spirit of Amos' condemnation of the exploitation of the poor by the rich and powerful, even if the festivals and weights and measures are not our own. Then as now, basic dishonesty often wore the cloak of respectability — the wealthy and greedy merchants scrupulously observed religious feasts (v 5). Then as now, exploitation was a matter of real suffering and death for the victims. Then as now, the perpetrators ignored the fact that their profit was gained through inflicting

human misery. Then as now, this grave harm in human society —
and God's order — was caused by placing greater value on money
and profit than on life and people.

Responsorial Psalm: Psalm 113:1-2, 4-6, 7-8
For most of its history, the nation of Israel was poor and subject
to domination by more powerful peoples. This song arises from this
sense of poverty and helplessness, but it affirms that the poor are
God's special, chosen ones. Response: "Praise the Lord who lifts up
the poor."

Second Reading: 1 Timothy 2:1-8
The Christian life is based on prayer; and all prayer is in union
with Christ, the one representative of humankind before the Father.
This passage is striking and challenging because the writer commands first of all prayer for worldly authorities, most of whom are
indifferent or antagonistic toward Christian goals. The Church as
the body of Christ cannot fail to stand as representative of *all*
humanity before God.

Questions for thought, discussion, and prayer:
1.   How can you — as an individual, as a family, as a community, as
a parish — make better use of this world's goods to bring about
God's kingdom?

2.   Re-evaluate your own prayer in the light of Paul's word.

TWENTY-SIXTH SUNDAY OF THE YEAR — YEAR C

THE GREAT ABYSS

Gospel: Luke 16:19-31
A common theme in religious thought around the time of Jesus
was that God's final judgment would bring about a reversal of
earthly situations. We see this in the beatitudes (Mt 5:1-12; Lk
6:20-26). In fact, this parable seems to be a concrete exemplification
of the blessings and curses of Lk 6:20-26. There are many similar
stories not only in Jewish but also in other near-eastern literature.
As Luke recounts it, moral behavior — good or evil acts — in it-

self has little to do with the ultimate destiny of these two persons. It is not what they do but what they are that counts. (After all, what you do flows from what you are.) Those who are lost in their own wealth are lost, period. Those who truly hunger will be filled in God's banquet simply because they are empty and open.

The rich man, suffering the consequences of his immersion in this world's wealth, gives a frightening example of his blind inability to repent. He still considers others — Lazarus specifically — only as instruments for carrying out his own desires.

Finally, the search for signs (e.g., someone coming from the dead) is not a sincere seeking for truth but a subterfuge to avoid it. True repentance comes from listening to and hearing the word that is already present and available.

First Reading: Amos 6:1, 4-7

Amos lived in Judah around the middle of the eighth century B.C.E., at a time when there was a great social gulf between the rich and the poor, in times when the wealthy had many possibilities of greater profit, and the poor could only grow poorer. Amos, a desert-dwelling shepherd extremely sensitive to this injustice and exploitation, condemns those who wallow in the false security of luxury. His prophecy is not merely an expression of envy of the have-nots toward the haves. Rather, he profoundly laments that complacency in material abundance has made the nation blind to impending destruction that is already visible just down the road (vv 6-7).

Responsorial Psalm: Psalm 146:7, 8-9, 9-10

This psalm is a trustful hymn of praise to God who is faithful and concerned for his people. Response: "Praise the Lord, my soul!"

Second Reading: 1 Timothy 6:11-16

V 10, which is not included in the liturgical reading, would connect this reading to the others thematically. The virtues listed in vv 11-12 are the opposites of self-indulgent luxury. As humanly valuable as they are in themselves, these qualities find fulfillment when they lead beyond to union with Christ in his sacrificial death and resurrection. In view of the themes established by the other readings, it would seem that vv 17-19 should have been included as well.

Questions for thought, discussion, and prayer:
1. "The rich are damned by their own excesses" or "wealth is a sign of God's providence." Evaluate and discuss those statements in the light of the Scripture and your own experience.

2. Discuss the possibility of unseen Lazaruses on your own doorstep, and what you can do about them.

FAITH AND SERVICE

Gospel: Luke 17:5-10

A most common temptation of religious people is to feel that they have merited certain rights before God. It is easy to believe that God owes us something because we have suffered or have performed some work for him. This "business contract" view of religion is insidiously wrong and is the spiritual counterpart of the materialistic self-centeredness that was the object of the previous two weeks' readings.

In v 6, Jesus expresses the need for faith, but does not seem to answer the apostles' question of v 5. Yet he answers it in a subtle way in vv 7-10. Faith is based only on a sense of giftedness. It is an awareness that no matter what we do, we can never match or return what the Lord has already done for us. The work of ministry, being the Lord's servants, is not something we do in order to get something from God or even to please him or to try to win his favor. Rather, it is a response — always inadequate — to what God has undertaken on his own initiative. Ministry — to which all Christians are called — is never our own work, it is cooperating in God's work. True humility is a sense that, no matter how dedicated we may be, we are only sharing what God has abundantly blessed us with, and that even our best is not really and finally our own. Realizing our own uselessness does not mean groveling in the dirt, it is avoiding puffed-up self-importance. Proud and boastful people usually hide a lack of real accomplishment in their words; humble, conscientious, self-effacing workers can be detached from their own ideas of success and glory, and let accomplishments themselves speak.

First Reading: Habakkuk 1:2-3; 2:2-4

Many religious people feel that it is improper to question or, worse, complain to the Lord. We have to remember that God has broad shoulders to bear the lament and even the anger of those who are afflicted. Of course, the Lord is still the Lord. If we question him, we must be prepared to accept his answer, not ours. If we complain, we must still trust him to heal our hurt in his way, not ours. The last word of our prayer, whether we pray in perplexity or anger, must be "Your will be done." This prophet, writing around 600 B.C.E. on the eve of the destruction of Jerusalem and the exile to Babylon, lamented both internal corruption and external danger in Judah. He had ample reason to complain (1:2-3), but heard the answer that both faith and corruption carry the seeds of ultimate life and death (2:2-4).

Responsorial Psalm: Psalm 95:1-2, 6-7, 8-9
This psalm, a call to worship, reminds us that we must cast off all hardness of heart in the Lord's presence. Response: "If today you hear his voice, harden not your hearts."

Second Reading: 2 Timothy 1:6-8, 13-14
The reason for fidelity in the Lord's service is the gift of the Spirit who enables us to remain steadfast. This gift is not merely a possession, but a dynamic power both to have faith and to communicate faith despite obstacles.

Questions for thought, discussion, and prayer:
1. Discuss and evaluate evidence of religious sentiments contrary to the Gospel that may have crept into your own life and into various religious movements today.

2. Discuss the words "strong, loving, and wise" (2 Tm 1:7) as qualities of ministry.

TWENTY-EIGHTH SUNDAY OF THE YEAR — YEAR C

THE POWER OF GRATITUDE

Gospel: Luke 17:11-19
There is more to this story than a casual reading will uncover. Coming immediately after last week's reading on faith and humility in God's service based on a sense of giftedness, this incident can be seen to continue the lesson by concrete example. The natural and obvious response to a gift received is often the right one. Yet many

factors may impede this powerful sense of gratitude which motivates ministry.

In a sense, Jesus placed nine of the ten lepers in a dilemma. He commanded them as Jews to follow the law regarding leprosy and its cure (see Lv 13-14; leprosy referred to a variety of skin diseases, not all of equal seriousness.) Yet he was disappointed when they gave the written law priority over the inner law of gratitude and praise. The only one to return was a Samaritan who was not bound by law to go to the temple priests in Jerusalem. All received physical healing, but the salvation of v 19 refers to a restoration of wholeness for which the physical healing is a symbol. This faith, the natural consequence of true gratitude, enabled the cured man to have a sense of values and proper priorities.

Unfortunately, many practicing Christians resemble the nine Jewish lepers. They may keep all the rules and perform religious practices with devotion, but a spirit of gratitude is missing. Their faith is in the God of a business contract, not the God of a covenant of love. They are incapable of receiving inner healing because they are unaware even of what to ask for.

First Reading: 2 Kings 5:14-17

Read the whole story of Naaman in chapter 5. This is one of a series of "prophet stories" designed to demonstrate the superiority of Israel's God Yahweh over the gods of nature worshiped by their neighbors — and increasingly and alarmingly by the Israelites themselves (see 1 Kgs 17-19; 2 Kgs 2:4-5). The particular character of God is affirmed in this story: he is not bound to any natural process, nor is he linked to any particular person or dependent on a place. The prophet is simply the spokesperson for God; he is not the instrument that channels divine power in any magical or superstitious way.

Responsorial Psalm: Psalm 98:1, 2-3, 3-4

Underlying the above readings is a sense of the universality of God's power, presence, and love. Although God may choose nations and individuals for special missions, it is so that his favor might be shown to all. Response: "The Lord has revealed to the nations his saving power."

Second Reading: 2 Timothy 2:8-13

Paul is depicted as writing at the end of his life to his successor as resident leader of the Church of Ephesus (see 1 Tim 1:3). He points to the centrality of the Gospel message — union with Christ is death and glory. As his own life faithfully embodied this union, demonstrated in deed as well as word, so must his successor's — and so must every Christian's.

Questions for thought, discussion, and prayer:
1. What is the nature of the healing (or salvation) in v 19 of the Gospel?

2. Think about the relationships of the various characters in the Naaman story. How does their interaction accomplish God's will?

TWENTY-NINTH SUNDAY OF THE YEAR — YEAR C

PRAY FOR JUSTICE

Gospel: Luke 18:1-8
The concluding section of chapter 17 (vv 20-37) provokes some difficulties of understanding, particularly if the reader insists on dead literalism of interpretation. Jesus' basic intention, however, was to counter the materialistic and nationalistic preconceptions about the nature of God's kingdom (vv 20-21) in the light of what he had already said. The reign of God is not subject to external control or judgment on the basis of things we can readily observe. It is a matter of deeply internal acceptance of God's rule. Note that Jesus was far more aloof about the "whens" and the "wheres" than some latter-day prophets like to admit. And these words lead to prayer.
The little parable of today's reading is a humorous story. (Too bad our sensitivities are so dull that we have to be told that!) The simple message is that God is going to be more responsive to our needs than we usually are ourselves. "Praying always" is closely linked to faith and to what we must pray for — justice. It means petitioning God to do what he already wills to do. Thus it involves changing ourselves so that we can allow God to exercise his concern in us. Much of what we call prayer is not prayer at all, but self-centered wishful thinking. Do we have the faith to trust that God's answer to our prayer is better than what we could ever think to ask for?

First Reading: Exodus 17:8-13

Moses' gesture of prayer — as intercessor and mediator — is portrayed as decisive in winning victory in battle. The physical act itself is not a magical gesture that automatically works, yet the raised arms are seen to be essential to the outcome. This tells us something of the need for and the force of symbolism. As symbols, the raised arms embody and express the inner attitude of submission and perseverance so essential to true prayer. As visible to the combatants, they inspire courage; as raised to God, they express recognition of his lordship.

Responsorial Psalm: Psalm 121:1-2, 3-4, 5-6, 7-8

This song of pilgrims expresses assurance that God is with his people as they journey in and towards him. Response: "Our help is from the Lord who made heaven and earth."

Second Reading: 2 Timothy 3:14-4:2

The author counsels the young leader of the local church regarding the struggles he would face in the future to maintain the integrity of faith within the community that was in his charge. Those who would distort faith try to turn it into magical formulas to impart "hidden" wisdom or to manipulate supernatural powers. Religion is not a matter of trying to control God, but of accepting his lordship into our lives. Scripture, as the record of God's dealings with his people, invites us to explore the meaning and implications of allowing God to be the Lord of our lives in faith.

Questions for thought, discussion, and prayer:

1.   What is the relationship of faith to prayer? What is the motivation and result of persistence in prayer?

2.   How do external things — postures and words — embody the inner spirit of prayer? Can we say the same thing about works of charity?

THIRTIETH SUNDAY OF THE YEAR — YEAR C

JUSTIFICATION BEFORE GOD

Gospel: Luke 18:9-14

Many people might click their tongues self-righteously at the judge of last week's Gospel (18:2) who "respected neither God nor man." It's easy and tempting to look at someone and say, "Thank God I'm not like that!" And so today's story follows quite naturally after the previous one, even though they may seem quite different. They are both about the type of prayer that God hears. These two characters were at opposite poles of religious society. One, a pillar of the synagogue; the other, a professional crook. In this story, Jesus gives a variation on the "reversal of situation" paradox we spoke of regarding the rich man and Lazarus parable a few weeks ago. The positions of these men are reversed in an unexpected way — the interior of each is not what the exterior would seem to indicate. (This also continues the theme of chapter 17.)

What is wrong with the Pharisee's prayer? Count the number of "I's" and it should be obvious. The only time he takes his attention off himself is to heap scorn on the other man. This is no real prayer of thanks, but only an exercise in self-admiration.

No one can justify himself or herself before God. We are good only because of God's gift, not by our own efforts. We are all weak and sinful, and if we see ourselves with the eyes of truth, we shall find more cause for humility and shame than for pride. Justification (i.e. making right) is a gift which only the repentant sinner can receive.

First Reading: Sirach 35:12-14, 16-18

Comparison of the ways and the destiny of the wicked and the good is a favored teaching method in the Bible. Beginning with Cain and Abel (Gn 4:1-16), it is developed in the law (see Dt 11:26-28), the psalms (with Ps 1 setting the theme), wisdom literature (today's reading), and finds its way into the the teaching of Jesus, for example, the above parable. Sir 34:18-35:24 compares the prayer and sacrifice of the unjust and the just, the dishonestly wealthy and the upright person. The rich man's sacrifices are valueless because he is using the fruits of his exploitation of the poor to try to bribe God. The lament and generosity of the poor is acceptable in God's eyes and bears fruit.

Responsorial Psalm: Psalm 34:2-3, 17-18, 19, 23
Poverty and affliction are not good things in themselves, and are no particular cause for God's favor. Yet they can be the road to uprightness and openness that enable one to undersand and receive God's care. Response: "The Lord hears the cry of the poor."

Second Reading: 2 Timothy 4:6-8, 16-18
Paul is depicted as concluding this letter with what might be called "deathbed words" to his close disciple. He sees the end at hand (v 6), and is satisfied that he has accomplished his mission (vv 7-8). He forgives his enemies (v 16), and expresses confidence in God (vv 17-18). This hope is based not on any prideful sense of merit, but on an awareness that a life lived in union with Jesus cannot have an outcome apart from him.

Questions for thought, discussion, and prayer:
1.   Retell the Gospel in terms of today. If possible, dramatize it. What might these two characters say to each other?

2.   Discuss the various possible effects of hardship, poverty, and sickness on one's relationship with God.

THIRTY-FIRST SUNDAY OF THE YEAR — YEAR C

SALVATION HAS COME

Gospel: Luke 19:1-10
The concluding section of chapter 18, omitted between last Sunday's and today's reading, contains the same matter as the passages from Mark's Gospel read in Year B on the Twenty-Seventh, Twenty-Eighth, and Thirtieth Sundays.
Luke is the only evangelist who records this incident about the tax collector, Zacchaeus. Last Sunday's readings showed God's acceptance of the sinful tax collector who turned to him in repentance. Today's reading provides a concrete example of how this repentance is worked out in reality. It may begin, as so many healing contacts with Jesus do, in a tentative and curious, but not fully committed

way. But Jesus himself transforms the heart. How?

By simple, total, and unconditional acceptance of the sinner. Notice that Jesus did not say: "Zacchaeus, I'd stay at your house if only you'd mend your evil ways." No, he says only, "Hurry down, I mean to stay at your home today."

Then, in his act of welcome, Zacchaeus is transformed by Jesus' love. Unlike the rich man a few verses before (Lk 18:18-25), he is willing to empty himself of the worldly possessions that displace God's love. He is a grown-up example of accepting the kingdom as a small child would (Lk 18:15-17). All indications point to his having been a small man in every way before his encounter with Jesus. And Jesus characteristically leads him to true greatness of stature.

First Reading: Wisdom 11:22-12:1
Read at least chapters 11 and 12 of this book. The author sings of the mercy of God not only toward the Jews but also toward their enemies. This shows a remarkable development of religious outlook that occurred among Jewish communities living as a small minority among pagan peoples outside Israel when this book was written (first century B.C.E.). The Jewish people are seen not only as God's favored ones, but as the instruments of his salvation to all humanity. Truly, God did not make the world out of nothing; he made it out of his own love. And his love extends to all that he has made. If this love is not everywhere evident, it is our fault, not his. We are called to make his love a living reality in the world.

Responsorial Psalm: Psalm 145:1-2, 8-9, 10-11, 13, 14
This psalm praises God for his works of both creation and salvation of his people. Response: "I will praise your name for ever, my king and my God."

Second Reading: 2 Thessalonians 1:11-2:2
Some members of the Christian community at Thessalonica were expecting the second coming of Christ at any minute, so they used this as an excuse to drop out of normal life. Apparently their headstrong attitude and refusal to work was becoming a nuisance in the community as well as an added reason for the pagans to persecute the Christians. Paul's advice is equally applicable today. We simply do not know the time of the Lord's return, and the only pos-

sible attitude is one of continuing our lives as normal — but in a spirit of watchfulness and prayer.

Questions for thought, discussion, and prayer:
1.   Try to put yourself in Zacchaeus' place, and describe how you would feel about this Gospel event.

2.   How should we live now in a state of readiness for the Lord's return?

THIRTY-SECOND SUNDAY OF THE YEAR — YEAR C

THE GOD OF THE LIVING

Gospel: Luke 20:27-38
A long section in the Gospel narrative is omitted from the Sunday readings. Of course, the entry into Jerusalem (Lk 19:28-40) is read on Passion/Palm Sunday, but the rest of the material between last Sunday's Gospel and today's is simply omitted. This is a pity, but not quite as unfortunate as it may seem. Most of the parables and events are repeated in other Gospel accounts, and many find their way into Sunday readings for other years. (See the Twenty-Seventh, Twenty-Ninth, and Thirty-Third Sundays of Year A; and the Third Sunday of Lent, Year B.)
In answering the Sadducees' question about the resurrection, Jesus probed far more deeply into the reality than the question itself called for, as we have seen him do many times before. The Sadducees, who did not believe in a resurrection of the body after death, posed this question to show the absurdity of any real afterlife. Jesus, in turn, showed the absurdity of the question itself. He did not talk about the nature of life after death except to say that the details of it are beyond comprehension in terms of earthly life. We really have no idea what it means to be "like an angel." Jesus' main point is that God is the God of life, and he does not will what he has brought into being to face ultimate destruction.

First Reading: 2 Maccabees 7:1-2, 9-14
The Sadducees faithfully reflected the general lines of Jewish thought concerning life after death throughout most of the history

before the time of Jesus. The ancient Hebrew usually thought and spoke of death in terms of exile, deprivation, and suffering. One had a more real existence in one's progeny than in Sheol, the abode of the dead. Only two or three centuries before Jesus did certain Jewish sects begin to develop the concept of a bodily resurrection, and then it was a limited one. These seven unnamed brothers and their mother in 2 Maccabees, which was written very late in pre-Christian Jewish history, about 110 B.C.E., show strong evidence of the characteristics of this belief. The outlook, however, is still very limited. Life beyond death is assured only to those who are prepared to give up their lives in fidelity to the Lord. Resurrection, then, is the gift of life restored to those faithful who surrender their own lives as a gift to God.

The number seven is an image of completeness and of divine blessing. This story is more likely an allegory representing Jerusalem and her children under persecution, rather than a strictly factual account. It was probably quite popular among the Pharisees of Jesus' day to express their belief. The Sadducees' story in the Gospel, also concerning seven brothers, seems designed as a pointed rebuttal.

Responsorial Psalm: Psalm 17:1, 5-6, 8, 15
This psalm is the confident prayer of someone being persued by personal enemies, or it may be the prayer of the whole nation of Israel under persecution. V 15 may reflect some undefined hope in a life after death, but more likely refers to the collective hope of Israel in the restoration of the kingdom in its former glory. Response: "Lord, when your glory appears, my joy will be full."

Second Reading: 2 Thessalonians 2:16-3:5
Paul reminds his hearers that the Christian life is characterized by confident hope in the midst of struggle. The "confused and evil men" were encouraging disorderly conduct by teaching that the time of fulfillment was already at hand, so there would be no use working. Paul notes that the missionary effort is not yet completed — not all have received the word of the Lord. In this work he asks for prayer.

Questions for thought, discussion, and prayer:
1. What kind of objections do you encounter against taking the promise of the resurrection seriously? How can you respond to them?

2. What is the basis of your own personal hope in the resurrection?

DO NOT BE MISLED

Gospel: Luke 21:5-19

As seen through the eyes and pen of Luke, Jesus' teachings show the relationship of earthly things to the kingdom. Wealth and possessions have value only insofar as they are used for the re-establishment of God's order on earth. To the extent that we grasp material goods and power for personal gain, and to the extent that we exploit people for the sake of our own selfish ends, to that extent our final end is emptiness and death.

These words about the destruction of Jerusalem (and the end of the world) must be read in the light of the whole attitude toward the things of this world conveyed by Luke's portrait of Jesus. All things are passing, and must yield to the full reality of God's kingdom. Therefore the followers of Jesus will have their sights fixed on what is beyond the temporal parade — whether of delight, pleasure, and accomplishment or of suffering, persecution, and failure. Just as we are not to put our hearts into wealth and power, so we should not fear trial and pain. If we look to the ultimate reality, no passing turmoil or trap can harm us in the long run.

Jesus' words look beyond the superficialities of the disciples' question — and our own questions as well. "When" is not important. What is important is that we learn to see beyond flashy and impressive appearances, and probe the substance of all things in the light of God's design.

First Reading: Malachi 3:19-20

This prophet spoke originally to a people who were struggling to rebuild their fortunes and nationhood after return from exile (about 455 B.C.E.). Read the whole book; it's very short. Evidently many of the new returnees were more concerned about their own fortunes than the restoration of the nation itself, and the prophet saw in this the seeds of further destruction. Yet he was hopeful that the Lord would send a leader to restore the covenant with God as the basis for nationhood, as in days of old. This hope was realized to a certain extent in the reform of Nehemiah, described in the books of Ezra and Nehemiah. However, we can see that the fullness of the Lord's restoration of his people, as Malachi prophesied it, took place in the coming of Christ.

Responsorial Psalm: Psalm 98:5-6, 7-8, 9

In the Jewish Scriptures military victory and successful political rule were often seen as images of God's power and dominion. This hymn of praise recognizes God's lordship over all people and things. Response: "The Lord comes to rule the earth with justice."

Second Reading: 2 Thessalonians 3:7-12

The letters to the Christian community at Thessalonica are among the earliest works of Paul, and therefore the oldest parts of the Christian Scriptures. Both letters discuss the second coming of Christ, and so this reading is pertinent to the other readings. Although Paul mistakenly assumes that this final coming would occur within his own lifetime, he is equally emphatic that it would not occur immediately, and should not provide an excuse for idle behavior.

Questions for thought, discussion, and prayer:
1. Would it be more proper to speak of "preparing for the coming of Christ" or "making his kingdom come"? Discuss the difference between these two expressions.

2. How do these words of Jesus speak to the situation of your own life today?

SOLEMNITY OF CHRIST THE KING — YEAR C
(THIRTY-FOURTH OR LAST SUNDAY OF THE YEAR)

THE CRUCIFIED KING

Gospel: Luke 23:35-43

The heart of the Gospel is the paradox of the cross — Jesus fulfilled in his total self his basic teaching: "he who would lose his life will save it." Representatives of all humankind — the common people, the leaders, the soldiers, and even a criminal who shares his crucifixion — failed to comprehend the mystery, and threw his own words back at him.

But the penitent thief recognizes something beyond appearances here. He comes at the end of a long list of outcasts and sinners in the Gospel accounts who found life in Jesus — prostitutes, lepers, tax collectors, as well as characters in parables: the prodigal son, unjust steward, and Lazarus the beggar. The thief's prayer (v 42) is more than an affirmation of Jesus' innocence. In an act of faith that we cannot fully comprehend, he is moved to acknowledge Jesus' lordship not in spite of but because of the cross. He is the first to follow literally the way of the cross, and so becomes the first to share explicitly in the glory of the kingdom.

Nothing is said here about the nature of the kingdom except that it consists in accepting Jesus' lordship. Paradise was an old Persian word for the king's garden, and was often used to describe humanity's original state as well as the promised state of heaven. But paradise is more than any place; it is to be with Jesus.

First Reading: 2 Samuel 5:1-3

David's kingship came from a hard-won struggle. The Biblical accounts clearly depict his reign as the result of God's will, but that did not make the achievement automatic or effortless. This reading gives us the third anointing of David, which signified his kingship over all Israel, thereby uniting as one nation the distinct regions of Israel and Judah. Anointing was both a sign of God's authority shared with the king and an act of acceptance of this authority by the people. The first anointing, by the prophet Samuel (1 Sm 16:12-13) set David apart for his kingly role. A second anointing (2 Sm 2:14) acknowledged his rule over Judah.

Responsorial Psalm: Psalm 122:1-2, 3-4, 4-5

This joyful psalm expresses pride and gratitude at the privilege of being under God's orderly rule. "I rejoiced when I heard them say: let us go to the house of the Lord."

Second Reading: Colossians 1:12-20

Early Christianity experienced many attempts to fuse faith in Christ with various pagan beliefs and practices. Cultural adaptations in forms of expression and worship were always necessary — and still are. But doctrines were also proposed that threatened the center of faith-life. This was the problem in community at Colossae. Pagan influences led the Christians to view Christ as only one among many "ruler spirits." In response, the author of this letter strongly asserted the absolute lordship of Christ over all creation.

This reading in all likelihood quotes a hymn that would have been commonly used in the liturgy at this time.

Questions for thought, discussion, and prayer:
1. What does Christ's lordship mean to you?

2. Put yourself in the place of the repentant thief, and talk about your feelings at that moment.

ALL YEARS
OTHER SOLEMNITIES
AND FEASTS

A REVEALING LIGHT
TO THE GENTILES

Gospel: Luke 2:22-40

This feast is closely connected to the Epiphany. In the meeting with Simeon and Anna, Jesus is recognized as the Messiah and revealed through their proclamation. The words of Simeon's canticle, "a revealing light to the Gentiles," associated this feast with light very early in the Church's history — candles were carried in procession representing Christ as the light of all people. From this the tradition of blessing candles on this day developed, hence the name, "Candlemas."

The occasion of this feast is in obedience to the law requiring a mother's purification after childbirth (Lv 12:2-8) and the ransom of the first born (Ex 13:11-13; 22:28-29). This is Jesus' first entry into the temple, a recognition of the presence of God in his person, and an anticipation of his mission as Messiah, to be himself the new temple of God's dwelling in humanity.

First Reading: Malachi 3:1-4

The prophet who wrote under the pen-name Malachi (my messenger) spoke to the situation after the return from exile (fifth century B.C.E.), when the temple was being rebuilt. Because political leadership had been destroyed, it was up to the priestly caste to unify and govern the people. This book addressed the corruption among the priests as well as the infidelity of the people. The possibilities of real leadership to create a strong nation appeared bleak, so the prophet expressed the hope that the Lord himself would rule the people. This messianic expectation was fulfilled in Christ.

Responsorial Psalm: Psalm 24:7, 8, 9, 10

This psalm served as a liturgical entry song, to prepare the people for worship in the temple. Response: "Who is this king of glory? It is the Lord!"

Second Reading: Hebrews 2:14-18

The author of this letter begins by asserting that Jesus is superior over the angels precisely because of his humanity. He is exalted by God because he, as God's Son, humbled himself to become a man (2:5-10). In this way alone could he become one with those in need of salvation (2:11-17). By God becoming a human the gap between human beings and God could be bridged. Jesus is the true high priest because he is in a unique position as mediator.

Questions for thought, discussion, and prayer:

1. How can one rise above the limitation of law by fulfilling it?

2. What does the belief that Jesus is both God and man mean to you?

SOLEMNITY OF ST. JOSEPH, HUSBAND OF MARY — MARCH 19

SON OF DAVID

Gospel: Matthew 1:16, 18-21, 24

See the commentary on the Gospel for the Fourth Sunday of Advent, Year A, page 27.

Alternative Gospel: Luke 2:41-51

See the commentary on the Gospel for the Feast of the Holy Family (Sunday in the Octave of Christmas), Year C, page 247.

First Reading: 2 Samuel 7:4-5, 12-14, 16

David's concern to build a temple was countered in Nathan's prophecy by the Lord's assurance that the future of his dynasty would be secure. In actual fact, it wasn't. The kingdom split in two after Solomon (930 B.C.E.), and the northern kingdom (Israel) was destroyed in 722 while the southern kingdom (Judah) lasted until the Babylonian exile in 597. This promise then was seen as the basis for a messianic hope that extended beyond the limitations of earthly kingship.

Responsorial Psalm: Psalm 89:2-3, 4-5, 27, 29

This psalm expands upon the promises made to David in 2 Sam 7. Response: "The son of David will live for ever."

Second Reading: Romans 4:13, 16-18, 22

The importance of faith is that it corresponds to God's way of revealing himself. If God's covenant were a contract, then the fulfillment of certain conditions would be the proper response. But the covenant is essentially a promise, a freely given gift on God's initiative. The only proper response is faith — a receptivity that does not seek to control. Through Christ the promise made to Abraham — that he would be the father of many nations — would be fulfilled.

Questions for thought, discussion, and prayer:
1.   Faith may be less a matter of certainty in truths than of steadfast trust in situations of uncertainty. Discuss the pros and cons of this statement.

2.   How do you think Joseph felt in his dilemma? How can he be a model for your own life?

SOLEMNITY OF THE ANNUNCIATION OF OUR LORD — MARCH 25

THE SON OF THE MOST HIGH GOD

Gospel: Luke 1:26-38

This passage is also used in celebrating the Solemnity of the Immaculate Conception, but since the Annunciation is considered a feast of the Lord rather than of Mary, we will concentrate on what this Gospel event says about Jesus.

The overshadowing of the Holy Spirit recalls both the Spirit of God (the mighty wind) hovering over the waters to bring forth life in Genesis (1:1-2) and the cloud as the manifestation of God's presence in Exodus (40:34-35). This affirms God as the source of this new life, and that the child will bring a new life-filled and spirit-giving presence into the world.

The messianic expectation in the Jewish Scriptures is the source of the titles the angel uses to announce who the child will be. "Great dignity" and "Son of the Most High" were titles of kings (see 2 Sam 7:8-16; Ps 2:7; 29:1; 82:6; 89:7), and looked forward to the Messiah as the perfect king. David's throne as extending to the house of

Jacob promises unity between the northern tribes (Jacob corresponds to Israel) and southern tribe of Judah, which had been divided since the death of Solomon (930 B.C.E.). This is an image of unity of all peoples of the earth. (See also the commentary on the Gospel for Solemnity of the Immaculate Conception and the Fourth Sunday of Advent, Year B.)

First Reading: Isaiah 7:10-14
King Ahaz, a descendant of David, found his throne threatened because of his infidelity to the Lord (see 2 Kgs 16), and capped this infidelity with unbelief in refusing to ask for a sign from God. The Immanuel (which means God-with-us) referred to by Isaiah is probably Ahaz's own son, Hezekiah, who reigned as a good king and sought to return the nation to the ways of the Lord (see 2 Kgs 18-20). The remembrance of the good kings in the line of David became the image in which the messianic hopes were built — hopes that were fulfilled in Jesus, the true Immanuel. (See also the commentary on the first reading for the Fourth Sunday of Advent, Year A.)

Responsorial Psalm: Psalm 40:7-8, 8-9, 10, 11
God has turned the psalmist's song from lamentation to gratitude, and the psalmist in turn pledges obedience to the Lord. Response: "Here am I, Lord, I come to do your will."

Second Reading: Hebrews 10:4-10
This passage quotes psalm 40 concerning the type of sacrifice that is truly pleasing to God. When reduced to its essentials, sacrifice is an attitude of the heart, not merely the giving up of a material thing. The one complete sacrifice is unwavering obedience, of which Jesus Christ is the perfect model. (See also the commentary on the second reading for the Fourth Sunday of Advent, Year C.)

Questions for thought, discussion, and prayer:
1. How do you fulfill obedience to God in your life? How can you grow more perfect in obedience to God?

2. What sort of hope do you have in the Lord? What do you mean when you call him Savior?

TO PREPARE THE LORD'S WAY

In celebrating the birth of John the Baptist, we are looking backward to the Jewish prophetic tradition as summed up in John, and at the same time looking forward toward Christ whose herald John was. There are two sets of readings, for the vigil and the day itself, and we will consider both sets together.

The GOSPEL readings (vigil, Lk 1:5-17; day Lk 1:57-66, 80) give us Luke's account of the annunciation and birth of John. Although he may well have been a relative of Jesus, the events are told in a way that is obviously symbolic. Details are presented only as signs of God's deeper works of salvation, and anticipate the fullness of salvation in Christ. Other persons in the Jewish scriptural history have similar birth stories, accompanied by wonderful events: Isaac (Gn 18:1-15; 21:1-9), Samson (Jdgs 13), and Samuel (1 Sam 1 and 2). These individuals marked significant turning points in Israel's history, but were not themselves outstanding leaders.

Zechariah's song (vv 68-79), which is omitted from these readings, stands at the heart of the daily morning prayer of the Church, and sums up the prophetic expectation for the Messiah.

Both FIRST READINGS describe the call of the prophet to announce God's word. Jeremiah's experience (vigil, Jer 1:4-10) was that the power of God's word overcame his youthful weakness. This reading alludes to the eternity of God's plan (v 5) and the insertion of God's word into the present moment through the prophet (v 9-10). The second "servant song" of Isaiah (day, Is 49:1-6) speaks of the effectiveness of God's word to accomplish his will.

The RESPONSORIAL PSALMS speak of God's support of his faithful servant (vigil, Psalm 71:1-2, 3-4, 5-6, 15, 17; Response: "Since my mother's womb you have been my strength") and inner penetration of his word into the very heart of his servant (day, Psalm 139:1-3, 13-14, 14-15; Response: "I praise you for I am wonderfully made").

The SECOND READINGS define the mission of the prophet as yielding to the greater reality of Christ's presence. 1 Peter 1:8-12 (vigil) points to the activity of the Spirit in the prophets' search to reveal the fullness of God's favor to come. Acts 13:22-26 (day), an excerpt from Paul's first missionary sermon, looks to John the Baptist's role as messenger who calls attention to the fullness of the message, and then diminishes himself before it.

Questions for thought, discussion, and prayer:
1.   What can John's calling tell us about the vocation of the Christian today?

2.   Discuss the relationship between humility and boldness in proclaiming the message of Christ.

SOLEMNITY OF SAINTS PETER AND PAUL, APOSTLES — JUNE 29

THE FOUNDATION OF THE KINGDOM

It is both fitting and difficult to celebrate these two apostles in the same liturgical moment. Together they are the foundation of the infant Church, yet in temperament and ministry they are nearly opposites. Peter, the impetuous braggart who could be counted on only to back out when the chips were down, yet who always repented and persevered, became the foundation "rock" of the Church. Paul, the most Jewish of Jews, had the insight to realize that the early Christian Church had to give up its "Jewishness" — in laws and practice, not in roots and heritage — if it was to be truly universal; and he had the courage to maintain his conviction even in face of strong and sometimes violent opposition.

The readings of the vigil seem to speak more of the call and mission of these apostles, while the Mass of the day concentrates on their primal position as apostles.

VIGIL MASS

Gospel: John 21:15-19
The love demanded by Jesus is not mere attachment and affection, but the enduring love of total commitment and fidelity. The

threefold question and answer echoes the threefold denial during Christ's passion (see Jn 18:17-22) but also underscores the importance of the moment in itself. The consequence of this love is the mission of the apostles, which is not to do their own will, but to fulfill God's will in imitation of Jesus the Master (vv 18-19).

First Reading: Acts 3:1-10

The dramatic character of this cure could obscure its important lesson about the apostolic ministry, namely, that the working of God's power requires the utmost attention and care on the part of the minister. It was God, not Peter and John, who healed the man. Yet, without their care for the person before them, and without their total concentration and conviction, the cure would not have taken place (read carefully vv 4-7). God accomplishes his will through the apostles (and we are all called to be apostles), but this is not a by-product of some other activity or a sideline occupation. The fulfillment of God's will demands that we care deeply and intensely about it.

Responsorial Psalm: Psalm 19:2-3, 4-5

This psalm reinforces the sense of apostolic mission — God makes himself known to all humanity through his works. Response: "Their message goes out through all the earth."

Second Reading: Galatians 1:11-20

In Paul's description of his own call and sending as an apostle, he repeats the theme of the Gospel: his task is to pass on what he has received — the apostle's mission originates in the call and sending forth by Christ, it is not undertaken on one's own initiative.

MASS OF THE DAY

Gospel: Matthew 16:13-19

This passage is often used as a proof text for the primacy of the Pope. It may well be that, but to stop there is to set aside rich insight into our own participation in the mission of the Church. The "power of the keys" is rightly understood as referring to the authority of Peter and his successors in the ministry of leading and unifying the Church, but it also provides us with an image of the mission of the whole Church, ourselves included. The Church is the doorway to God's kingdom. Each of us as a member of the Church has the power to unlock that doorway — to welcome all we meet, by our spirit of love and forgiveness, into association with us in the kingdom. But we can also close the door of the kingdom to others, excluding them by our attitudes of superiority, prejudice, selfishness, or negligence. As Christians, we have the power to open or to lock the door of God's kingdom. By our own words and actions we cannot help but exercise this power — one way or the other.

First Reading: Acts 12:1-11
The liberation of Peter from prison echoes many events of Jewish history (the deliverance of Joseph, Gn 39:21-41:57; the three young men, Dn 3; and Daniel, Dn 6) that consciously reflect the paschal liberation (Ex 12:42). Peter now undergoes the same trial and deliverance as his Master, and in his own person becomes a sign of God's deliverance of his people.

Responsorial Psalm: Psalm 34:2-3, 4-5, 6-7, 8-9
This psalm, in the words of one being unjustly persecuted, echoes hope for deliverance and freedom. Response: "The angel of the Lord will rescue those who fear him."

Second Reading: 2 Timothy 4:6-8, 17-18
Paul is writing from prison at the end of his life. The only deliverance he can expect is death, and he confidently proclaims that it is the greatest deliverance of all. The death of the Christian who has lived and worked in union with the death of Christ through baptism is true release to freedom and glory.

Questions for thought, discussion, and prayer:
1.   Discuss the qualities of people you know who are exemplary apostles in the light of these readings.

2.   Discuss the differences and similarities between Peter and Paul.

THE GLORY OF THE SON OF MAN

Gospel: Matthew 17:1-9, Year A; Mark 9:2-10, Year B; Luke 9:28-36, Year C.

The Gospel reading for this feast is the same as that of the Second Sunday of Lent in the same year. Please refer to that commentary.

This day is the anniversary of the first explosion of the atomic bomb by one nation against another, by the United States over Hiroshima, Japan, August 6, 1945. It would be timely and important to devote Bible study time to probing what this Gospel event — and the whole Gospel message — can say to that event which ushered in the threat of nuclear conflagration that has since hovered over humankind.

First Reading: Daniel 7:9-10, 13-14

The visions of the book of Daniel represent nations and historical events of the time of the author (about 165 B.C.E.) as well as previous history (such as the Babylonian exile, 587-538 B.C.E.). The book was written during a time of bitter persecution, and served to strengthen the faith of the Jewish people that God would deliver them. The "apocalyptic" style of the writing, characterized by wildly symbolic visions, was very common at that time, and on into the first century after Jesus. The book of Revelation is a Christian example of the same type of writing.

The "son of man" of this vision represents no definite person, but rather personifies the re-establishment of a kingdom under a king, and emphasizes that this would be God's doing, not a human endeavor. As such, the vision does foreshadow Jesus as the Messiah, and Jesus applied the title, Son of Man, to himself. (See also the commentary on the first reading for the Solemnity of Christ the King, Year B.)

Responsorial Psalm: Psalm 97:1-2, 5-6, 9

This psalm of divine judgment recalls the cloud, light and darkness, and power of the manifestation of God's presence of Ex 19:16-19, which is also displayed in the transfiguration of Jesus. Response: "The Lord is king, the most high over all the earth."

Second Reading: 2 Peter 1:16-19

The second letter of Peter claims to have been written by the apostle himself, but most commentators regard it as the latest of the Christian scriptural writings, dating around 100 to 140 C.E. There is considerable evidence to support this, such as the reference to Paul's writings as "Scripture" (3:16), indicating that they were already part of a tradition handed down from the past. Even if written at a later date by someone who wished to claim Peter's authority, and even if its "eyewitness" claim is several generations removed, this letter has still been accepted as an inspired writing by the Church from the very early times.

One of the situations the author faced was a denial of the second coming of Christ because of the long delay since his resurrection. He appeals to the apostolic witness of the transfiguration to show that Jesus already possessed the glory to be revealed in his second coming. The author assumes that his readers are already familiar with the account of the transfiguration found in the Gospels.

Questions for thought, discussion, and prayer:
1. Discuss the meaning of the word "passage" as found in Lk 9:31.

2. What was in Peter's mind in Lk 9:33?

SOLEMNITY OF THE ASSUMPTION — AUGUST 15

A WOMAN CLOTHED
WITH THE SUN

The assumption of Mary, body and soul, into heaven — as defined in Catholic dogma — is not found explicitly in Scripture, but has been a part of Christian faith-tradition from the earliest centuries. This feast emphasizes the "cosmic" dimensions of Mary's role in God's plan of salvation. We do not celebrate her exaltation in the sense of a removal from us, but as the fulfillment of what we all are called to be.

There are different readings for the vigil and daytime Masses.

Gospel: Luke 11:27-28
This brief passage sets the theme for the whole feast: Mary is blessed, not in the fact of her physical motherhood so much as because she perfectly received God's word and cherished it so that it might grow into perfect obedience. Just as Mary's relationship with God was not the automatic result of God's call, so our relationship with God is forged in obedience to his word.

First Reading: 1 Chronicles 15:3-4, 15, 16; 16:1-2
This passage retells the story of bringing the ark of the covenant to Jerusalem after the Lord had brought David victory over Israel's enemies. This ark — a container with the tablets of the law inside — was looked upon as the sign of God's presence among his people. This reading, therefore, alludes to Mary as the ark of the new covenant, insofar as she received into herself the Word of God in fullness in the person of God the Son. The bringing of the ark to Jerusalem suggests Mary's assumption into heaven, to the new and eternal Jerusalem (see Rev 21-22).

Responsorial Psalm: Psalm 132:6-7, 9-10, 13-14
This song accompanied the ark in its ascent to Jerusalem. Response: "Lord, go up to the place of your rest, you and the ark of your holiness."

Second Reading: 1 Corinthians 15:54-57
This passage concludes Paul's teaching on the resurrection as found in 1 Cor 15. This is a hymn of victory and praise for all who have attained the final state of being with Christ. (See also the commentary on the second reading for the Eighth Sunday of the Year, Year C.)

Gospel: Luke 1:39-56
The Gospel fittingly narrates the pregnant Mary's visit to her cousin Elizabeth in the hill country of Jerusalem — a passage which suggests the entry of the ark into Jerusalem of the vigil's first read-

ing. Even the infant's leaping in Elizabeth's womb recalls the singers and dancers before the ark. Mary's hymn is a victory song in which she speaks for all who can claim a share in God's saving power — the poor and weak, the powerless and oppressed, who alone can be the recipients of God's work because they do not trust in themselves. (See also the commentary on the Gospel for the Fourth Sunday of Advent, Year C.)

First Reading: Revelation 11:19; 12:1-6, 10
The woman of this reading refers to the people of Israel from whom Christ came, and the new people of God suffering persecution. Mary, as the mother of Jesus, sums up the role of the Jewish people in bringing forth the Messiah, and is the image of the Church which continues his presence.

Responsorial Psalm: Psalm 45:10, 11, 12, 16
This is a wedding song of the king, and it points to the final union of Christ as bridegroom with the Church as bride. (See Rev 21:2; 22:7.) Response: "The queen stands at your right hand, arrayed in gold."

Second Reading: 1 Corinthians 15:20-26
Paul here speaks of Jesus Christ as the first born from the dead to new life. It is fitting that his mother share this resurrection, not only as a personal glory, but as a further sign of hope for us. (See also the commentary on the second reading of the Solemnity of Christ the King, Year A.)

Questions for thought, discussion, and prayer:
1. How is Mary the model for your own life?

2. Discuss the title, "Mary, Mother of the Church."

LIFTED UP
ON THE CROSS

Ancient traditions place the finding of the true cross of Jesus in Jerusalem on this date, probably about 325 C.E. by St. Helena, mother of the Roman Emperor Constantine. Substantial evidence indicates that by 400 C.E., a feast commemorating the holy cross was celebrated in Jerusalem, and very shortly thereafter it became one of the major feasts throughout the whole eastern Church. Although it began to be celebrated in the Christian west in the seventh and eighth centuries, this feast never attained in the Roman Rite the prominence it had in the east.

Gospel: John 3:13-17
    These concluding verses from Jesus' conversation with Nicodemus look backward to the incident recounted in the first reading, and forward to the crucifixion. John's Gospel views the cross primarily as the manifestation of God's glory in Christ, and therefore its meaning is not so much a sacrificial appeasement, but the sign of faith. In the crucifixion, the Son of Man is "lifted up" to be recognized as the suffering servant (see Is 52:13-53:12), and this must be the basis of all faith in him.

First Reading: Numbers 21:4-9
    This event, along with many others in Jewish history (for example, Ex 7:8-13 and 1 Kgs 18), contains traces of a primitive acceptance of magic and superstition, but also succeeds in rising above this base, materialistic appeal. It is clear that faith and repentance on the part of the people is the important thing in this story, not any magical powers that the bronze serpent might possess. Much later in history (Wis 16:6-7), the bronze serpent is portrayed as a sign of God's salvation.

Responsorial Psalm: Psalm 78:1-2, 34-35, 36-37, 38
    This lengthy psalm recalls the history of God's saving works in order to recognize the same works happening now. Response: "Do not forget the works of the Lord!"

Second Reading: Philippians 2:6-11

This is an ancient hymn to the death and glorification of Jesus. It probably dates from before anything that Paul himself wrote, and was very likely a part of the eucharistic liturgy in some areas. The humility of God the Son and the glorification of the Son of Man are inseparable and balanced elements in the meaning of Jesus. This song contemplates this mystery of suffering and raising up. (See also the commentary on the second reading for Passion Sunday, Year A.)

Questions for thought, discussion, and prayer:

1.   What part does the cross play in your own personal life of faith?

2.   How is Christ a model of "self-emptying"? To what purpose does one empty oneself?

SOLEMNITY OF ALL SAINTS — NOVEMBER 1

THE MULTITUDE

Gospel: Matthew 5:1-12

Today's Gospel takes us back to the basic charter of the kingdom of God. The beatitudes emphasize that the kingdom is not something achieved by human effort or even according to the best of human designs or expectations, but is solely the work of God in those who are open to him. The kingdom belongs to the poor, the weak, the compassionate, and the non-violent because they are the ones who can let God rule in their world. But it would be a mistake to think that these characteristics imply passivity or timidity. It takes passion and strength to be so devoted to truth, justice, and love as to withstand persecution. It takes courage to face squarely one's own inner poverty.

As the foundation of the kingdom, these beatitudes take flesh in the lives of the saints. The beauty of this feast is that it enables us to recognize the great diversity in the lives of those who grasped the kingdom through fidelity to the spirit of the beatitudes. The saints are important to us because they show us how real people in real-life situations have put Jesus' teaching into practice. (See also the commentary on the Gospel of the Fourth Sunday of the Year, Year A.)

First Reading: Revelation 7:2-4, 9-14

One of the themes of the book of Revelation is that the final kingdom would involve the re-establishment of the twelve tribes of Israel as the new Jerusalem. The early Christians, even those of pagan origin, were aware that they were heirs in faith of God's promise to the Israelites, and so saw themselves as the new People of God. The 144,000 speaks of a symbolic but organized multitude — not merely a limited number, but not a faceless crowd either. The mark on the forehead (the image is from Ez 9:4-6) indicates God's protection, but also refers to the sacramental seal of baptism and confirmation in the Spirit (see 2 Cor 1:22; Eph 1:13; 4:30). The "trial" of v 14 refers especially to the persecutions of Nero, but more broadly expresses the trials that all Christians must face (see Mt 5:10-12).

Responsorial Psalm: Psalm 24:1-2, 3-4, 5-6

This psalm was sung as worshipers entered the temple in procession, and so it speaks of the qualities of heart needed for faithful worship as the Lord's people. Response: "Lord, this is the people that longs to see your face."

Second Reading: 1 John 3:1-3

The first letter of John is based on a strong awareness of what communion with God as his children sharing his life means. Being one with God is incompatible with sin and hatred, but this relationship is something that is in a state of growth. Our present reality leads to what we will become. Recognizing who we are as God's children now is the faith that gives birth to hope in eternal fulfillment. (See also the commentary on the second reading for the Fourth Sunday of Easter, Year B.)

Questions for thought, discussion, and prayer:
1.   Who are your favorite saints? How did they in their lives exemplify the message of these readings?

2.   Who are present-day saints who are examples of what it means to be a Christian living for God's kingdom? What qualities in their lives show it?

* * *

ALL SOULS AND
THE MOTHER CHURCH

Whenever All Souls Day falls on a Sunday, the following Sunday is the Feast of the Dedication of the Basilica of St. John Lateran. Each of these days in its own way is an invitation to reflect on the meaning of God's people gathered to be church.

All Souls reminds us that we are still one with those who have gone before us into eternal life, and in particular that we can and must realize that unity by prayer and commendation of them to the Lord. We are not perfect, and neither were they in their lifetimes. Therefore we still owe them love and support in Christ's name, even beyond the grave.

The Basilica of St. John Lateran in Rome is the "Mother Church" of all churches throughout the world because it is the Cathedral of Rome. It, not St. Peter's, is properly the Pope's own church. And so it is very fitting that we commemorate the day of its dedication, which took place in the fourth century, because we are celebrating an important aspect of our heritage as God's people.

The readings for both days may be chosen from a great variety found in the Masses for the dead (for All Souls) and the common of the dedication of a church. This gives us an opportunity to look at a large number of Scripture passages as they relate to a common subject — the mystery of death and our identity as one people united in Christ.

* * *

ALL SOULS DAY — NOVEMBER 2

GOSPEL

Seventeen different Gospel passages are presented for our selection. Several of them are simply the accounts of the death and resurrection of Jesus (Mk 15:33-39; 16:1-6; and Lk 23:44-49;

24:1-6). More significant, concerning our share in the risen life of
Jesus, is the promise and foretaste of the resurrection. In conjunction with his discourse on the eucharist, Jesus assures us that he will
raise up those who are truly his own (Jn 6:37-40). As a prelude to
the raising of Lazarus, he affirms Martha's faith in the final resurrection in union with him (Jn 11:17-27), and on the cross he promises paradise to the thief who repents (Lk 23:33, 39-43). In the
raising of the widow's son (Lk 7:11-17) and of Lazarus (Jn
11:32-45), we have not mere words of promise but actual events
which embody that promise.

The rest of the Gospel readings speak in some way of the
Christian life as it leads to eternal life. The beatitudes (Mt 5:1-12)
give the constitution of the earthly kingdom of God to be fulfilled in
eternity. The kingdom demands childlike acceptance, and in Christ
the burdens of living his life in this world are light (Mt 11:25-30).
But it is clear that the kingdom as built here and now is imperfect
and passing — this is a time of assiduous preparation (Mt 25:1-13)
and watchfulness (Lk 12:35-40). The kingdom begins in the present
moment by sharing Jesus' life, and this is based on recognition of
him where he is truly found, in the "least" brothers and sisters (Mt
25:31-46). Our life in him is continually nourished by faith in Jesus
as the bread of life, and this faith focuses on the eucharist (Lk
24:13-35 and Jn 6:51-58). Living in Jesus means day-by-day union
with his death to bring forth the fruit of new life (Jn 12:23-28), acceptance of him, not merely as pointing the way but as being the
Way itself (Jn 14:1-6), in fulfillment of his prayer for his followers
(Jn 17:24-26).

FIRST READING

There is a choice among seven from the Hebrew Scriptures,
each of which shows some stage in the development of Jewish
thought and faith in afterlife. During most of the time before Christ,
only a vague idea of afterlife is found: and "abode of the dead"
called Sheol, whose inhabitants had only a shadowy existence.
God's favor or disfavor was understood in terms of the present life
only. However, as hard times and tragedies befell the Jewish people,
ideas of life beyond this life began to emerge. Isaiah saw this as eternal restoration of the nation — death destroyed and the whole people
would live forever (Is 25:6-9). Jeremiah experienced the almost total
destruction of the nation, yet in the day-after-day rising of the sun
he saw a sign of hope for renewal (Lam 3:17-26). Job in the depths
of personal tragedy looked to God for vindication (Job 19:1, 23-27).

It was only late (second and first centuries B.C.E.) in wisdom writings that strong ideas of personal immortality began to emerge, especially as a solution to the all-too-apparent injustices of this life (Wis 3:1-9; and Wis 4:7-14). This afterlife as comprising both reward for the just and punishment for the wicked (Dn 12:1-3) and the value of prayer and sacrifice for the dead, as well as faith in a future resurrection of the body (2 Mac 12:43-46) put the finishing touches on Jewish revelation and paved the way for Jesus' teaching.

SECOND READING

Eighteen different readings from the non-Gospel Christian Scriptures constitute the field of choice and also give evidence of a development of understanding during the first generations of Christian faith. The apostolic preaching (Acts 10:34-43) focuses on Christ's resurrection as the source of forgiveness. Paul's earliest letter (1 Th 4:13-18) addresses the concern that the dead would be excluded from taking part in Christ's final coming, then expected very soon. Later, writing from prison (Phil 3:20-21), Paul begins to unfold his teaching that Christ is the pattern for the Christian who will be transformed into his likeness. In Corinthians, Paul envisions Christ as having fought in our name and won victory over death (1 Cor 15:20-24, 25-28; and 15:51-57), and faith in this victory will be the criterion for judgment (2 Cor 5:1, 6-10). Romans explores further implications of this union with Christ's death and resurrection in the Spirit: as source of reconciliation (Rom 5:5-11; and 5:17-21), as patterned in the Christian through baptism (Rom 6:3-9), and fulfilled in the Spirit who makes us heirs with Christ (Rom 8:14-23) and therefore inseparable from him (Rom 8:31-35, 37-39). Christ is Lord of all, dead and living (Rom 14:7-12). At the end of his life, Paul expresses to Timothy his hope in God's fidelity (2 Tim 2:8-13). John sees eternity primarily as the completion of the relationship with God — family life and love in him — that is begun now (1 Jn 3:1-2; and 3:14-16). One brief passage from Revelation (Rev 14:13) echoes the readings from Hebrew wisdom noted above; another (20:11-21:1) looks back to the Daniel reading, while the third (21:1-7) displays an exalted view of heaven as the new Jerusalem and the bride of Christ.

Questions for thought, discussion, and prayer:

1. How does praying for the dead express our faith that the bonds of relationships formed here are not broken by death?

2. How is Jesus' death and resurrection the model for our own death and resurrection as his followers?

FEAST OF THE DEDICATION OF ST. JOHN LATERAN — NOVEMBER 9

GOSPEL
The choice is among four. The temple was the center of worship of the Jews. Jesus affirms its worth by driving out the merchants and money changers who profane it (Jn 2:13-22), but goes beyond it by establishing a worship "in spirit and truth" that is not dependent on the temple or on any particular place (Jn 4:19-24). The church building is not the house of God but the home of his people, a home in which the sinner especially finds welcome, repentance, and a new life (Lk 19:1-10). All who gather for worship must first seek reconciliation, or their worship is valueless (Mt 5:23-24).

FIRST READING
The six selections convey various aspects of Jewish faith and worship relating to God's dwelling with his people: a location or a building signifying God's presence (Gn 28:11-18; 2 Chr 5:6-10, 13-6:2; and Ez 43:1-2, 4-7), the altar as central point of worship (1 Mac 4:52-59), and a realization that God transcends any particular place (1 Kgs 8:22-23, 27-30; and Is 56:1, 6-7).

SECOND READING
These four selections affirm that God's people themselves, not any particular place, make up his favored dwelling (1 Cor 3:9-13, 16-17; and 1 Pet 2:4-9). Thus all people everywhere are invited to be God's home (Eph 2:19-22) where the new covenant in Jesus' blood is continued (Heb 12:18-19, 22-24).

Questions for thought, discussion, and prayer:
1. How is a building symbolic of the people who gather there?

2. Where do you personally feel closest to God? Why?

SOLEMNITY OF THE IMMACULATE CONCEPTION — DECEMBER 8

YOU HAVE FOUND FAVOR WITH GOD

Gospel: Luke 1:26-38

This is the same Gospel passage that is read on the Solemnity of the Annunciation, but as it relates to this feast, it sheds light on Mary's position in God's order of salvation. We should pay particular attention to the angel's words to Mary and to her response.

The angel's greeting echoes Zeph 3:14-16, in which the prophet is speaking to Jerusalem (see also Zech 9:9). This means that Mary herself is to be the new Jerusalem, having the privilege of bearing the Lord within her womb. That this should take place in Nazareth of Galilee, a territory that was despised by proper Jews as almost pagan (see Jn 1:46; 7:41), already indicates God's favor toward the lowly and the rejected in his concern to extend salvation to all.

The word "favor" in the phrases "Rejoice, O highly favored daughter" ("Hail, full of grace") and "You have found favor with God" ("Blessed are you among women") is an expression from the Jewish Scriptures describing the personal attraction of a man toward a woman which is fulfilled in the marriage relationship (see Ruth 2:2, 10, 13; Prov 5:19; 7:5; 18:22; Song of Songs 8:10). God is desiring a faithful wife; Israel as a nation has proven unfaithful, and Mary is the symbol of his taking a new and hitherto rejected people to himself. (See also the commentary on the Gospel for the Solemnity of the Annunciation and the Fourth Sunday of Advent, Year B.)

First Reading: Genesis 3:9-15, 20

This account of God confronting Adam and Eve with their sin reveals a basic human tendency that locks us into our sinfulness and prevents our release: our failure to face our responsibility for our own actions. The three curses uttered by God — to the serpent (vv 14-15), to the woman (v 16), and to the man (vv 17-19) — speak more of the consequences of sin than of punishment for it. The refusal to face guilt constructively and seek reconciliation results in alienation from the rest of the created order, from our fellow human beings, and from God himself. But even in his curse, God leaves the door open for restoration (v 15) — a restoration that was signaled in the openness of Mary to be the recipient of God's favor. (See also the commentary for the Tenth Sunday of Year B.)

Responsorial Psalm: Psalm 98:1, 2-3, 3-4
This psalm bursts with praise for both the creative work and saving presence of God. It probably originated as a song of the faithful Jews flushed with new freedom returning home from exile. Response: "Sing to the Lord a new song, for he has done marvelous deeds."

Second Reading: Ephesians 1:3-6, 11-12
The whole letter to the Ephesians speaks of the restoration of all humanity in Christ. God's will does not limit salvation to a single "chosen people." To speak of his choice as predestination (v 12) is not to restrict salvation to a select few, but to rejoice that he has chosen us so that "all might praise" (v 6).
See also the commentary on the second reading for the Second Sunday after Christmas.

Questions for thought, discussion, and prayer:
1. Does considering Mary as conceived without sin make her closer to you or more removed? Why?

2. How do you find hope in the negative consequences of sin in the world today?